England Aft

☆ENGLAND☆ AFTER DARK

Geoffrey Beattie

WEIDENFELD AND NICOLSON · LONDON

Published in Great Britain by
George Weidenfeld & Nicolson Limited
91 Clapham High Street
London SW4 7TA

ISBN 0 297 81137 1

Typeset at The Spartan Press Ltd,
Lymington, Hants
Printed in Great Britain by The Guernsey Press Co. Ltd, C.I.

For Rod Johnson, nightclub proprietor, who understands what England can be like after dark, and yet stays sensible.

Contents

Acknowledgments

This book would not have been possible without a good deal of cooperation, and a great deal of patience on the part of many people – as the reader will surely discover. I thank all those who allowed me to share part of their after dark experiences. John Course, Northern Features Editor of The *Guardian*, encouraged me to develop the idea of a series about life in England after dark. Without such encouragement, books of this kind would be impossible – at least for me. So he receives my warmest thanks. The 'Grassroots' page of the *Guardian*, which John edits, allowed me the space to report back what I found out there, and for that I am truly grateful. *Marie Claire* magazine suggested that I spend a night out with the Vice Squad, and printed the article resulting from that experience; *The Sunday Telegraph* Colour Magazine did likewise with the night out with the commuters from Grimsby. I thank them for two very good ideas indeed. And then it is back to the ordinary punters. Patrick Maloney, Jenny Brough, Mick Mills and Steve Baxendale suggested things, offered advice, introduced me to people and, in addition, kept me out of trouble. They know exactly how important they were. And then there was Rod Johnson, nightclub proprietor. I think that it is true to say that Rod has taught me a good deal about life in England today after dark. He has also taught me the secret of having a quiet word, about being in control, and that the word 'nice' still has some meaning out there. It is for this and much, much more that I would like to dedicate this book to him.

Introduction

This is the England most of us do not know. This is England after dark. For this book, I have ventured into the kingdom of the night to report back on what life is really like in England today when most of us have retired for the evening. I went out on patrol with the Vice Squad in Central London around Park Lane and Paddington, where the WPCs have to wear enough layers so that the 'toms' with AIDS cannot bite right through their clothing and infect them. One tom, who was HIV positive, cut her wrists in front of the WPCs and flicked the blood at them to keep them away. Another tom was arrested and charged. 'How much do you weigh, Deborah?' asked Alison, the young WPC. 'Eleven stone. Would you believe it? If you look at my first charge sheet, I was nine and a half stone. I've put on a bit of weight in the last few years,' explained Deborah. 'Do you want me to be kind?' asked Alison – 'I'll put ten and a half stone down on the form.' I went to a club and watched a transvestite, or a very manly woman, devour some unsuspecting punter, but was she a tranvestite? And was he that naive? Who was fooling whom? And why was anybody really interested?

I travelled through the night down from Grimsby to London with a crane operator who commutes to London every week for work, in order to see for myself what life is really like for those that have decided to get on their bike. We left Grimsby at 3.15 am in February in a blizzard. The crane operator could hardly keep his eyes open, and he informed me that he's had loads of accidents. He shaves while he's driving to keep himself awake. But sometimes it doesn't work. A number of years ago he broke his spine in an accident and spent a year off work. 'It's just the law of averages though,' he said philosophically – 'you're bound to have a smash going up and down this road all the time. I think I've been pretty lucky so far.'

1

I watched an air hostess get herself ready for work in the wee small hours, for that morning's run to Ibiza. She was trying to put any thought of accidents to the very back of her mind. Very sensibly. She knew that she had one hour to make herself look 'presentable'. She had to be out of her house at 4.00 am at the latest. 'I'm useless without my face on,' she explained as she applied her make-up. 'I leak my real feelings far too easily without it.'

I spent a night with the Fire Brigade, and ended up being caught in an inferno with the Red Watch of Rivelin Fire Station in Sheffield. The inferno was routine and forgotten a moment later by the firemen. They were the first firemen on the scene at the Hillsborough disaster in Sheffield. That was not forgotten quite so quickly. They tried to cope in their own way – 'The funniest thing about Hillsborough is that all the lads went out that night quite independently and got absolutely bladdered. We only discovered that we'd all done it the next day when we all came in with hangovers.'

I went out on a raid, code-named 'Operation Donkey', with a team of highly professional private investigators to catch a pub landlord on the fiddle. Just another job for them, as we stood in the pub trying to blend in with the seventeen-year-old regulars. We ended up catching the barmaid as well, with forty-five quid stuffed down her knickers. It just wasn't her night. I stayed on as the CID arrived to interview the landlord and barmaid, and two joiners arrived to change all the locks in the place. The landlady meanwhile got quietly drunk behind the bar.

I travelled on a coach from Sheffield to Manchester with some style merchants, now into Acid House. 'I'm only a snob about two things,' said one style merchant called Thomas with a pony tail and ripped jeans – 'women, food and wine.' I asked Thomas about the drug Ecstasy. 'Look, put it like this, you can get an awful lot of lager for twenty-five quid. I was approached a couple of weeks ago in a club, and this guy asked me if I wanted to buy some 'Windowpane'. I told him that I'd never heard of it – Windowlene yes, but Windowpane? Acid House isn't about drugs, it's about staying ahead of the pack.' The next day, I called into one of the shops where the style merchants get their clothes. It was the afternoon and daylight outside, but dark in the shop. All the profits of the shop go to supporting a variety of stray cats. Then I went to watch some heavy metal fans try to stay ahead of their particular pack by playing imaginary guitars in the air.

They had hangers-on, just like their heroes. 'There are some ace air guitarists in this club,' explained one of the regulars. I went to the Deadmill on St Walpurga's day, and tried to understand what was going on amongst all the weirdness.

I found myself in a Working Mens' Club, listening to a joke about farting that went on for nearly fifteen minutes. 'That was absolutely disgusting,' said the straight man in the group as the funny man appeared to fart. 'I know, it weren't one of my best.' 'You've got to learn to control your body, you've got to squeeze your bum a bit tighter', said the straight man – 'It works, you know, it saves you getting bubbles all down your stockings, or having to put your trousers inside your socks.' I listened to nurses and their fellas on a night out, and then witnessed the brides-to-be show at a club in Sheffield. The brides-to-be were festooned with inflated durex and pictures cut out of men's sex magazines, with captions cut out of newspapers pinned below – 'What a whopper!' and 'A right Charlie!' I found a club in Rotherham where beer and lager were sold for twenty pence a pint. Judge Michael Walton at Sheffield Crown Court had said that such a policy was 'disgraceful' and 'an anti-social act' when he sentenced two youths to nine months at a young offenders' institution for robbing a taxi driver, having drunk approximately twelve pints of the cheap beer. I say approximately because they couldn't remember exactly how many pints they'd drunk. But the judge needn't have worried. The owners had new plans for the club anyway – 'An Ibizan club right in the centre of Rotherham.' They didn't say if Judge Michael Walton would be invited to the opening.

I tried to learn about the threat of the dark. I watched Barry, who was small and fat, and who had several teeth missing after being beaten up in Sheffield Station one night, learn commando-style self-defence on a squash court. The only casualty of the night, however, was when someone slid on the smooth surface of the court. I met Bob, who is a big time club owner, who had a rigid view of the world. There were guys you had to take seriously, then there were muppets. I was a muppet. Down in the Midlands, Don, who has worked as a bouncer for twenty five years, explained how violence in clubs had changed over that period, and how the violent punters were getting craftier. In clubs with metal detectors on the door to detect knives, they now carry splinters of glass with insulating tape wrapped around the end. Don said that he had never felt so wary at work as he did at the present time. I went for a drink in Britain's roughest boozer, a title conferred on this particular public house by The *Sun* newspaper. I didn't get glassed, but I didn't get bored either, and then I went home and reflected on the nature of threat. Whilst watching my back, of course.

I spent the night with a security guard working in another northern city, who was signing on the dole as well. He was terrified of having to call the police in the event of trouble because they might catch him fiddling. He was an ex-soldier with experience in Northern Ireland, and a black belt in karate. He carried a *nunchaku* around with him to help him sort any trouble. 'I'm a great Bruce Lee fan,' he explained. 'Just as well I suppose.' I went to Stoke-on-Trent to see what life was like on the night-shift in the Potteries, where everything is done on a piece-work basis. And there I found some Pakistanis manning the kilns in the face of some blatant racism. I talked to a young architect designing for the future, who explained the problems in selling taste to the ordinary punter. I then confronted a number of individuals whose lives didn't make that much sense to me, including the dynamic ex-chairman of the Monday Club students. This organisation wanted a ban on all further immigration coupled with a policy of further repatriation. The ex-chairman's name was Sanwar Ali, and he was born in Bangladesh.

I went in search of that great media stereotype – the lager lout – and found them everywhere – Manchester Airport, Majorca (some corner of a foreign field that is forever England, and therefore more than qualifying for this book) and nowhere. I learned the limited vocabulary of those who like to watch American Pit Bull Terriers fight. 'Awesome,' they say about the dogs that manage to kill. Then I found myself among the audience at some championship boxing. This was not awesome. I then went out on a sting with a professional arm wrestler and bare knuckle fist fighter, who was. He drove a pink XR3. 'It's not pink,' he said rather forcefully – 'it's purple or, to be more technical, metallic amethyst.' I still don't agree.

A number of people in England after dark were in altered states of various sorts. I went ghost hunting in the Stretford end of Manchester, and even though I never managed to talk to a spirit, I heard them talking about me. It was almost reassuring, especially when they got my name wrong. More reassuring at least than a lot of what I saw after dark in England today. The Charismatic Christians that I bumped into explained to me what it is like to be 'slain by the holy spirit'. A number have apparently found themselves stuck to radiators when this happens. It seems that the Holy Spirit likes to travel along cold metal. A professional cyclist then talked to me at length about drug abuse in that particular sport. For light relief, I went to see a stage hypnotist and watched as some poor girl tried to lay some very large, square eggs. I needed to relax so I took myself off to an Electro Crystal Therapist, only to be told that I had a very bright aura around my head and shoulders, but that I was dead from the waist down. I then went looking for the nobs – at a country club, at the Grand Hotel in Brighton, at a university ball, at High Table in Cambridge. They were very elusive. The nobs always are. For contrast, I travelled to Garston in Liverpool to spend the night with an eighty-six-year-old pensioner living alone in a block of flats, infested with cockroaches. She needed a wheelchair to get about, and yet she was given a flat on the first floor. She only gets out when someone arrives to take her out. She kept making jokes about her see-through nightie, and said that she was looking for a toy boy. I had to tell her that I couldn't oblige. She couldn't go anywhere under her own steam. A young triathlete I met couldn't stop.

I was becoming acclimatized to the culture of the dark. I was learning the rules. I knew the score. I wanted to finish the book off by working on the door of some club for a week. The view from the inside. I was fed up with just being a muppet. So I set off to be inteviewed for a job as a bouncer one bright afternoon – in some little office just opposite the skating rink and next door to the Cee Bee (busy, busy, busy) variety agency. I went armed with my new found knowledge, and all of my list of contacts. I was gong to be treated seriously. I had, after all, managed to survive out there in England after dark.

I didn't, however, get the job.

★ 1 ★
Love is in the air

A Night Out With The Vice Squad

It was 10.30 pm. We were in Park Lane. It was Ascot Week, and the nobs were out in force. The nobs and the prostitutes both. 'Like bees round a honey pot,' said Alison, a twenty-four-year-old WPC who was sitting in the back of the unmarked Bedford van, with three others – one other young WPC, Cath, and two young male officers. The girls were in uniform, the men in plain clothes. There was room for about ten in the van, but we were still all sweltering in the heat. We had been in the van since 6.00 pm. The nobs in the pavement cafes looked very cool indeed. Alison surveyed the Rollers and the Porsches parked at odd angles up every available inch of pavement. 'The toms can smell the money around here,' she said. And at that precise moment, as if on cue, two girls – one with fluffy blond hair and one with long straight blond hair – turned the corner and headed towards the back of the Hilton hotel. Both wore high heels and very short and tight black skirts, it was almost like a uniform. 'Look – two toms – Samantha and Adele,' said Alison. 'Adele's from Leeds originally. She's alright, never makes any fuss when she's arrested. Samantha, on the other hand, is a right pain.' The van started to reverse. Adele and Samantha looked up, spotted the van, and turned and ran. Alison, Cath, and Simon, one of the male officers, jumped out of the van and ran after them. The nobs of Park Lane scattered at this unseemly sight. Despite the high heels, the toms managed to escape. 'They'll be back,' said Alison, puffing a lot. 'We'll catch up with them later.' Alison got her breath back. 'Normally we wear tee shirts, jeans and trainers just like the men, it makes running after the toms that bit easier. But sometimes like tonight we wear normal uniform. We never dress up as toms, that would be entrapment, but we've still been propositioned whilst we've been carrying out surveillance work dressed in our jeans and tee shirts. That just shows how bad some of these areas are.'

7

We set off round the block. I was out on patrol with the 'B' team of the Street Offences section of the Vice Squad. The Vice Squad, or to give it its proper name, the Central Area Clubs and Vice Office, is responsible for gaming and licensing of casinos in Central London, obscene publications, brothels, hostess clubs, and the never ending stream of common prostitutes plying their trade on the streets of the capital. 'The whole spectrum of vice,' Chief Superintendent McBride, the head of The Vice Squad, had explained to me earlier that evening. 'From dealing with new building work in casinos to seizing obscene videos, that's the breadth of our job.'

'What's the biggest vice problem in Central London?' I had enquired. There was a long pause. 'Now, you're asking,' said Superintendent McBride. 'Some would say, I suppose, the drug problem in night clubs. Others would go for the hard-core porn that comes into the country, especially the kiddie porn or the heavy sado-masochistic stuff because of its likely effect on some people. It's not that pleasant to watch a vagina being sewn up in glorious colour. But I suppose if you asked an ordinary member of the public who lives in Paddington or tries to go for a meal in Shepherd's Market, they'd say the biggest problem was prostitution. There's a huge amount of inconvenience caused by all these girls actually working on the street. And worse than inconvenience. It means really that these are no-go areas for ordinary respectable girls, because any normal girl has a fair chance of being approached by a kerb crawler in these areas. We can never hope to eradicate the problem, of course. The best that we can hope for is to control it somehow, or if you're being slightly more cynical to displace it from one area to another. Soho, for example, has improved greatly over the past few years. Westminster Council have been marvellous in this respect in terms of their policy towards the licensing of sex establishments. The number of girls working the streets in Soho has also dropped dramatically. But, of course, you could say that they've just moved elsewhere.

'The girls still working in Soho, by the way, are often "clippers". They're different from ordinary prostitutes – they take your money and they don't do the business! They say that they need a hundred quid to book the room or whatever, they take your hundred quid and you don't see them again. Sometimes with a really gullible punter their friend will then turn up and say that the first girl has run into a spot of trouble, but that they can have sex with them instead, but they'll need a further hundred quid as deposit, and then they scarper as well. It's a service reserved almost exclusively for tourists. Older toms sometimes get into it, when they recognize that it's an even easier way to make money. We have to try to control this as well as ordinary prostitution. We have sixty-six members of the Vice Squad, including myself, to deal with the whole spectrum of vice, and twenty-four members of the Street Offences Squad, which deals with street prostitution and street brothels. Not a lot of manpower for such a big problem. Five of the constables in the Street Offences Squad are women, by the way.'

Two of the women, Alison and Cath, were out that night with the 'B' team of the Street Offences Squad, or the 'tom squad', as they prefer to call it. That night they weren't interested in the clippers of Soho. It was the more abundant common prostitutes of Park Lane and Paddington that they were after. Alison explained the critical differences between the girls working in these two areas. 'Park Lane has the up-market toms, the Paddington girls are very much the dross. A Paddington girl will charge fifteen to twenty quid for a hand shandy, you know a hand job with a condom of course, and perhaps twenty-five for a blow job. In Park Lane prices start at around fifty quid for a hand shandy, then it's up to sixty-five for a blow job, and £150–£200 for the full works. Some of them can even manage three punters in an hour. Not surprisingly, the girls in Park Lane can make a packet. Another important difference between the girls working the two areas is that girls working the Paddington area get taken to Paddington Green Police Station and ultimately to Marylebone Magistrates' Court, where the average fine is £75 plus costs. Girls from Park Lane, on the other hand, usually end up in West End Central Police Station then Marlborough Street Magistrates' Court with average fines of £25 plus costs. The high-class toms have it a lot easier than the rest. Some of the girls working Park Lane can pick up £800 a night,' she added somewhat wistfully.

I had to ask Alison at this point how much she was earning a year. '£13,000 a year, and it's almost permanent nights,' she replied. 'We work seven nights then four days, then five nights and three days in a rota. On days we often carry out surveillance work on the telephone boxes where the girls' numbers are stuck up – you know, "Half Hour of Hell with Madame Pain", ring this number. Anyone caught sticking these numbers up gets done for criminal damage. The hours we work can interfere with social life quite a bit. I suppose some of the girls that we arrest must think that we're crazy doing what we do for the money we earn, but that's life, I suppose. The girls working Park Lane and Shepherd's Market tell us as much. We can chat to them. But the girls in the Paddington area are very different to this. There are girls with AIDS still working on the streets in Paddington. Loads of them are druggies. Their ponces have them on the streets working for the money to support their habit.' Cath interrupted – 'Last winter I was bitten by one of the girls working Paddington, when we tried to arrest her. I knew that she was HIV positive. It was just as well that it was the winter time because I had a lot of layers on. She didn't quite manage to bite through them all. I dread what would have happened if this had taken place on a warm night like tonight. We always wear gloves when we search the girls from Paddington, you have to be very careful.' 'Last week we arrested another tom who's HIV positive in Sussex Gardens in the Paddington area, and she cut her wrists right in front of us and started flicking the blood at us warning us not to go near her. She's really violent. We had to handcuff her in the end,' said Alison.

The unmarked van now made its way through the very narrow streets of Shepherd's Market. The driver, Sergeant Terry Falcao, a lightly built officer whose parents come from Goa, skilfully edged the van between the Corniches and the Porsches. A lot of the women at the pavement cafes and restaurants wore hats, having spent the day at Ascot. The men wore deep tans and Rolexes. Cath hummed 'Summertime, and the living is easy', unselfconsciously, and without deliberately trying to be funny. She then started to wrestle the young male constable, Simon, beside her. 'I feel a bit better for having got that little bit of violence out of my system.' Alison just laughed – 'they call me the gentle giant, I'm much bigger than Cath, I'm five foot eight, and she's only five five, but she's a lot tougher than me. She's a year older than me as well, but she looks about sixteen. If she takes hold of a suspect, though, she just doesn't let go, no matter what.' Simon nodded – 'I can vouch for that.'

Cath rather suddenly stopped singing and started pointing and shouting – 'On the right!' All eyes shot out to the right side of the vehicle. The vehicle, however, mysteriously veered towards the left. 'That's left, she's on the right.' And we could just about see the back of a pair of high heels turn the corner. The van roared around the block.

'But I didn't see that girl soliciting', I protested. 'She's a known common prostitute,' said Cath. 'She was loitering for prostitution, what else do you think she was doing out here? We can arrest a tom once we see her loitering if she's had two cautions in the past year for either loitering for the purposes of prostitution or for soliciting, or if she's been convicted in the past year as a common prostitute.' The van roared several times around the block, but she had mysteriously disappeared. 'I think that it was Barbara from Huddersfield,' said Cath. 'She's in my little book.' 'But how could you tell from just a rear view, from the merest glimpse of high heels as they made off into the distance?' I asked. 'Don't worry, we get to know them very well during our six months with vice, and them us. Some of them even claim that they can tell the engine noise of both of our two unmarked vans. They scamper off as soon as they hear them without even looking up.'

'Do you ever make mistakes?' I asked. 'Hardly ever,' said Alison. 'Sometimes,' said Simon simultaneously. They both laughed. 'What about that night we saw this woman standing in the street in Shepherd's Market all tarted up, and she turned out to be the chairperson of the local housing association, and I was just about to give her a caution. That could have been a little bit embarrassing.' 'You see the beauty of it is,' said Alison, 'if it is just a normal girl, when you have a word with her she'll leave the area. Only if she's a tom, will she still continue to hang about. And you have to give two cautions before you arrest them.'

We drove back to Shepherd's Market. A beautiful black girl in a very tight black dress stood at the edge of the pavement. 'That's Sandra,' said Alison. Alison waved out at her, and Sandra waved back. 'She's such a nice girl, I don't know why she's a tom. We arrested her last night.' They drove up to her. 'What are you doing, Sandra?' 'I'm waiting for a taxi, honest to God,' she replied. 'Well make sure you get the next one. Go home!' said Alison. And we drove on. Just around the corner, we came across this young girl with bleached blond hair. She was accompanied by an old Middle Eastern man in a brown sports jacket and brown trousers. Terry, the driver, pointed their way. 'She was standing by that telephone box outside the Hilton earlier. They don't exactly look right together. Does anyone know her? No? We'll stop them anyway.'

Cath took the girl to one side of the pavement, Simon kept her male escort on the other side. Cath went through the contents of her handbag. Alison was just about to explain to me exactly what Cath was

11

looking for, when her face suddenly erupted in a smile. 'Eureka! See what Cath's come up with – a bumper packet of condoms – a twelve pack. If she was just going out with her boyfriend, she wouldn't need that many. We find packs of thirty in their bags sometimes – industrial packs we call them. Cath will just do her Aunty Cath bit and give her a good talking to. Then she'll give her a caution, and tell her to clear off.' And sure enough a few minutes later the girl strode off. Her escort hurried off in the opposite direction. 'He claimed that he was an Egyptian diplomat,' said Simon when he got back into the van. 'No, I didn't check. But I think that being stopped will probably cool his ardour for the night anyway.'

We drove back along our well-worn circuit, back towards Park Lane, watching every single girl or pair of girls and every couple to check their level of incongruity. I was trying to be helpful and pointed towards a very incongruous couple going into the Hilton. She was about half his age and easily twice his size. I say easily because his seventy or so years had almost bent him double, which diminished his stature even further. But the Vice Squad were not impressed by my observations. 'She's not a tom, she's just bloody clever,' somebody said. I then pointed to this very tarty looking girl walking down the street arm-in-arm with some guy. 'What about her?' I eagerly suggested. 'That, by the way, is a transvestite,' explained Alison. 'He's called the best bum in Shepherds Market. He may importune but he can't solicit or loiter for the purposes of prostitution.' We left the best bum in Shepherd's Market alone that night.

The streets are very narrow around Shepherd's Market, and we soon drove into something of a traffic jam with a Saab blocking the path of our van. Rather unfortunately, as it turned out for the driver of the Saab. Simon had time to scrutinize the woman in the front seat. 'Well, well, well, that's Joanna Wickham in that car.' A little too late Joanna recognized our van. It was Simon's turn to interview the driver. Simon came back smiling. 'The driver said that she just jumped into his car. He claims that he was just driving home. I had to point out that this was slightly out of his way, about ten miles out of his way to be exact. He's acutely embarrassed by the way. Joanna didn't look too pleased either tonight. We've just cost her a few quid. He's had a verbal warning for kerbcrawling and he may get a letter to his home saying just that. He'll have some explaining to do to his wife then.'

I discovered that a man can be done for kerbcrawling, if he is simply accompanying a known common prostitute. The man in the Saab seemed equally surprised by the news.

The first arrest of the night followed soon after this. Again we were heading round the back of the Hilton. 'The Hilton car park is a great place for toms, there's so many places to hide,' explained Cath. Alison was the first to spot the tom who had forgotten to hide. The van pulled over towards this lone solitary figure. The girl on the pavement with the bright blond hair and the tight black dress just smiled vacantly. The door of the van was opened for her. She climbed in, with considerable difficulty because her dress was so tight. She laughed as she got into the back. 'My hair always gives me away. I just didn't see you coming tonight, but I bet you could see me a mile off. God, it's sweltering in this van.' Alison greeted her like an old friend. 'Remember the time, Deborah, you hid behind that wall in the Hilton car park with another tom, and all I could see was your hair sticking up. I knew it was you right away, it's such a lovely colour. How's it been tonight?'

'Well, I were really worried before you came along,' said Deborah. 'This big black man passed me a short while ago, and I thought that I were going to be mugged. I were really clinging on to my handbag. I were really frightened. I were almost relieved to get arrested tonight. I'd be quite pleased really, if it wasn't so bloody hot in the cruiser.' I could tell by Deborah's dialect that she was from Yorkshire. She was not, however, prepared to answer any questions about her background. 'My mum would have a heart attack if she knew what I were doing down here.' We drove back to West End Central Police Station. The charge room was very busy, although Deborah appeared to be the only tom who had been brought in. Most of those who had been arrested eyed her up. She had looked better out on the street. Alison filled in the charge sheet. 'How much do you weigh, Deborah?' asked Alison. Deborah grimaced. 'Eleven stone, would you believe it? If you look at my first charge sheet, I was nine and a half stone. I've put on a bit of weight in the last few years.' 'Do you want me to be kind?' asked Alison. 'I'll put ten and a half stone down on the form.' A sergeant arrived to charge Deborah formally . He asked all of his questions in a mock-Shakespearian style. It was probably as much a result of the repetitive nature of the routine, as because he had an audience that particular night. 'Do you know this lady to be a common prostitute?' he asked of the arresting officer. 'Not that common, thank you very much,' interrupted Deborah. Deborah was most concerned as to whether her court appearance would be fixed for the following day, when a tube strike was scheduled, or the day after that. The sergeant agreed to put her on the court schedule for the day after the strike. They chatted away like old friends. Most prostitutes get arrested three times a week, it really is an integral part of the job.

'It's a pleasure doing business with you,' said the station sergeant. Deborah tried to break the monotony by being provocative. 'Why can't we just pay the fines at the station? That's what I want to know,' said Deborah as she was preparing to leave. 'Without all the messing about of having to go to court. Some people say that prostitution should be legalized so that the government could tax us. But they get their tax anyway through the fines. It's probably more efficient at the moment. How else would they do it, have a little tax man in the room with the girls counting all the comings and goings. I just wish that we could pay the fines here to save a lot of bother.'

Deborah was escorted out. It had taken two constables about forty-five minutes to do all the paperwork for Deborah's arrest. 'See you all soon,' shouted Deborah jauntily as she left. All the PCs waved back rather wearily.

It had been a long night and it was far from over. 'It's time for refs,' said Alison. We made our way up to the empty station canteen for refreshments. It was 12.30 am. Alison settled for a cold sausage roll and a blackcurrant drink, Cath had a cup of tea. This was the natural dip in the night's activity. It was a good time for some questions. 'Why the police as a career?' I asked. Alison, it turns out, had wanted to be a WPC since she was twelve. 'My brother's a prison officer, and that may have had something to do with it. It's still a man's world in the police and you have to be twice as good as the average male PC to be accepted. I always knew this but I still wanted to join.' Nevertheless, she had started working as a clerical officer in the DHSS when she was seventeen. 'Why Vice of all things?' I asked. 'Basically because you're left on your own a lot and you can use your own initiative. I like that way of working.'

Cath had started her working life in the bakery department of Tesco's. She, too, had worked as a clerical officer for the DHSS, but not in the same office as Alison. Originally she had been rejected as too short for the police, but the height restrictions were changed. 'It's stupid anyway,' said Alison joining in, 'because the bigger you are the more likely a bloke is to take a crack at you. I've had my ankle broken by a bloke I was arresting when he tried to do a runner. He also gave me a smack in the eye. He probably thought I was fair game because of my size. He was eventually caught and charged with GBH. He got eighty hours community service for it, which makes you a little sick.' Unlike Alison, Cath never really intended to get into Vice. She had been working very happily from Bow Street Station on a community unit in Covent Garden, when a request went out for some volunteers for the Vice squad. Unfortunately, she was off that day, and so she was nominated. 'But funnily enough, I really quite enjoyed it, and I've put in for a further six months on vice, and I've got it as well,' said Cath. 'There's no particular training for this job. You just pick it up as you go along. I picked it up very quickly.'

'What about its effects on your social life?' I asked. Both said that the worst aspect of the work for social life was the hours. 'You end up hanging about with guys from the Force,' said Alison. 'The Vice Squad does, however, make you emotionally hard and a little bit cynical about human nature, but you could say that about all police work. It does change you, believe me, and makes relationships with people who haven't been through all this that bit more difficult. Anyway, we're both young, free and single at the moment.'

It was time to leave the empty staff canteen. The van now headed for Paddington, and the down-market side of the business. The banter in the van seemed to stop. Talk now turned to the working girls and their motives. 'I don't know how they can do it,' said Alison. 'Most of them will take home a lot more than the money. There are still girls working Paddington who will do it without a durex – only because, of course, they've got all the diseases already.' 'And imagine standing about in winter,' said Cathy, 'with just a short skirt and some skimpy clothes on waiting for some old bloke to come along. It gives a new meaning to the term "frozen assets".' And everyone laughed, but the constant humour was starting to feel a little forced. 'Toms end up in a right mess, with their ponces and all the rest of it,' said Alison. 'You know, I've never met one nice ponce, they're nearly all nasty bastards. We arrested one tom last week and she had nine inch bruises all over her body where her ponce had beaten her up with a scaffolding bar. The week before, we arrested one tom who had all

15

her teeth knocked out by her ponce and he had kept her locked up in a cupboard all weekend. He took her out once, just the once, and that was to rape her, and one of the other toms that worked for him actually held her down. I can't understand the mentality of these people. You hear the toms boasting about which ponce is looking after them, and the ponces treat them like shit. You feel sorry for some of the toms though. Their ponces persuade them to come down from Birmingham or wherever, and then they get them working on the streets. The ponces take all the money and leave them sometimes with a tenner for a hotel room. Most of the girls are absolutely terrified of the ponces. One thing that I've learned is that ponces never make idle threats. Since I've been working for the Vice Squad we haven't had a tom killed, at least not by a ponce, but we've had everything up to that. We arrested one sixteen-year-old ponce last week. The girls who worked for him were much older than him, but still terrified of him.'

I asked what this ponce was like. Simon leant over from the front seat. 'To be absolutely frank, he was a right horrible little shit bag, believe me. He had a string of previous convictions – for robbery, GBH, you name it. One girl who was working for him had just had an abortion, and was feeling a little tender. So what did this little shit head do? Boot her between the legs, that's what. He threatened to set fire to one of the other girls. A right little charmer.'

A certain gloom was setting in, as we cruised towards Paddington. Suddenly a call came on the radio informing us of an attempted burglary in the area. A white male carrying a crowbar was seen running away from the scene. Our van roared off in pursuit. 'Try Paddington station,' cried Alison. The van, with no identifying features to tell other motorists that this was indeed a police van, and with no siren or warning lights, shot across the oncoming traffic. I closed my eyes. 'Miami Vice' was never like this. A riot shield in the back of the van clanked up against the side of the vehicle. Alison was thrown off the back seat. Eventually, we got to Paddington Station. We raced across the concourse. There was no sign of the man with the crowbar. Simon checked the toilet. He didn't find anyone with a crowbar, what he found instead was a young smartly dressed man in his mid-twenties with a carrier bag. He appeared to be loitering down there. The young man left after a few minutes. We made our way back to the van and drove off. A hundred yards further along, the van pulled into the side of the road above the station. Simon told us to keep watching the man with the carrier bag. And sure enough, the man with the carrier bag walked in a great loop, and then started to make his way back to the toilets, as if drawn by some invisible force. 'I find it bloody horrible,' said Alison. 'We catch them at it all the time. You see two pairs of legs in the same toilet and you know what's going on.' Simon headed back to the station. The man with the carrier bag didn't look that surprised. He admitted that he had been importuning, gave Simon his address in Surrey, and then he started to cry. He begged Simon not to report him, in between great sobs.

We left him crying on the station platform. We drove off. The banter in the van, and the incessant humour, had now dried up. Alison soon spotted another girl whom she recognized. The girl looked about fifteen, she was standing on the edge of the pavement chatting to a black youth in an Adidas tracksuit with a cap saying 'New York' perched jauntily on his head. The black youth was well known to the squad, apparently he spends a lot of his time hanging around prostitutes, and he had been previously picked up on a drugs charge. We pulled up beside them. Sergeant Falcao threatened to do him for kerbcrawling. 'Don't make me laugh,' said the youth as he adjusted and readjusted the cap on his head. 'I know the score.' And just to show that he did indeed know the score and wasn't intimidated in the slightest by the police, he started speaking more forcefully to the sergeant and he began to jab the narrow buffer of air between them with his finger as he spoke. Cath talked to the young girl. Suddenly, a passer-by ran up. 'Are you the law? Well then, you might just like to know that someone's just taken a shot at me from that window over there. I think it was an air gun, but I'm not sure. I'm not hanging about to find out.' He hurried off. I thought that I noticed the merest hint of a smile from the black youth. He was just told to go home. The van roared around the block, but the shooting, if indeed it had been shooting, had stopped. Sergeant Falcao shook his head. 'We haven't time to hang around here to find out.' We were back patrolling the streets.

A few streets further on, Alison recognized another tom, a black girl called Barbara talking to a black guy in a blue sweatshirt on a street corner. The van pulled up. The black girl cursed. Cath went to interview the girl, Simon the guy. Alison was relieved that it wasn't her turn. 'She's a right nutter,' said Alison. 'She's a drug addict with a big heroin problem. Last week she was arrested and she bit the arresting officer, and dug her nails right into him. Just look at her hands, she's got big open sores all over them. She picks at those sores when she's high. Normally when she works she wears long lace gloves. She must have forgotten them tonight. Can you imagine any punter wanting to be touched with those hands?' Barbara was just told to go home. Sergeant Falcao then called another unmarked police car up to stop and search the black guy. He thought that this guy might well be Barbara's drug connection, but he wanted him to think that any search was unconnected with the interview with the tom. 'To save her a beating,' explained Alison.

We made off around the corner only to be immediately confronted with the sight of a white girl with long dark hair reeling across the pavement. She looked drunk. She was shouting somewhat incoherently up at an open window. When she turned around, I could see that she had a large tattoo of a cobweb covering one side of her face. The van slowed, and Cath tried to get out, but unfortunately the driver decided to park some distance off. Cath nearly had a rather unfortunate accident right in front of the girl. The girl with the cobweb on her face, however, seemed totally oblivious. 'She needs a fix,' explained Alison. 'She's a tom and a heroin addict. She had a baby last year, and it was born an addict. Not the best start in life.' Alison's discourse was disturbed by the screaming of the girl with the cobweb on her face. She was wailing that she wanted to kill herself. Cath tried to calm her down. 'Have you had a fix lately?' she asked. 'No, that's the bloody problem.' 'Go home,' said Cath. And slowly and very painfully, the girl with the tattoo wobbled off. This time, it wasn't just the high heels that were making her gait unsteady.

We left the horrors of Paddington, and started to make our way back to Park Lane. The squad were still determined to catch Adele and Samantha. As we turned towards the Hilton, we spotted two other toms instead. Sharon from Derby was arrested, and her friend, Andrea, who wasn't known to the squad, collected her first caution. 'How many of these can I get before I'm nicked,' shouted Andrea after us. Nobody could be bothered to answer her. Sharon explained that she was an away-day girl. She was aiming to return to Derby that night on the Inter-city. Sergeant Falcao said that he thought this was unlikely, because there was a warrant out for her because she had failed to turn up at court a few weeks previously. Sharon said that this was a load of cobblers. 'I've had a bad night, and you're trying to make it worse. I've only made fifty quid so far, last night I made £330. I got £200 from one trick last night, from this businessman from what do you call it? . . . Dutchland.' I suggested 'Holland'. Sharon smoked and chatted away to the team all the way back to the station, just like old friends. When I found myself alone with Sharon, I asked her what she really thought of the squad. 'Some of them are alright but most of them are real bastards.' 'And the WPCs?' I asked. 'They can be the worst of all sometimes because they can really look down their noses at you because of what you do. I couldn't care a monkey's myself.' Sergeant Falcao returned, he had managed to trace the warrant. Sharon was told that she would have to spend the night in the cells. She just shrugged her shoulders – '*C'est la vie*', she said, trying to show us all what a cultured lady she really was.

'*C'est la vie*, as they said in Frenchieland, eh Sandra?' I suggested. Sandra didn't get the joke.

It was about 2.00 am. The squad would probably be on the street that night for a further two hours, because there were still so many toms about. Cath had a court appearance at 10.00 am the following morning. 'It's the hot weather,' explained Cath. 'They probably can't sleep, so they try to do a bit of overtime.' The squad trudged wearily back to the van. I left them and made my own way across central London. I spotted Adele and Samantha back outside the Hilton, and could only smile to myself as a black BMW pulled up beside them.

A *brief* encounter

She had the longest legs I've ever seen. The short black leather dress showed them off to perfection, the stockings were sheer and black. She knew how to dress to get a certain kind of attention. The legs went on for ever. The bouncer noticed them too. He was deaf and dumb. He mouthed something, and made a face. It reminded me of the face that Les Dawson always puts on when he meets a pretty girl. The face is all contorted, the mouth squeezed and protruding. With a single contortion of his mouth, he was trying to indicate that this girl had legs that went right up to her arm pits, and that he would not mind finding himself between them. It was a difficult enough pair of concepts for one facial contortion.

But she was a dream – about five foot eleven, long black wavy hair, and those legs. The man she was with seemed very plain in comparison – a smart grey suit, probably in his late twenties. But noticeably plain, noticeably ordinary beside her. He had just started chatting her up. The five pints of lager had persuaded him that he might just have a chance. He had just commented on her legs – he reasoned that it was a make or break kind of a night. He might get lucky, he might get his face slapped. What the hell! He had taken another gulp of his lager and jumped right in there. She had thanked him for his compliment. Thanked him! He stayed on the same track. 'Are you a model, then? You've certainly got the body for it.' She was flattered again. Every so often she tossed her long black hair, and straightened her skirt – to make sure that it was not riding up too far. It was already indecent enough. The deaf and dumb bouncer came along for another look. He made that Les Dawson facial expression again, this time accompanied by a certain hand and arm gesture. He wanted to break the message down this time into its component parts, to make sure that it was all understood. The tall girl noticed the arm gesture as well. She seemed pleased. That was the strange thing. She seemed easy to please. The man in the grey suit went off for two halves of lager. The tall girl eyed herself in the full length mirrors on the walls of the club. Two youngish men made their way out of the club – they'd had a disappointing night, they hadn't got one on, they hadn't even had a tickle all night. They were keen fishers of women, you see. The one on the right made some comment to her as he passed, his mate squeezed her ass. She smiled. Smiled? The deaf and dumb bouncer looked confused. She was too easy, far too easy. He looked my way and mouthed 'pro'. But I could see the question mark in his eyes. He knew all the girls from the escort agencies, all the girls from the massage parlours, all the good-time girls, and yet he didn't know her.

The man with the lager had returned. She sipped it delicately. It gave the man in the grey suit a chance to examine her breasts. He liked what he saw. He turned his back to the wall, and she leaned towards him. That way he could see over her shoulder and watch her ass from the rear. He had gone fishing here before, but he had never netted such a 'big un'. He seemed quite overcome with lust. But then he noticed her hands, as they moved towards his hair. They were very large. He commented on this – fairly loudly. Loud enough for people to hear, that is to say, loud enough for people who were already interested in the couple to hear. The deaf and dumb bouncer even managed to read his lips. The bouncer studied the hands as well. They were very large, but not just large, they were thick and veiny as well. The veiny hands played with the split ends of the man in the grey suit's hair. The man in the grey suit seemed to like the way that it felt.

It was the deaf and dumb bouncer who decided that this sensual apparition was not all that it seemed. 'It's a man,' he mouthed. He called one of his colleagues over, his friend told him not to be so daft. They called the owner of the club over for a second opinion. The three of them stood in a row debating the issue, trying to reach some conclusion. They started arguing about it. The owner went for a closer look. He came back smiling. 'It's a bird. Just look at the throat – no Adam's apple.' But I glanced in the mirror on the wall of the club and saw that I hadn't much of an Adam's apple either, neither did the club owner, for that matter. But it was temporarily irrelevant, this piece of evidence was now concealed as the man in the grey suit kissed his beautiful companion. Four feet away stood the owner of the club and two bouncers watching every sideways shift of the mouth, every lip movement, every tongue protrusion for some further evidence – one way or the other. Only one bouncer thought to look at the contented face of the man in the grey suit. 'Well he seems satisfied enough,' he added somewhat unnecessarily. But the look wasn't so much one of satisfaction, as one of bemusement. But was his look attributable to the fact that he had never been so lucky before? Or something else. His left hand started to explore the nether regions of the black leather mini-skirt. The owner of the club was convinced by this latter action. 'You're not telling me,' he said in his best man-of-the-people accent, 'that this bloke can't tell the difference. That bloke has been in here before. I can vouch for him. If it was a bloke he was kissing, he'd have realized before now. For God's sake, how long does it take before you can tell?'

There was a long pause, only filled by the frantic mouth activity of the couple a few feet away. When it had ended, the deaf and dumb bouncer again mouthed, 'It's a man.'

The space between the courting couple and the mirror had been filled by two girls. They had emerged from the ladies' toilet, and their attention had been drawn to the couple, only because the female was significantly taller than the man. The girl was pushing her head down into the man's. It was a sight which would attract your attention, it looked sort of passionate. When the girl had surfaced for air, however, their interest had changed. 'That's a bloke there – dressed up. Look at the jaw on him. That's a transvestite. I think it's bloody disgusting. Somebody should tell that poor bloke that's kissing him.' 'You're only jealous because you haven't scored,' said her friend, and then they both laughed. 'What are we doing wrong, if blokes can score in here with ordinary, normal fellas, and we bloody well can't?'

They raised their voices a little more. They were going to put the tall female in the black leather mini-skirt to a critical test. Trial by water. Their loud talk was going to douse the passion of the two in front of them. If she came over and thumped them then she really was an ordinary female angered by their ridiculous comments. Or alternatively she was an aggressive male who had thought through this bit already. But they nevertheless proceeded to pour their scornful comments all over the courting couple. It was a modern form of witch-hunting.

But neither of the courting couple moved, except against each other, and more and more passionately at that. 'I think it's bloody disgusting,' said the taller of the two females in the green dress again. 'That poor bloke doesn't have a clue. I think that he must be pissed out of his brain.' 'I'm going to do something about it,' said her friend. She was wearing a black dress and was showing a little cleavage. She tugged it downwards, so that she was showing a little more cleavage. 'That should do the trick,' she said in a certain self-satisfied manner.

The courting couple had started to walk hand-in-hand towards the dance floor and past the pair of females. The tall female in the leather dress walked first. As her companion passed the pair of females, the one with the readjusted cleavage leaned forward and touched the man. 'Excuse me, did I go to school with you?' The man in the grey suit shook his head. 'Are you sure, you don't remember me? I was the spotty one in the fourth form.' He shook his head again. She was clearly having no success, so she came straight out with it. 'That's a fella you're with, you know that, don't you? You're kissing a fella.' But the man in the grey suit just squeezed his companion's hand, and walked on towards the dance floor. Strangely, he didn't reply to the accusation. Perhaps, he thought that it was just too ludicrous – just the bitchy comments of a spotty schoolgirl grown up and still not having much luck. The girl with the readjusted cleavage just started to squeal – 'Ugh, I think that it's bloody disgusting. I think the management should do something about it.'

But the owner of the club still wasn't convinced. 'What does she want me to do? Stick my hand up her skirt, like Crocodile Dundee? I know a girl who wears size eleven in shoes, and she's got the hands to go with it. What does that prove?' He then went and explained to the deaf-and-dumb bouncer about the absence of an Adam's apple. He needed to use a good deal of sign language. But the message got through eventually, and a potential crisis was averted. This was a club founded on the principle of good old-fashioned, red-blooded activity after all. A cattle market perhaps, but nothing perverted.

The courting couple danced and retired to one of those dark private corners that all nightclubs have. The bouncer went back to making his Les Dawson mouth contortions. He fancied the tall bird again. Even the girl in the black dress admitted that she had probably been wrong, as she pressed up against some fella on the dance floor. She was having more luck at last. 'We've all learned a valuable lesson,' said the owner of the club in his man-of-the-people philosopher's style – 'don't jump to hasty conclusions. I was right again. It just proves that you should weigh up all the evidence, before you make any decision.'

Later that night, I saw the girl in the leather mini skirt leaving the club, quite alone. The smile which seemed to have been pasted to her lips all that evening had disappeared. I also saw the man in the grey suit being sick in the empty toilet a few minutes later. But then again, I've got no stomach for lager either.

★ 2 ★
Getting on your bike

The Commuters

It was the middle of the night. A quarter past three to be exact, in a village called Holton le Clay, just outside Grimsby. The snow was falling heavily and the wind from the North Sea whipped it right across the road. It was a very good night for snow drifts, but very little else. Dave Cowley opened the front door of his little semi, the wind blasted him in the face. 'Bloody hell,' he said. He'd left his wife wrapped up in bed, in the middle of her eight-hour sleep cycle. He was in the middle of his sleep cycle as well, and that was why it felt distinctly odd to be up and about. He pushed out through the blizzard, and into his mini-van. The temperature was way below freezing. Luckily the van started first time. But the snow was starting to lie. 'That's all I bloody need,' he said, as he roared off, 'I'll have to push it a bit now with this bad weather, or I'll get caught up in the traffic, as I get near London.'

His housing estate was asleep, Holton le Clay was asleep, all of Grimsby was asleep. Nothing at all stirred. 'That's the bloody problem basically, it's dead up here now. The fishing industry's been killed off, and Grimsby was the fishing industry. Don't ask me why it died, that's political, and I'm not into politics, especially at this time of the bloody morning. But I've always been one of those that got on their bike basically. Just as well really.'

Dave made his way through the town, and into a cul-de-sac with more warm semis. There was one light on in the whole street. 'That'll be George,' he said. Dave pulled up. There was a slight delay as George made his way slowly through the blizzard and loaded his gear into the back of the van, between the portable bed and the empty buckets. 'The bed's in the back in case I can't find anywhere to kip tonight,' said Dave. 'I'm moving on to a new site today in Mansell Street near Tower Bridge. I haven't got any digs lined up yet.'

George got into the van beside him, he was bleary-eyed and shivering. He wrapped himself in his donkey jacket. 'Wake me when I get to London,' he said. George was fifty-five years old, 'and I feel it, I'm getting too old for this bloody game.' This game being commuting from Grimsby to London for work on a building site. Dave and George were both crane operators for the 'Expanded Piling Company' of Grimsby. George had been commuting like this on and off since 1957, Dave since 1971. 'But there's been one big change in the past five years,' said Dave. 'There's more blokes having to do it now. You'll see when we get on to the A1. You used to be able to do the 180 miles in two hours, but now the traffic is terrible near London. It takes nearer four hours now. You have to leave earlier and earlier to get there on time. It's dead in the North, that's the basic reason.'

'When I started out,' explained George 'you used to go down for a month or six weeks at a time. I never saw my kids grow up. I prefer coming home for weekends, but all this travelling is very hard on you. It's worse when you're travelling on your own though. This morning we're going in convoy with a couple of lads from Hull – they had to leave home at half two this morning.'

And sure enough, through the blizzard you could just about make out the other little 'Expanded Piling Company' van, with the snow settling in layers on its roof. Dave screwed his eyes up even tighter to try to see the van through the snow on the windscreen. 'And the worst thing is that with this weather we're gong to have to push it all the way there,' he said.

Dave was thirty-eight, but he looked in fact much older. He had been getting on his bike for the past seventeen years. He did it, he said, for the job security. It cost him his first marriage. 'She found somebody else while I was away. But she wasn't a patch on Sheila, my second wife anyway. Sheila is more independent, she needs to be. She understands why I have to work away. Most building sites, you see, operate on a hire and fire basis. One week you've got a job, the next you're out. With this company, you've got a bit of security.'

For a basic week of 50 hours, Dave took home around £200. 'But the hours can stretch a bit. I've had to work a 20-hour day before now, and once I had to work 27 hours on the trot. It can be risky work mind. One time my crane nearly tipped over on the Cenotaph, it's risky enough even without these long hours. But I've made as much as £400 in one week, absolutely fantastic wages by Grimsby standards, so I can't really complain. But you don't get money like that every week.'

With wages like that, he had been able to buy a three-bedroom semi in Holton le Clay for around £32,000. 'You'd get nothing in London for that kind of money,' he said, 'and don't forget within a few miles of my house I've got both countryside and seaside – Cleethorpes is only six miles away. I wouldn't swap it for the world. But,' he added after a moment's contemplation, 'the sea is a bit shitty around here, and to be honest if it wasn't for the people from Sheffield and Rotherham, no-one would come to Cleethorpes for their holiday. I only go there for some decent fish and chips. But I'd never move to London. It's a horrible place, it's too fast and too expensive. I'm a big bloke, but when I go down the street, everybody's flying past me.' George stirred for a second and said 'the people are all like ants, the way they pour out of the tube stations and that. Just like ants.' He curled up again, and his eyes closed – 'five days a week in London is plenty, believe me.' Dave took over again, 'but that's where the money is basically. If I'd bought a house in London when I first started working there, I'd be one of them now, I suppose – the rich. But I've left it a bit late. For me it's up and down this bloody road, week-in, week-out.' Dave squinted even harder at the windscreen, trying to follow the white line in the centre as it wound its way through the sleeping Lincolnshire countryside.

'The main problem with this job,' said Dave, 'is the travelling. I've had a few scrapes already. In 1976 I was off work for a year when I broke my spine in an accident on black ice. I was in hospital for four months. The bloke who found me just said, "I thought you were dead mate." I said, "Well, I'm bloody well not." I've never been so happy in my life to see the inside of a hospital. In '84 on the way back from London I went straight into a woman doing a three-point turn right in the middle of the road. There was a three-tier wedding cake in the back of her car, after the smash it was just a trifle.' He guffawed with laughter, but George didn't stir. 'But luckily she wasn't hurt. Six weeks after that I rolled my car right over a hedge and into the grounds of a detention centre. My son Jason was beside me and he fell out of the car, luckily he wasn't hurt. There wasn't a straight panel on the side of the car though. I'd just bought it as well, but I hadn't got round to insuring it yet. It's just the law of averages though. You're bound to have a smash going up and down this road all the time. I think I've been pretty lucky so far. One of my best pals was killed a few months ago, I guess his luck just ran out. I've worked out a few ways of keeping myself awake on the drive – I'll sing at the top of my voice, or talk to myself. Who cares if people think I'm a nutter. Sometimes I have a shave when I'm driving, with an electric razor. I don't shave all week when I'm down in London. So when you start pulling your beard off with this thing, it keeps you awake alright. At times I'll drive really daft to keep myself awake. There's nothing more boring than driving slowly.'

The blizzard stopped rather abruptly, as we headed toward the A1. The road was dry now as Dave started to accelerate. I couldn't stop thinking about his sojourn in hospital, as we started to drive faster and faster.

'It's not a bad life,' said Dave. 'In addition to your wages, you get £12.36 a day subsistence allowance. That's not bad – it's a quid over what most firms pay. You can usually get a bed-and-breakfast for around £14 a day in London in the Kings Cross area. The only problem is that we're out in the morning before breakfast and back in the evening after tea. We get fish and chips most nights, or a kebab. We live on that kind of food. Nearly everyone prefers working out of London, up in Morecambe you can get bed and breakfast and an evening meal for £8, which is very reasonable.' 'And a cup of tea for 15 pence,' added George. 'In London it sets you back about 25 pence.' George shut his eyes again. 'The only problem is,' continued Dave, 'all the work is down in London. They're always pulling office blocks down and putting up new ones. I've built all sorts – the Lloyds bank building – that's a real space oddity, the extension to the Covent Garden Opera House. I've even drilled a hole in the House of Commons car park. I don't talk about my work much at home, and Sheila has only been to London a couple of times, so she's never really seen anything I've built. There's too much to be crammed into a weekend to have time to talk about it. We have to do the shopping at weekends, and visit all our relatives. My dad has farmer's lung disease, and if I don't take him out, then he doesn't get out. It's as simple as that. And Sheila often says that some things that you're dying to tell each other about during the week just seem trivial by the time the weekend comes around. Sheila would like me to work at home but she knows the score about the job situation up in Grimsby. Once you couldn't move down at the docks early in the morning, now you can drive straight through any time of the day or night. That says it all. You either go in search of work, or you stay on the dole and commit Hari Kari, and I don't fancy that somehow.'

We passed Lincoln Cathedral at around 4.30 am. Lincoln slept.

'I'm going to a new site today and I don't know what it's going to be like. If I can't get digs, I'll have to just kip down where I can – in the site office or whatever. I always say that after a few pints it doesn't really matter anyway. The truth is I don't even go out drinking much in London these days. After a day at work I'm too knackered. We used to go up Soho and that sort of thing – into the sex shops. When I was looking at this magazine once, this bloke came up behind me and said, "this ain't a library mate." I'm big, but he was huge, so I legged it. But I'm getting too old for that sort of thing now. I usually go to bed before 10.00. I bring a little portable telly with me and that's about it. Sometimes I'll go round some model shops in the evening – that's my hobby, you see. Now and again the blokes will bring a blue video to watch in the site office, but I'm more content with a good fishing book to tell you the truth.'

The A1 got noticeably busier near Leicester. It was, however, still pitch black. 'The other problem with this journey is that there are so few transport cafes open all night. But luckily there's one around here – time for a cup of tea,' he said and we pulled into Truckers restaurant. The other 'Expanded Piling Company' van was already sitting outside. Inside sat another Dave, who was a foreman, with Mark and Jim. Nobody talked, and somewhat incongruously the TV in the corner was broadcasting an American news programme about the Republican Primaries. 'You know, I'd prefer to work anywhere in the country except London,' said Dave the foreman – 'anywhere.' This was followed by a long silence.

We left the cafe at 5.45, and got back on to the A1. The road was starting to fill up. Dave still pushed the pace along. Dawn started to creep up as we entered Hertfordshire at around 6.20. Ten minutes later the A1 was solid traffic. London was still twenty-nine miles off. 'Five years ago this road would have been empty at this time,' said Dave, overtaking another mini-van full of workers. 'To miss the traffic jams now, we'd have to leave at 2.00 in the morning.' George started to wake up. 'Do you know what you're building at the moment George?' asked Dave. 'No, but it's probably an office block, they're all office blocks – going up or coming down. It's always the bloody same.'

We started to drive through Mill Hill, it was now 6.45. A green Mercedes, with a personalized number plate, raced the van at some lights, and finding itself unable to leave the van behind, simply cut right in front of it. Dave muttered something, you could see that he hadn't really got the energy to shout anything stronger. 'It's like this,' said Dave, surveying the posh houses of Mill Hill. 'There's so much money floating about down here. I was on a job where they offered the residents £30,000 each not to complain about the noise. Thirty grand a piece. Straight up. There are some Cockneys on the site, and they're all the same – they've all got their heads screwed on alright. And look at all those wanted criminals on the Costa del Sol, they're all bloody Cockneys. They don't just go for the odd grand, they go for the whole bloody lot. They think big down here, that's why all the bloody money in the country has ended up down here. It's nothing to do with effort. Nobody worked harder than the Grimsby fishermen, and look what they got for their trouble.' George just squinted out at the roads paved with gold and litter, before getting out of the van at his site at Tower Bridge. 'See you on Friday,' he said.

It was now 7.25 am as we pulled into Mansell Street. It was still freezing, but thankfully there was no snow. I made my excuses and retired to bed. Dave started a day's work.

The Air Stewardess

The line on her face looked longer and deeper than she had remembered. Deep furrowed brows and she wasn't frowning, laughter lines and she wasn't laughing. She most definitely was not laughing at this time of the night. And a large red spot right on the tip of her nose. She tried different combinations of lights in the bathroom to see if it might improve this visage in front of her. It didn't. It was 3.00 am.

She ate breakfast with her eyes closed. Her flight on that particular morning was due to leave from Manchester airport for Ibiza at 6 am. 'Ibiza again,' she said. 'I really don't like early morning flights to that place, I'm sorry but that island does seem to attract a certain type at the moment.' I told her that was where I had been for my holidays last year. She shrugged. 'It's too early in the morning for diplomacy, I'm afraid, far too early. I'm useless without my face on anyway, I leak my real feelings far too easily.'

29

Angela had to be at the airport for 4.30 am, luckily she lives with her parents in Cheshire so she doesn't have to leave home before 4.00 am. Her brother gets up at that time to take her to the airport. 'I'm one of the lucky ones, some of the girls travel from different parts of Wales to Manchester airport for this very glamorous job,' she said with the merest hint of a smile that nevertheless leaked a great deal. 'I've got exactly one hour to make myself look "presentable" for work. It's a wonderful word, isn't it? All things to all people I sometimes think – reassuring professional to the over-anxious first-time flyers, challenge and disciplinarian to the lager louts, bubbling bimbo to the old hands of a flight crew. But today of all days I don't feel like it – any of it.'

She went back to the bathroom and squeezed her spot, but it stubbornly refused to pop. It just got redder. 'Damn,' she said. It was 3.20. The hour was slipping past.

She'd had a lot of late departures recently and her working day seemed to have been extended – distended out of all recognition. It was already a twelve-hour day on a flight to Tenerife. With the airline she was currently working for there was no time for a meal on the stopover – she had to tidy the litter off the seats, check all the sick bags and the magazines in the backs of seats, and restock the range of toiletries laid out in the toilet. She also had to total the sales from the bar and the sales of the Duty Free's. 'So much for glamour,' she said. And then there were sometimes the delays on top of all this. The passengers, of course, complained bitterly whenever they occurred. Just occasionally Angela had started to snap back. 'I want to get home as well, you know. I've a home to go to just like you.' But most of the time she kept her frustration under some control. 'The passengers never seem to realize that you hate delays as much as they do. It's strange really but they're so self-centred, so caught up with just seeing the problem from their own point of view.'

She started to splash cold water over her face. Flicking through her mind at that precise moment was the type of passengers that she would encounter on that morning's flight. 'With the airline I'm currently working for there are a lot of rowdies, I'm afraid. Six o'clock isn't so bad though,' she said. 'They'll probably not have been up all night drinking. Any earlier and you can be pretty sure that they would have been. But you can never be sure – part of the excitement of the job really.'

She opened her make-up box. 'I go on automatic pilot really. It takes me a good twenty-five minutes to put it all on and transform myself into the cool professional that I know that I have to be. The most basic aspect of the make-up is that it has to project the company image, and somehow blend in with the uniform. This is more difficult than you might think. Take British Airways, for example, that company's uniform is navy blue and grey with a touch of red in it. It's difficult to get colours that don't clash with that. Pink or ruby red lipstick is okay. Or take Orion with its dark brown uniform. You can't wear brown eye shadow with that, you have to wear vivid colours otherwise you look really washed out. You can wear creamy-coloured eye shadow with orangey red lipstick. You have to use a lot of moisturizer if you're an air stewardess because of the air condition-ing, and then, of course, you have to use a lot of powder otherwise your skin looks really greasy. It's really a bit of a science getting the make-up exactly right, and getting the colours to coordinate with the colour of the uniform. Getting your skin to look exactly right whilst you're on board is a science in itself. Of course, nearly all women know a bit about make-up, but unlike them we can't afford to get it wrong.'

'All air stewardesses know that make-up works. When I get up at 3 o'clock for early morning flights, I usually think to myself that I look absolutely foul. After I've got all my make-up on, I usually feel that I don't look so bad after all. But it's not just about looking slightly better. I always think that if you look well groomed, then you look as if you've got self-control and self-respect. If you haven't got self-respect then you can't expect others to respect you – that's my philosophy. To be honest, without make-up I don't think that I'd be able to face the passengers in the morning, or any other time of day for that matter. In fact, I don't think that I'd be able to do the job at all. Of course, the make-up that we put on in the course of our job isn't necessarily what we'd choose to wear if we had any choice in the matter. It's always a certain type of look that you have to aim for – a bit of a dolly bird image, if you ask me. But the one advantage of this is that all the girls are pretty uniform that way. One doesn't stand out from the crowd then – you're not going to be singled out for special attention or, more realistically, special hassle during the flight. We all look a bit the same – as if we're essentially in control of ourselves and the situation. I think that's why the passengers respond so well to us. Of course,

31

people make jokes about make-up – that its very good for disguising the effects of a hangover, but if you're an air stewardess you can't go to work with a hangover. If there is an accident, you can have a blood sample taken, and if you had been drinking, even the night before, you could end up being held partially responsible for whatever went wrong.

'When I'm putting my make-up on like now, I usually run through all the questions that are going to be asked in the pre-flight briefing. You can be asked anything about First Aid, or aspects of passenger safety or passenger care. You can even be asked about the technical aspects of the aircraft that you're set to fly on. The briefing is run by the senior cabin crew member, and I still get nervous about briefings – in case you're asked a question that you just can't answer. Some senior cabin crew staff really like to stamp their air of authority on the briefing, to show you who's boss. And consequently some of these briefings can be really quite fraught. Although I've been pushed for time in the past, I'd never turn up at the briefing without make-up. It just wouldn't be professional. How could you try to look calm and composed and professional without your make-up?'

Time was running on, and the make-up was now fully applied. Angela was starting to smile more, but I got the impression, although perhaps it was just my imagination, that each smile was starting to say less and less. She had been slowly transmogrifying into the cool, calm professional. 'About this time I usually start to feel a little better, able to face the day for the first time.'

It was 4.00 am. Her brother stumbled down the stairs and bundled himself into his car, ready for the drive to the airport. He hadn't shaved and certainly hadn't combed his hair. Angela hadn't got a hair out of place. She noticed the contrast as well – 'He'd go to work like that, you know, if you let him. But that's the basic difference between the two of us. I'm the professional,' she said.

The Routines of the Fire Brigade

'There's a lot of routine in this job,' explained Temporary Sub-Officer Woodhouse, the officer in charge of Red Watch at Rivelin Fire Station in Sheffield. 'An awful lot of routine. A lot of people join the Fire Service for the excitement, of course, and they can be a little disappointed by all the routine. But you have to be in a state of preparedness all the time and that is where the routine comes in. You need routine.'

It was 7.00 pm on a Sunday night, and we were sitting discussing the work of the Fire Brigade in Rivelin Fire Station, or rather we were sitting discussing the routine. Rivelin is a fairly small station on the Manchester side of Sheffield. It has just one pumping appliance, called a 'water ladder'. This is the type of fire engine that carries its own water supply, and has a 13.5 metre extension ladder. On this particular shift there were six men to operate the appliance (the minimum is five). One was the officer in charge – Temporary Sub-Officer Woodhouse. Then there was the driver who is also the pump operator, then there were the two firemen assigned to wear the breathing apparatus in the case of a fire. They're called the 'BAs'. One of the others had the job of running the hose out at any fire, the responsibility of the final member of the team was to operate the entry control board on the pump – to keep a record of all BAs who enter premises during a fire, and to keep a check on how much air is left in their cylinders.

The station may be fairly small, but it had been described to me as 'a moderately busy station' by Divisional Officer Ian Travis, Deputy Divisional Commander of the Sheffield Fire Service. It had 1,740 call-outs last year, that is nearly five calls a day to punctuate the routine. But the call-outs don't necessarily space themselves out nice and evenly. As Divisional Officer Travis pointed out, 'Many shifts come and go without a single incident, and then there is just the routine.'

Sub-Officer Woodhouse went through it with me. 'On nights the routine starts at 17.58 with a parade, where the previous watch is dismissed and the new watch inspected. After that, all kit is loaded into the fire appliance. Then it is time for the checks. The driver checks the vehicle – the oil, the water, petrol, the horns, the lights. The BAs check their equipment to make sure that it is all in proper working order. Then we do situation drills for an hour from 18.30 to 19.30. We work through situations that we may have to confront – like, say, someone is trapped on the second floor of a tower block and you can only bring the ladders so close – that sort of thing. Then from 19.30 to 20.15 we do the cleaning of the station, followed by an hour's fitness training from 20.15 to 21.15. Here we have a multi-gym and we insist that all firemen use it daily. We also like to encourage games like volleyball, because we think it helps with a team spirit, but unfortunately we don't have a net here at the moment. Then we have supper and stand down. Any time after 23.00, the men can retire to bed. On Sundays, we have the parade and the checks and the cleaning, but stand down is at 19.30 instead of 21.15. The men can play snooker or watch television, but they can't retire until after 23.00.'

That particular night, they were all watching a video. The Fire Station almost seemed deserted. Just six men in one room, the rest of the station empty. 'Sundays tend to be very quiet,' said Sub-Officer Woodhouse 'You should have come on a Friday. Things tend to get a bit busy after closing time. We have all these chip pans going up in flames, when people who have had a little too much to drink decide that they want a fry-up. On Sundays everybody goes to bed early. We could have a very quiet night tonight.'

I wandered around the empty station. The bar had a metal grille across it. The order from the Chief Fire Officer of Sheffield is that anyone called upon to drive the fire engine must not drink any alcohol at all. As, in theory, they could all be called upon to do this, alcohol is banned. One fireman let himself into the bar with a key to buy three cans of Pepsi. There were no takers for the snooker. I was bored already. I wandered along to the dormitory. Officers have rooms of their own with bunks that pull out, and all ordinary firemen sleep in the dormitory on what I couldn't help but notice were fairly rudimentary bunks. Temporary Leading fireman John Jubb found me examining the hard plastic-covered mattresses of the bunks in the dormitory. 'The public often think that being a fireman is pretty easy, because you can sleep on the job between 11.30 pm and 7.00 am, but I always think that it's not like really deep sleeping. The best way to explain it is it's like trying to have a kip on your settee at home, but you know that you have to get up in half an hour. It's a very light sleep, and even when you've had eight hours, it feels more like two.' John stretched out on the bunk. 'This is some people's image of firemen. They see firemen resting and they think that it's a right cushy number. They don't see the other bits.'

I had to remind myself that the man on the bunk had six months earlier been very much involved with one of the other bits, when he carried out a spectacular save of a man threatening to jump from a railway bridge in Sheffield. He had to creep up behind him, sixty feet up, and pull him back to safety. 'The guy had gone, mentally,' said John. 'The police threatened him with a strait-jacket, when they got hold of him, if he didn't calm down.' For his act of bravery John was awarded the Chief Fire Officer's commendation – the highest award for bravery in the Fire Service. But that was six months ago. Now it was just another Sunday night with that night's routine over, and boredom just setting in. I expressed my regret at not having come on a Friday night. I expressed my deeper regret at not having come six months ago.

Suddenly the alarm went. Now, this was not as dramatic as I had anticipated. Every time the telephone rang in the station, it was accompanied by a strange sound which I had already taken to be the fire alarm. The strange warbling sound of the actual alarm seemed less urgent by comparison. But John was up off the bed and running. 'We're on,' he shouted as he ran down the corridor. A computer print-out with the exact location and grid reference was handed to the driver. An easy-to-follow, and home-made map of the vicinity of the fire was pulled out of the files. This map had all entry points and the position of all fire hydrants marked on it, as well as the location of all kidney patients on dialysis machines. I couldn't, for the life of me, think why this was relevant. John noticed my perplexed expression. 'If we use hydrants near where patients on dialysis machines live, it messes up their water supply, it can leave too much sediment in the water. So we avoid those hydrants, if we can.' This was all shouted in my direction as we ran towards the fire engine.

We raced across Sheffield to Southey Green, which falls within another station's patch. Cars dived out of our way – for the most part that is. Two teenagers in an Austin Allegro blocked our path for vital seconds. The fire engine from Rivelin was first on the scene, two pumps have to attend any house fire. A lone police car marked the spot. 'It's a hoax,' said John as we pulled up. There was no sign of any flames or even any smoke, at that stage. Then John noticed the blackened curtains upstairs in the bedroom upstairs. 'No it isn't. We're on.' The BAs entered the house and made their way tentatively upstairs. 'It's quite a small fire,' explained John, 'but you always have to be ready for the unexpected. You can always have a Calor Gas heater explode with the heat. And remember up there the BAs won't be able to see any-thing, it will be just black. They have to make sure that no-one is trapped up there.'

I entered the downstairs room – very tentatively. There was no sign of any fire, just a few large ornaments resting in a pile, as if they had been knocked over or at least heaped rather hastily. A hose led upstairs, and John motioned that I should follow it up. I moved cautiously keeping an attentive eye out for any Calor Gas heaters that might have been sitting about the place. It wasn't until I rounded the bend in the stairs that I could see that we were not trespassing without just cause, for it was here that I met a wall of thick black smoke. People talk about a blanket of smoke, but that sounds too reassuring, even though blankets can suffocate you. This was a wall – impregnable, solid with clearly defined boundaries. As I walked headlong into it, one of the firemen in breathing apparatus, emerging out of the gloom like some creature from another planet, motioned to the space between the floor and the bottom of the wall. This was where I was to put my head and try to breathe. From the floor I watched the proceedings, as the two BAs systematically searched the room. There were no signs of any flames, but then again there were no signs of anything. You could not see your hand in front of you. Divisional Officer Travis had earlier explained to me that it was quite possible for a fireman to walk into a room with a fire in one corner and not be able to find his way out, without a pre-planned search routine. The pre-planned search routine is also necessary to find any people in the room. It had been pointed out to me that children will sometimes hide in wardrobes to get away from the flames. Firemen have to look everywhere in a systematic fashion and to be able to find their way back out as well.

It had seemed incredible at the time to hear that firemen might be unable to find their way back out of a normal-sized room. Now I believed it. It had also been explained to me that the BAs always work in teams, and I could now see why this was essential. A couple of firemen had earlier made the comment that in films like *The Towering Inferno* or in TV programmes like 'London's Burning', fire is always depicted by a lot of flames and very little smoke. The reality is somewhat different. The reality is the thickest, blackest fog that you have ever seen. The reality is air that you cannot breathe. The reality is not good film.

The firemen were now ventilating the room, and chucking some bits of charred furniture out of the window to be dampened down outside. The salvage sheet was sent up to collect other bits and pieces. A cuddly toy dog with large eyes sat in one corner. It had escaped the flames, and the salvage sheet. Its plastic eyes seem to have melted. The effects of this were that it looked as if it might have been crying. The BAs removed their helmets. They looked as if they might have been crying as well, with the exertion and the smoke that still clung to the room. The whole thing had taken about thirteen minutes, but the intense heat and the sheer physical exertion of wearing that equipment meant that rivers of sweat ran off them. John Jubb had pointed out that in the case of fires on the moors just outside Sheffield, firemen can find themselves grafting for fifteen hours at a time. 'You should see the sweat then, this is nothing.'

We hung about in the charred bedroom, which was still being ventilated, whilst the officer-in-charge interviewed the occupier of the house downstairs about how the fire had started. Apparently it had been started by her son playing with matches on the bed. She came up to inspect the damage, and just shook her head when she viewed what had once been a bedroom. John pointed out the professionalism of the whole thing. 'Just look at the floor, just notice that you're not paddling about in pools of water. The minimum amount of water was used to put the fire out. Inexperienced firemen use too much water. They just want to stand outside and squirt water into the building. But you have to go inside and locate the fire. And don't forget only 40% of the damage in a fire is caused by the fire itself, 60% is caused by the smoke and the water used to put it out. We put this fire out whilst causing the minimum of damage.' The occupier still looked devastated. 'You can never tell how people are going to react in a fire,' said John. 'Some want to put the fire out for you. Others want to run away and hide.' This one just stood looking confused as we made our way back to the fire engine.

This was a small, very routine fire from the Fire Service's point of view. The statistics told me that the call came in at 20.07, and that the fire engine got to the scene at 20.13. This fire was identified as a Class C risk, which means that one pump has to be at the scene within eight to ten minutes. We had made it in good time, despite the lads in the Allegro. The stop time on this particular fire, that is the time when it was clear that no further appliances were necessary at the scene, was 20.26. The fire appliance returned to the station at 20.39. The whole thing was routine and hardly worth comment. A few words on the way back to the station, nothing more. John told the story about being at a fire the previous week where the smoke was thicker than tonight's. He found a man asleep in the room, who then woke up and demanded to know why firemen were trespassing in his house. Apparently, he'd had quite a bit to drink.

We got back to the station. Two shoes were lying in the middle of the floor and a cold sausage roll sat on one side, testifying to our great speed in leaving the station. I looked in a mirror and discovered that my face was black, as were my hands. 'The first thing that you do when you get back is wash,' said John. I wanted to relive the excitement of the holocaust that I had been through. John looked nonchalant, some might say bored. Some incidents do, however, get them talking. It turned out that Red Watch from Rivelin Fire Station were the first firemen on the scene at the Hillsborough disaster. 'We talked about Hillsborough for months afterwards,' said Sub-Officer Woodhouse. 'That you couldn't forget. I kept seeing the face of this particular lad that I was trying to revive every time I tried to go to sleep. The funniest thing about Hillsborough is that all the lads went out that night quite independently and got absolutely bladdered. We only discovered that we had all done it the next day when we all came in with hangovers. Stones brewery must have done very well out of it.'

But that Sunday night was not the stuff out of which memories are made, or jokes. There was another house fire at 12.09, a stand-by at 4.26 and a road traffic accident at 8.22 am. This meant a disturbed night's sleep for six individuals, and very little else, but thankfully it did mean a good night's sleep for the rest of us.

Operation Donkey

This was an operation that I could not afford to miss, the private eye from *SYLJEN* had told me on the phone. An undercover operation to catch a landlord of a pub engaged in some big fiddles. 'It's top secret, we've code-named it "operation donkey", by the way,' he said. 'We're calling it that because a donkey doesn't do much work, and doesn't earn its keep, just like this pub really. But in the case of the pub we know why, the landlord's got his hand in the till a bit too deep.'

The plan was simple – I was going to accompany four members of the security agency as they carried out their surveillance of the pub on a particular Friday evening. They had already carried out surveillance on one previous evening that week and collected some fairly conclusive evidence of the fiddles being operated. So had the company that owned the pub – a routine stock check the previous week had revealed that the pub was £1,750 down, the pub was losing around £400 a week. This was to be the final surveillance, and the plan was that at 11.00 pm there would be a huge raid involving the local CID, directors of the company, accountants, stock controllers, in fact everybody remotely connected with the place. 'It will be quite an evening,' the private eye had said on the phone. 'Oh and by the way, wear a leather jacket in case the evening turns nasty.'

We were to meet at Pond Street bus station near Sheffield city centre at 8.30 pm. 'Why half eight?' I enquired. 'Do you have to have a pre-raid meeting to coordinate the action between yourselves and the police?' 'Oh no,' said the private eye. 'Sue's bus gets in then, she's one of the team.' So half eight it was. I was expecting the team to be made up of Sue and three burly men – in leather jackets presumably. However, the sex ratio was quite the reverse – one burly man and three women. 'Men respond better to women in an aggro situation,' explained Sue when she eventually got off the bus.

The pub was in Doncaster so I thought that we would head immediately for the M1, but instead we set off from Pond Street station and headed for Hyde Park flats. Were we going to pick up some heavies from the flats to take on the job? Heavies that might come well tooled up and ready for action? Is that why they couldn't meet the rest of us in the town centre? Well, not quite, we had gone to the flats for some cheap petrol. 'I always come here,' said Patrick the private eye. 'The petrol's cheap and I collect the stamps.'

Now it was time for the M1. Surely? But no, there was one last detour – up to the Makro hypermarket. It was now just after 9.00 pm. I'd no idea what we were doing there. What had this to do with 'operation donkey'? A child of about six passed by wearing a green super-hero's cape. Green? I was feeling even more puzzled. We waited for about twenty minutes. Was this the secret rendez-vous point? Were we going to be joined by the heavies here instead? At last Patrick emerged. 'I needed some batteries,' he said. 'I've got some new fancy tape-recorders today with hidden microphones, the works. The only problem is that I forgot the batteries. The queue at the check-out was terrible.'

We were off, at last. Dire Straits sang on the car stereo, 'Money for nothing and the chicks for free.' 'Yeah, money for *nothing*,' I repeated after each verse. We pulled into Doncaster at around 9.50. I was still humming the song. 'Are you trying to give the game away or something?' asked Patrick. 'Sing something else for God's sake.' And, of course, the more I tried to think of a different song to sing, the more this particular one stuck in my mind. So I tried singing it in a quieter and quieter voice. 'They'll think you're a nutter, if you keep this up,' Patrick warned, as we made our way round to the pub. He was busy trying to get the batteries into his new tape-recorder in the meantime.

The plan was simple – I was to accompany Patrick and Sue in the upstairs bar, Jenny and Janet were to mount their surveillance downstairs. 'Just act natural,' said Patrick, as we went in. 'We've got to blend in to the surroundings, so we can keep a close eye on what they're all up to. We're going to record everything on tape as well, to really nail them.'

That, at least, was the plan. The first problem became clear as soon as we entered the place. The upstairs bar was full of under-age drinkers. The average age was about seventeen. That, unfortunately, wasn't the only problem, the bar also functioned as a disco on Friday and Saturday nights. The music was deafening. 'So much for the brand-new tape recorders,' said Patrick. We were about to order a drink when we encountered yet another problem – we all wanted Britvic orange. 'That's no bloody good,' said Patrick. 'Somebody's going to have to drink beer or a short or it will look ridiculous – out for a big night and all supping Britvic orange.' So we took turns at having the beer. The landlord was working downstairs that particular night. In the upstairs bar there was the landlady, two barmen, and a barmaid. All were under surveillance, and we in turn were under surveillance from them. They watched our every movement from the moment we entered. Even the seventeen-year-olds with their tongues lapping each others' tonsils had started watching us, trying to work out what we were doing there. Two men and a woman, only one drinking alcohol at any one time. Which two were the couple? Who was the gooseberry? 'Blend in,' said Patrick, as he started to sway to the music. For one awful moment I thought that the landlady might ask us to leave.

'Now watch the barmaid closely,' said Patrick. 'Look there she goes – £1.21 rung up as 21p.' Sue nodded her head, I unfortunately missed it. 'You've not quick enough,' said Patrick. 'Stand with your back to the bar, so it looks as if I'm talking to you. That way you'll be of some use.' The landlady and bar staff were getting increasingly suspicious. One of the barmen even rotated the little section at the top of the till around so that Patrick couldn't read the sums being rung up. Patrick found an immediate solution. 'These disco places are full of mirrors, if I look in that one over there I can still see what he's ringing up.'

Groups were wandering in off the street – the place was filling up. But my position at the bar had been fixed for the night and I was under strict instructions not to move. One group of lads wanted to get past and they politely asked me to move, but we were in the very best position for watching the tills, so I couldn't. 'Excuse me, mate,' one said. 'Can I get past?' 'Sorry, but I can't,' I had to reply. 'What?' the youth was looking extremely perplexed. 'You can't? What do you mean, you can't?' 'I just can't. I'm waiting for some-body and I said that I'd see her in this exact spot. If I move she might miss me.' It was the best that I could think of on the spur of the moment. It didn't, however, really satisfy the youth, who reached around me to the bar and proceeded to scowl at me for the rest of the evening. So far I hadn't made a particularly good job of blending in. Patrick was trying harder – he was swaying at a greater angle to the music now and was bumping into the other customers as he did so.

It was now 10.55, five minutes to go. 'Oh, by the way,' said Patrick 'the police won't be coming. We had a long meeting with them today, but they weren't that interested. They said, "Give us a call if you discover anything, preferably after nine o'clock in the morning." We're on our own. It's a pity you forgot to wear your leather jacket.'

I started trying to locate all the fire exits, in case I had to make a run for it. Patrick meanwhile nipped downstairs to have a look at the landlord. Sue seemed to be falling asleep. Patrick came back up, beaming. 'He's only a little bloke with a beer gut, thank God for that. When I saw the landlady, who's tall, I thought that we might have a bit of a problem. Get ready, it's nearly zero hour.'

I was waiting for the big raid, but at 11.00 all that happened was one lone individual wearing glasses and a pin-striped suit walked up to the bar, said something to the barmaid, and then went behind the bar. He proceeded to lock the till. The landlady looked quite puzzled by it all. The remaining customers didn't notice. 'That's it – go, go, go,' said Patrick. I was rooted to the spot with embarrassment.

Suddenly, Jenny entered, accompanied by a youngish man in a sweater who turned out to be one of the directors of the company that owned the pub. The staff were told to sit quietly in different parts of the room and not to confer. The few customers that remained still didn't notice anything. Patrick was asking them to leave. 'Drink up and make your way out *please*.' 'I've ordered a taxi, I have to wait for it here,' came the reply. 'Well wait outside, *please*.'

I could see the face of the barmaid. She looked extremely anxious, and she asked if she could go to the toilet. 'I'm sorry, but you can't,' said Jenny. I felt like reassuring her, I wanted to explain that the purpose of the raid was to catch the landlord at his fiddles. But it was time for her to be questioned. Behind the bar there was a a scene of frenetic activity as the stock controller moved various bottles around, and accountants emptied the tills. Loud banging noises were coming from outside. Patrick could see that I was puzzled. 'They've brought two joiners along to change all the locks. After tonight the landlord and landlady won't be allowed back into the pub. They'll be out of a job and evicted from their flat above the pub as soon as possible.' With the banging still going on in the background, the barmaid was told that she had been observed with the 'latest technology' under-ringing at the bar. She was asked if she had taken any money. Quietly, she said that she had. She was then asked if she had any of this money still on her. She nodded. How much? Forty-five pounds. Where? 'In my tights, under my trousers. I needed the money for a gas bill that I couldn't pay.' Jenny asked her if she needed to go to the toilet to get it back out. She said that she did, and she was led away to the nearest toilet. 'I have to get home to my baby-sitter tonight, please,' she said quietly as she left. Patrick whispered in my ear, 'What a night for her to help herself. Now that's what I call bad timing – caught because the landlord was too greedy. I feel a bit sorry for her. When I went downstairs to see how big the landlord was, she lifted my drink. But when I got back and she realized her mistake, she gave me another one immediately. Probably a decent sort of girl really.'

One of the two barmen from the upstairs bar was next. He denied everything. 'I want a pub from this company. Do you think that I'm going to screw my chances for a stupid drink?' The argument was long and protracted. Finally, he agreed to admit something. 'Alright. I've had a couple of lemonades for nothing.' Jenny pounced. 'Okay, you've had a couple of drinks for nothing. How many?' 'I said lemonades, not drinks, lemonades aren't drinks.' 'Look,' said Jenny, 'you were seen putting 21p in the till for a double pernod and lemonade.' 'No, I didn't. I put in £1.77.' The till roll was then read out. 'There's no £1.77 in the last hour.' 'Okay, I must have rung in the wrong number, perhaps £1.70. It's easy to do. Have you ever worked behind a bar?' 'Yes I have,' said Jenny.

I made my way down to the stock room. There, one director of the company, two accountants and a stock controller were checking both the stock and the night's takings. The landlord just looked on, his face becoming more and more flushed. 'He actually bought us a drink downstairs,' said Jenny, 'or rather he gave us a drink. I don't think he actually bought any. He asked if we were going on to a party, because we bought eight cans of lager. We bought them because we wanted to see how much he would ring up – he rang up £1.06 instead of £7.20. He only rang up one fifty pence drink correctly all night, everything else was under-rung. He kept saying to the customers, "keep the money rolling in, come on loadsa money." You know why, it was all going into his bleedin' pockets, that's why. We had him.'

The landlady meanwhile was kept behind the bar. There didn't seem to be much evidence against her personally, but from her vantage point she had to watch as her livelihood and home were systematically taken away from her. She seemed quite stunned as the two joiners whistled as they methodically changed all the locks in the place. It was now 1.30 am. The CID had arrived to take a statement from the barmaid, whose baby-sitter had to wait. 'They'll get the statements of the landlord tomorrow. The stock is well down,' said Patrick. 'Nobody minds a bit of fiddling, but he just went too far, that's all.'

I asked the two workmen if they got many jobs like this one. They told me that they were definitely on the increase, but they liked the work because they were on double time. They then went back to their whistling. I was sure I recognized the tune, as I made my way out into Doncaster town centre on a cold frosty, spring morning. Oh yeah, it was a song about microwave ovens and colour TVs, and one line repeated many times – 'money for nothing'. That night I knew all about dire straits.

★ 3 ★
All dressed up and nowhere to go

The Ultimate Trip

'I'm really sort of bored with nightclubs in Sheffield basically,' said Dom, sitting in his office in the centre of Sheffield, where he works as a self-employed graphic designer. A rather well-thumbed copy of the *Modern American Poster* sat prominently on the desk in this little box of an office. The room was heated by an electric fire with just one bar on. The small room was very cold. Dom was dressed in a sort of distinctive tan colour, right from his cap down. He stood out from the crowd alright. His speech was also quite distinctive, he liked to drawl on the last syllables of words – 'really' and 'basically' seemed to go on forever. Some 'House' music went on interminably in the background. 'Sheffield doesn't provide an exciting enough night scene, so we travel to Nottingham or Manchester for a night out. House Music is the current big thing, it's the most exciting thing to happen, since punk. The only thing to happen in my opinion. My partner Chris and I organize "The Beat Route" – the ultimate trip, we like to say. We take a group to a club in a different town – there and back by coach for about a fiver, including the admission to the club. It's one long party, in the coach we have in-transit sounds from Graeme Park and Winston and Parrot. 'Yes, *the* Graeme Park and *the* Winston and Parrot,' said one of Dom's friends.

I was none the wiser.

'We go to the clubs with the top DJs, we'll follow them around to hear the best sounds. This is the scene today with House Music, you know – the cult of the DJ. My partner and I make about eighty quid if we manage to fill the coach. Tomorrow night we're going to the Hacienda in Manchester, it's really hot. One girl is coming up from Covent Garden to go on the trip. She'll be back in Sheffield for about half three in the morning, then she'll catch the first train to London

44

and be at work for 10 am. This is serious business – really exciting. The bus leaves at 8.30, so don't be late.'

There followed a night of nervous planning about dress. 'It's going to be Acid House music,' said a friend, 'so wear a fluorescent shirt or a Smiley tee shirt.' But what kind of fluorescent shirt, or what kind of Smiley tee shirt? I had already learned that Dom regularly forks out £15 for a pair of socks, and Chris £20 for a toothbrush ('well, it's a Paul Smith toothbrush, well worth it and instantly recognizable, if you're in the know'). This level of expenditure on socks and toothbrushes shocked me a little, especially when I learned that Chris, the better off of the two, earns about nine grand a year as the manager of a cinema in Sheffield. Chris' underpants cost more than his weekly rent. Here were men with an eye for detail, and some not insignificant dedication to what they currently thought was fashionable. So what kind of buttons should there be on the shirt that I would wear? And how many rips should there be in the tee shirt, or my jeans? I went off to sleep pondering such important issues.

The following night was late night shopping in Sheffield, and the town was positively heaving, but despite this I could still spot Dom's crowd congregated in front of the City Hall from some considerable distance. It might have been the hats and caps, it might even have been Dom's satin shirt with the wing collar and his leatherette jacket. 'Seventies retro,' whispered one devotee – 'very cool, very cool indeed. Old Dom does it again, always ahead of the crowd. And just look at that hat – brown corduroy, it takes real style to wear a hat like that. Wow, *brown* corduroy.' I nearly told her that I'd just got some brown corduroy trousers from Next, and that I was thinking of lending them to Dom to go with the hat, but I decided to keep my mouth shut. It was as if she could read my thoughts. 'We're the opposite of Townies, you know. We're into style, fashion, X-cess, with a capital "X". We're individualists – the opposite of Townies, who all buy the same old boring blazer from Next.' I nodded in agreement before hurriedly boarding the coach.

Now, Acid House has got a lot of publicity from the tabloids because of the apparently heavy reliance on drugs in this particular cult. So like any self-respecting scoop, I was keeping an eagle eye out for any little tablets changing hands or any little pellets being surreptitiously popped into the mouth. But the only thing that I could see being popped into the mouth were rather large bottles of

Lambrusco, and some rather smaller bottles of Bell's whisky and Gordon's gin. I called Dom over and asked where all the Ecstasy tabs were. 'Oh, we don't bother with that stuff here. The whole drug thing's been really exaggerated. I wouldn't even know where to get hold of any. A friend of mine tried to score some Ecstasy in a club a few weeks ago, but all they got for their twenty quid was a Valium. I know why people believe it – when you see some of the dancers in the Hacienda, you'll wonder what they're on as well. But they're not so different, Chris always says that they look as if they're just squeezing an orange box. So, if you want to dance and fit in, just pretend you're squeezing an orange box, and you'll be okay.'

Our conversation was rather suddenly disrupted by the first song of the specially commissioned tape of House music. It was one of those songs whose words were rather easy to learn. 'Boolie hoolie, boolie hoolie, boolie hoolie.' The volume was intense. I was being deafened and we hadn't even made it past Sheffield Wednesday's ground in Hillsborough yet. The atmosphere was building up, people kept changing seats. I was joined by Thomas. 'I'm not into all this Seventies retro stuff, I'm into any clothes that go with my hair, basically.' His hair was in a pony tail, which was set off with an expensive black leather jacket and ripped jeans. His knee, clearly visible through one of the large rips, was bleeding profusely. I wondered for a moment whether the cut was functioning as a fashion accessory. I asked him whether, like Dom, he would consider paying £15 for a pair of socks. He looked at me as if I was personally responsible for the hole in his knee. 'Look,' he said, grabbing my attention by biting the top off a bottle of lager, 'I'm only a snob about two things – women, food and wine.' I was dying to point out that this was actually three things, but I couldn't stop thinking about what he'd just done to the bottle of lager. Thomas continued, 'When I go to clubs, I always eat in restaurants. That way the management knows you're a good punter. I eat in the Millionaire's club in Manchester and Mr Craig's in Leeds. There the food is out of this world, but when I was there last week, I was too pissed to eat.' Now the problem here was that none of this sounded terribly nouveau, quite the opposite in fact. I was wondering why Thomas needed to travel all that way to a new club, like the Hacienda, when his concerns were so, well, basic. He seemed to anticipate my question. 'I'm barred from Josephines, by the way, the top club in Sheffield, because of my appearance.'

My musings were disturbed again by Thomas. 'Time for wee wee,' he suddenly cried. Now, I'm not that familiar with Acid House slang. *The Longman Register of New Words*, that I'd just been sent to review, informed me that Acid House dancers were called 'ecstatics' or 'shoomers', but what was this 'wee wee' that they were all now chanting. I asked Thomas about the mantra. 'Let me show you,' he said as he and three friends got off the bus and proceeded to urinate on its wheels. 'It's only the men who ever do this,' said one female devotee in 1940s' gear, 'it's all that lager. We're hardly even out of Sheffield yet, they'll need to stop again before they get to the club.'

'That's better,' said Thomas, when he got back to his seat. 'Now what do you want to know about Acid House? About where it came from? It's like this, when I was a DJ, I was playing Acid House music three years ago. It's basically funky music, and boring funky music at that. The truth is I can't stand the bloody music. If some other producer worked on these records they'd be able to do a lot more with them. But that's just my opinion.' I wanted to point out that almost everyone I spoke to had claimed that they, and they alone, were the first to play Acid House music in Britain, but bottle after bottle was being passed from the back of the bus for Thomas to take the top off with his teeth, and this ritual was somehow inhibiting any provocative questions that I might have liked to ask.

Instead, I stuck to more innocuous questions, like asking Thomas what he did for a living. 'I own a small engineering company,' came the immediate reply. 'What kind of engineering company, exactly?' I asked. 'Well, um, a domestic appliances company – I fix broken vacuum cleaners. I call my firm – the Sheffield Vac Hospital, not bad eh? Our motto is that your vac can be broken, even without you realizing it. I supply free safety and efficiency checks – there's usually something wrong with them in the end. But I really want to get in to selling credit, then you can sell anything – cars, holidays, the lot. All my mates are entrepreneurs – see that guy over there, he's a top entrepreneur. Did you see 'The Clothes Show' when it had these sun glasses on with the flashing lights – £4.95 they were. He's selling them for four quid. He's got the brains, you see.'

A different tune was now playing. This one had more elaborate lyrics – 'You want this party started right.' I asked Thomas about the drug Ecstasy. He said, 'Look, put it like this, you can get an awful lot of lager for twenty-five quid. I was approached a couple of weeks ago in a club, and this guy asked me if I wanted to buy some "Windowpane". I told him that I'd never heard of it – Windowlene yes, but Windowpane? Acid House isn't about drugs, it's about staying ahead of the pack. I organize coachtrips to clubs as well, you know, but more up-market clubs. I don't make a fortune, but it's a start.' And on that note Thomas disappeared to the back of the bus because there was a queue of bottles waiting to be opened.

Chris, the co-organizer, made his way over, and started telling me about a friend who had just paid £750 for a suit and £195 for a shirt. The friend in question was a hairdresser. 'He had a real Northern accent, and they laughed at him in this trendy shop, until he produced his wad of notes. Just imagine their faces.' I could see that there was real power for Chris in this – something to keep inside your coat more deadly than any concealed weapon. 'The assistants just froze, you should have seen their faces, he killed them stone dead.'

The group on the bus kept drinking and chatting and changing seats – all one long party, and we weren't even there yet. Josie sat beside me. 'Do you want to know why I come on these trips?' she drawled in that awfully trendy way, before inserting the usual inordinately long pause . . . 'It makes me forget.' There was another significant and very meaningful pause. 'Do you know what it makes me forget?' I shook my head. 'The way everyone is so oriented towards money today in Thatcher's Britain. You just can't get away from it no matter how far out you go.'

And we both would have laughed at this double entendre, if it hadn't been quite so uncool.

So much bad taste

It's a shop that's easy to miss. It's beside a trendy wine bar, and your eyes are already on the customers in their black berets sipping the Chardonnay before you realize that you've just passed a shop with no name. What sort of a shop is it that doesn't need to advertise? I was thinking aloud, but some people heard me.

'It's a junk shop run by this old eccentric woman, who's got this thing about cats. She's absolutely brilliant, everyone calls her Auntie Hilda,' said one young woman with a black beret and a green gabardine. The young lady slipped her Ray-Bans off. 'I got the gabardine there. What do you think? I must say that I think that it's absolutely mega. I got it in Auntie Hilda's shop – for a quid. I'm afraid that she doesn't have much concept of the value of stylish clothes. The sunglasses, though, cost me an absolute bomb, £150 would you believe?'

I said that it was indeed hard to believe. She was, however, making the most of the sunglasses as she twiddled them this way and that. The bright metallic sunglasses were glinting and winking at all the trendies huddled in their little noisy groups, and the glasses seemed to be saying, 'Just look at me, look what my master can afford.' A few sunglasses seemed to be winking back. Their owner continued, 'I'd only been in the shop once before when I was looking for some clothes for a bad-taste party. I got some glittery platform soles for fifty pence, a purple polyester shirt with a fly-away collar for fifty pence, and some lurex tights for fifty pence. Everything seems to be fifty pence. I looked amazingly bad, and for just one pound fifty. I also spotted this gabardine when I was in the shop, which is very stylish, very chic.'

Very, Frank bloody Spencer, I thought to myself, silently this time, and slipped away.

I entered the shop behind two more style merchants who immediately started rummaging through one of the piles of clothes. One wore a Thirties' man's jacket over what I can only guess was a shrunken liberty bodice. Within a few seconds, she had managed to find a green velour top, with one of those huge collars that friends of Lieutenant Kojak like to wear, a purple velour top from the same period, and a pink man's shirt, all of which evidently met with both her and her friend's approval. 'That's one pound fifty,' said Auntie Hilda, 'all good quality stuff, hardly worn, the money goes to feed the cats, you know, love. I'm not looking to make a profit from any of it. I've got twenty-seven cats out the back, and five at home. They need a lot of feeding, and every little bit helps.'

'Wow,' said the girl in the liberty bodice, after a slight delay which indicated that she had been so caught up in the search through the piles of goodies in the shop that she had hardly been attending to what Auntie Hilda had been saying. The delay had been made even more incongruous by the 'wow', which usually indicates something of great concern and great immediacy. 'I've got one little tabby cat, and that's a handful, I don't know how you cope,' she drawled eventually, whilst pushing her new acquisitions into her bag. 'It's my life,' said Auntie Hilda. The girl in the liberty bodice now wanted to look through the pile of blouses behind the counter. 'Is it bad taste, that you're looking for, or are you going for style?' asked Auntie Hilda. 'Style,' said the style merchant, slightly put out by the question. 'Then what about this one?' said Auntie Hilda, clearly with an eye for style, if the style merchant's avaricious look was anything to go by.

I waited for the two trendies to leave, before I tentatively approached Auntie Hilda. The first question was the one that I had been dying to ask. 'How can you tell the difference between the bad-taste clothes and the others?' Auntie Hilda gave a very loud laugh as if I was just a little daft. 'Any platform shoes are bad taste, and all the really bright clothes are bad taste. This bright purple dress from the early seventies is bad taste, this other purple dress is style.' I studied the dresses closely, they both had very large flaps as collars, and a very odd, sort of flared shape, but I said that I thought that I could detect some difference between them. 'It's like this,' continued Auntie Hilda, 'my shop isn't upmarket, and there aren't many of these shops left. There are shops in town that are so posh that you can't get anything under ten pounds. Here you can get a good suit for five pounds, and a dress for a pound. All the profits go to my cats. Some of my customers are going to bad-taste parties, but I get a lot of students and ordinary people as well.'

One of the ordinary people had just entered the shop. She wore a blue woollen dress, *circa* 1959, and carried a walking stick. I noticed that the dress was not bright blue. She was in her mid-thirties. 'Anything new in, Hilda?' she asked, as she rummaged through the pile of cast-offs. 'I'm desperately trying to give up smoking, again,' she told Hilda. 'Some of these cures for smoking are more dangerous than smoking itself, did you know that Hilda? I've heard some of these cures are like a poison. It's too dangerous, far too dangerous. I only smoke for my nerves, and my nerves are all shattered – gone. I've always been bad with my nerves.'

Meanwhile one young female student had entered the shop and had started browsing through the piles of books. Here lay *The Tears of Venus*, *The Old June Weather*, *A Man of His Time*, and *Once is not Enough*. 'Some right classics,' said Auntie Hilda. 'Just pay me what you want for them,' she said to the girl. 'All the money's for cat food.' The lady with the bad nerves and the blue dress had in the meantime wandered out, mumbling to herself. A young woman with a child then entered the shop and hurriedly flicked through the rack of dresses, with just a hint of embarrassment. She found nothing, and left quickly.

'I know all of my regular customers by name,' said Auntie Hilda. 'In fact I call my cats after my customers. The customers have heard me calling the cats by their names, but they never seem to bother. Perhaps they think that it's just a coincidence. I've got so many cats now, though, that I've started just calling them all "puss"'.

Auntie Hilda, who is seventy one, has been running this shop in Sheffield for twenty-eight years with her common-law husband, Matt. 'Everybody thought we were man and wife,' she said, 'but my real husband still lives in Sheffield, and he still talks to me. He's eighty eight.' She and Matt were very happy, she said, until Matt was mugged. 'He used to go out to the pub every night. Well, men like a bit of a social life, don't they? The police brought him home at three o'clock in the morning. He had no wallet, no watch and hardly any clothes left on him. They found him in the centre of town in a puddle. It had been pouring with rain. How he got into the centre of town, I don't know. He only drank at the corner of the street. He was in a right state when they brought him home, I can tell you.' And Hilda produced one of her great infectious laughs.

And then a somewhat different expression swept her face. 'After he got mugged, he turned a little bit funny, very peculiar, I'm afraid. He had to go into a home eventually. I still see him once a week, when I can. We both loved the cats, you know. I used to live out the back of the shop, but it's too dangerous around here with all the break-ins. I had to move away.'

Now Hilda is alone with the cats. 'They're all I've got left, they're my life,' she said. 'I don't bother with holidays or anything like that. The first time that I had been on a train since I was eighteen was two years ago, when my son took me to London. The time before that it was a steam train that I was on. I've never been to the theatre in my life, but I did once see *The Sound of Music* in the cinema. Basically I never go out. When I finish in the shop I get the bus home and I draw the blinds. I shut myself in with my cats. I never visit people, and even though I've got a lovely next-door neighbour who's eighty I never go to see her. I explained to her when I first moved there that I don't neighbour. She said that she could understand that.'

'All of my customers tell me that I've got a great sense of humour, even if I am a bit of a loner. People come to see me after they've been to the Samaritans, and say that they feel much better after talking to me. Because I spend so much time on my own, people think that I'm a bit eccentric, but I love meeting people in the shop. And I think that when you spend so much time on your own, you learn to sense things. You can end up on a different plane from everybody else. I feel that I'm very psychic. I can tell a lot about people from the first meeting.'

I asked her what she made of me on the basis of first impressions. It's the kind of question, of course, that you usually regret asking before you've even finished formulating it. 'Well, I thought that you looked a bit like a con man, when you first came in. But as soon as you started talking, I realized that you weren't anything of the sort. No con man talks like that.'

I wasn't sure whether this was a compliment or not. Hilda continued regardless. 'You can get so much information about people that way. There are some lovely customers that come in here. Full of life and full of joy. There's this group going to a bad-taste party in Dronfield tonight. They'll have a lovely time. But some of my customers are a little sad. They've had it hard. I never complain about my own life. My customers joke with me that I should look after myself better. I had hypothermia last winter because I wouldn't eat. You see, I never cook a dinner in the week, I just have a sandwich. I had one chop for Christmas, just ask my butcher – he lives down the road from me. One or two of my customers know me very well, and they were bringing me meat sandwiches to eat, but they joked that I was probably taking the meat out of the sandwiches and feeding it to the cats, which was exactly what I was doing. Some of my customers know me alright. The problem is that my cats get through twenty tins of cat food a day, which can work out a bit expensive. They're feral cats, you see, wild cats. The Cats' Protection League won't give you any support if you look after wild cats. I don't understand why. They need looking after just like any other cat. I started feeding the cats when they used to live in the grounds of the Sheffield Royal Hospital, which used to be just down the road, before it was pulled down. The boiler men used to feed the cats before they left. After they left, it was my responsibility. I always thought that if I didn't feed them, then who would?'

I wanted to say that exactly the same thing could be said of Hilda herself, but she was far too busy to listen, as she extracted a purple waist-coat from below a pile of second-hand shirts for a young man with green hair and a ring through his nose.

The waist-coat was bright purple, but I wasn't sure if it mattered any longer.

Heavy Metal – Anthrax lives!

It was just after 11.00 pm on a Friday night, and I was looking for a club called Rebels. 'A club for extraverts' said the owner, Steve, on the phone. 'A club for headbangers,' said everyone else. You know the kind of guys with long limp hair, *circa* 1969, playing imaginary guitars, and girls, well I wasn't sure about the girls. But I knew they were still into Led Zeppelin, sorry Led Zep, and Deep Purple, twenty years on. Youth cults may come and go, but this one seems to have endured, or the pause button had got jammed, one or the other.

I'd received detailed instructions on how to get there – 'near where Woolworth's used to be, but it's not there anymore. There's also a kebab waggon on the corner, some nights, at least,' said the owner on the phone. So I set out looking for a derelict shop that could potentially once have been a Woolies, and a kebab stall that may or may not be present.

However, my quest was easier than I imagined – I turned a corner and there indeed was a derelict shop and a kebab waggon, vibrating to loud music, which was being pumped out of an adjacent building. Three 'extraverts' were having a kebab and chips, they were also hopping from foot to foot to the music. Nevertheless, they somehow managed to get their chips into their mouths from every angle, most of them at least. The ketchup not surprisingly was everywhere. One suddenly sat his kebab and chips down carefully on the pavement, and started playing an imaginary guitar. I had never watched this spectacle with much interest before, but it does bear close examination. This one, I assumed, was playing lead guitar, on the basis of the pattern of his hand movements. He obviously knew the track inside out, he'd clearly 'played' it many times before. After the track had finished I tentatively approached, and asked him about it. 'I was just getting into the music, basically,' he said, in a surprisingly refined middle-class accent. His friend told him not to be so modest. 'He's an ace air guitarist. He's won competitions, you know, for his air guitaring. Did you see his mega finger work? He can play any Thrash Metal song absolutely brilliantly. He's one of the best, a real top-gun air guitarist.' I was impressed, who wouldn't be? I told them that I was going to Rebels, so they invited me to watch some more ace guitar playing later.

They went back to their kebabs, and I set off into the gloom and darkness. Rebels, you see, is at the very top of a building, up endless stairs with the walls all painted black and with a galaxy of silver crescent moons and stars painted on top. I could just about make out the old Led Zep classic 'Stairway to Heaven', as I trudged up the endless flight of stairs. A queue stretched down to meet me. It was my first chance to see the Heavy Metal Men and Women close up. The men seemed to fall into distinctively different categories: there were some bikers in leathers, some 'hippies' – one of whom who looked about twenty years old was wearing flares (although where he managed to get them from must remain a mystery – perhaps they were his father's) – and the rest seemed to be an assortment of Bon Jovi clones – jacket sleeves rolled up in the regulation way, tight bright trousers, and loud talk which sounded vaguely American. The Heavy Metal Women were all girls in what appeared to be a uniform of leather mini skirt, basque and torn T-shirt. The men, amazingly, seemed to be ignoring them.

'We're glam rockers,' explained Paula Gill, who was nineteen and from Rotherham. 'I've come in a big group of Glam Rockers tonight, by bus from Rotherham to Sheffield – we always get the half seven bus. Heavy Metal fans come from as far away as Manchester to this club, you know. It's the top spot. But there are a lot of different sorts of Heavy Metal fans. I'm into Bon Jovi and AC/DC and glam rock. To be honest, I'm a bit indifferent to the Thrash Metal groups like Anthrax and Slayler. It's mainly guys who like Thrash Metal anyway, and they tend to be a bit younger. Then, of course, there's the AORs that means the American Oriented Rock fans – fans of groups like Journey and Kiss. I get on okay with the AORs. Then you have your older fans who like Deep Purple and Hawkwind . . . Does that make it any clearer?'

I nodded and hoped that she wouldn't ask me to repeat any of it, by way of a test. Luckily the queue was moving to the top of the stairs. At the top stood two very casually dressed bouncers. One was massive.

His six foot six inch, twenty-one stone frame amply filled the casual Fred Perry shirt he was wearing. Somewhat incongruously he was sipping a cup of tea. 'We don't wear a DJ and dickie bow here,' said Mick Castledine, 'we go for the more casual approach, to blend in with our customers.' Mick has worked on doors for eighteen years and volunteered that Rebels was the quietest place that he'd ever worked. 'You get far more trouble from respectable people,' he said. 'The punters who come here are usually either really skinny kids or guys with big guts from all the beer, they don't want to fight. They also have to put up with a lot. They get picked on all the time because of how they look. They're really used to aggravation, and they hardly ever react to hassle.' 'And this club is too important to them to get barred from,' said his associate Steve Stokes. 'If they got barred from this place, they'd have nowhere else to go. This club is unique for these punters.'

I made my way tentatively on – I just followed the noise. Through the gloom, I could just about make out the shapes hunched over the imaginary guitars. Two bikers, one male, one female, who looked as if they were pushing forty, gave an exhibition of the old Teddy Boys'/ Hell's Angels' dance, thumbs in the pocket bending and twisting forward. Long, damp hair fell over their sweaty faces. It looked for all the world like an aerobics exercise from the 1980s, or a dance performed by Mud some time ago to their hit Tiger Feet (if my memory serves me correctly). I wanted to ask them if they were Mud fans. But before I got the chance, the record had changed, and they were gone. A Bon Jovi was on. 'Ace,' shouted a guy in a pair of leopard skin pants, with a red towelling band on each wrist. He played the first few chords as he strode on to the dance floor, simultaneously flicking his long, blond hair back. Ace rock star, ace air guitarist. His friends – all male – performed very similar actions. They stood in a circle performing to each other. The girls in the leather mini skirts in the meantime passed by unnoticed.

Around the dance floor were the spectators, all drinking from bottles. The customers carried their bottles of Newcastle Brown around with them, using their thumbs to block the hole at the top. The preferred mode of drinking was to shake the bottle up, with the thumb still blocking the top, to make it nice and gassy, and then pop it straight into the mouth. 'It's fun, and nobody gets the chance to pinch your drink,' said the manager – Ron Bromwich, who had just joined me, looking slightly out of place in a pink cardigan. 'That's currently the trendy way to drink it, but these things go in phases.'

It was now the turn of more Thrash Metal from the DJ – faster, louder, 'wilder,' said Ron. He wanted to show me one particular spectacle – a young black guy air guitaring. He seemed to be the only black person in the club. 'He's a fantastic player,' said Ron (although it took him about four attempts to get this message across, because of the incredible volume of the music filling the room). 'He plays bass air guitar. Just watch his incredible movements.' And sure enough something of a crowd had gathered around him to watch his bass playing. He was sweating profusely, and if my mother had been there she would have described him as 'sent', but where to? And how? 'There's no drugs in here,' said Ron, spotting my quizzical look. 'If we catch anybody smoking dope we take it off them and send them straight back to the bar. If we catch them a second time, they're barred, and that for them is really serious.'

I wandered off to the bar to look for the reformed dope fiends, and was approached by two females. They clearly had something to say to me, but no matter how hard I tried I just couldn't make out what they wanted. One of them, obviously more used to the extraordinary volume than me, managed somehow to make out my Belfast accent. She then told me, I think, that she was from Dublin. However, she may have said that she'd visited Dublin, or perhaps even that she'd like to visit Dublin. I just couldn't make it out. She also said something about 'Southern Belle', or it could have been 'Southern Bell'. I hadn't deciphered enough of the context to allow me to decide which. I kept pointing at my ears, meaning that I was going deaf and that there was no point at all in trying to communicate. One of the two girls must have interpreted this piece of non-verbal communication as meaning 'shout down the hole', because that's exactly what she proceeded to do. As all News of the World reporters say, I then made my excuses and left – to go outside to talk to the bouncers again in comparative peace and quiet.

Steve, the owner, joined us. Steve is the kind of man that you don't mess with. He himself started out as a bouncer, and it shows, and significantly he alone wore a DJ at Rebels. He controls the door at the club and lays down the door policy. He's had seventeen years experience of this kind of work and he says that he's learned a lot, some of it clearly the hard way. 'I had to sort some trouble in a nightclub in Doncaster that I worked in. The gypsies were command-eering the club. At the end of the night, they'd strip their shirts and shoes off, and fight in the middle of the floor for money. So I played them at their own game – if they wanted a fight, they got it. I took eleven professional lads with me from Sheffield, boxers, karate champions, all very tasty, and I employed a couple of the gypsies as well. We soon got it sorted. Here I only have two bouncers on at a time. That's all we need – two grown men who are very experienced at this sort of thing, and know how to get respect from the customers. In this club we specialize in volume for people who are basically extraverts. We have all sorts in here – doctors, nurses, teachers – who want to be a rebel one or two nights a week.'

'But what about all the air guitarists?' I enquired. 'Surely they're not all doctors and nurses.' 'Well I must say,' said Steve, 'that I don't really understand that particular part of it. What I do know is that the girls in here dress in basques and suspenders, with mini skirts up their ass, the lot, and the blokes don't bother them. And that makes running the club a lot easier. If there's any dope, it's taken off them, my bouncers are like sniffer dogs, you know. We video-record everything here, in case there's any trouble. We had our video-recorders installed long before most football clubs. I think we're the only club around here that gets the annual renewal of our license through the post, we never have to go to court to contest it. The punters – the extraverts – who come here are satisfied with the volume and the chance to dress up. We all like to live a dream.'

All this performing and silent guitar playing was clearly making some of the extraverts hungry, and in ones and twos they made their way to the little kitchen, just by the entrance, which Richard Speed hires off Steve for a fiver a night. A long queue formed as the bikers waited patiently in line with the AORs and the Thrash Metal Men and the assorted varieties of ace air guitarists and glam rockers. They queued patiently for liver sandwiches with onions for 45 pence, or egg sandwiches for 35 pence. The traditional 'Sorry, no credit' sign was replaced by 'Instant credit given to all customers over 90, and accompanied by both parents', pinned above the counter.

The ace air guitarists ate their 35-pence sandwiches quickly before making their way back to the dance floor for their next performance in front of their own fans. The bouncers just sipped their tea and thanked God for a quiet life.

A night at the Deadmill

'Come to the Deadmill, tonight,' said the girl with the bright red hair, 'if you dare, that is. It's Walpurgis night, when the witches riot in the company of demons and worship the devil. You'll be amazed and terrified. I'm a witch, by the way. Come and see.' And she was off, as suddenly as she had appeared – into the fog which had descended on to Sheffield on a spring afternoon, on the eve of St Walpurga's day, when all witches return from – well, wherever they return from.

It took me a while to realize that the Deadmill referred to was none other than the Leadmill, Sheffield's famous council-supported Arts Centre, so on a misty Walpurgis night I was off to see the appropriately named 'Sheffield Friday Show'. Well, at least it's an accurate name for a show on a Friday night, I thought to myself as I searched in vain for the front door. But it was a building without a door. On the eve of old whatshisname, nothing was to be what it at first appeared. I eventually tried round the back. It was only 8.00, but it was already getting dark. Through the gloom, I could just make out a girl dressed entirely in black with a shaved head and a pony-tail with a plastic spider clip in it. She was standing up against the wall, her wild eyes red and staring. I walked past her several times still looking for the door, her red eyes watched my every movement. Suddenly another apparition approached through the gloom. He was in black as well, and he also had a shaved head. 'Where the fucking hell have you been?' she screamed at him, immediately causing me to realize that the first apparition that I had been studying was a teenager who thought that she had been stood up. But it was clearly going to be a night for all things satanic and alternative, above the surface at least. I followed them into the dark, dungeon-like Deadmill.

There were about twenty people in the room, all sitting in something of a semi-circle, facing the stage. A young man with long hair and a pair of dungarees continuously swept the dusty floor in front of the stage. 'It's part of the pre-show,' whispered one of the regulars, who had sensed my obvious puzzlement. 'Some Friday nights it's all pre-show, the show itself never gets going, the pre-show is sometimes so fantastic. I think that because tonight is Walpurgis night and the theme is witchcraft and freaks, it might happen tonight.' I decided therefore to concentrate on the pre-show, as the young man came brushing, brushing, brushing my way. Yes, there did seem to be a rhythm to his strokes – groups of three, and twice three is six, and what do repetitions of six give you? No, not a well known Bingo number, old clickety click, but 666, the sign of the devil, satan. I wasn't going to miss a trick.

There were some holes in his dungarees, and as he approached I could quite clearly see his red underpants through them. Was this going to be significant? Like 666, or an inverted cross, were red underpants a symbol of the devil? I needed to see more, I wanted at least to understand the pre-show – red underpants, let me see – with holes! I was leaning forward for an even closer look, when something out of the corner of my eye grabbed my attention – an old hag was leering at me from about two feet away. And not just any old hag, but an old hag with dark pits instead of eyes, and fangs dripping blood. As I turned around, she swivelled away. I kept my eyes on her as she made her way through the audience, leering sideways on at unsuspecting individuals. One brave punk (for indeed there still are punks who attend the Leadmill, and hippies from first time around) shouted 'bite me, bite me' somewhat hysterically, and for one moment the old hag looked vaguely taken aback.

Things were definitely getting a bit weird, as they say. A Medusa figure with snakes as hair, black lipstick and a pair of Fifties sunglasses weaved closer. She stroked the hair of the girl in front, who nearly jumped out of her seat as a result. Now what was going on? Medusa looked as if she might wear this particular get-up most nights anyway – freak show, or no freak show, Walpurgis night or no Walpurgis night. Were these people actors and actresses? Or genuine witches? Or just a bunch of weirdos, given some artistic licence for the evening to practise their weirdness rather than their witchcraft?

It reminded me of some friends of mine who one afternoon consumed quite a quantity of LSD – more by mistake than by design. They did, however, remain sufficiently rational to recognize that they had no chance of successfully concealing their odd behaviour, so they thought that they'd bring it out into the open, and try to get it attributed to something quite different. By a stroke of luck, it just happened to be their university's Rag Day that particular Saturday, so they pretended that their odd behaviour was all part of the Rag Day fun. They handcuffed their legs together, and off they went into the centre of town, howling like wolves as they dragged each other along the city's wet, grimy streets. Eventually, and I do mean eventually, they made it to Rackhams, the very heart of the commercial city, if not the very heart of capitalism itself (I believe the drug was notorious for making the mundane appear especially significant). So right in the middle of their hallucinogenic experience they tried to drag each other on to a multi-coloured but very menacing escalator. They howled a good deal more as their three bodies piled on top of each other. The Rackhams customers, however, found the whole thing very amusing and proceeded to press coins into their hands. Apparently, it was one of the best received Rag stunts of all time. But, of course, it was no act.

My musings were shattered by loud swirling music. I recognized one of the musicians. He had passed me earlier, with a chalk white head and a hatchet gash down the middle of it. But what was even more interesting was the way that he held a cigarette. He held it with the lit end pointing inwards, the way that bouncers almost invariably hold cigarettes. It even looks hard. Were some of these ghouls not quite what they seemed? A witch passed by, very much in character, and asked me if I had any lovely toe nails for her? I laughed with embarrassment, but didn't answer. I didn't think that she required an answer. 'Well have you, my lovely?' she asked again, tugging at my hair this time. 'Sorry, I'm afraid I don't,' I replied, and she started to cackle very loudly. The guy next to me looked most uncomfortable. I heard him ask his girlfriend 'What the fuck's going on here?'

Suddenly a large man with a black cape, and a skull as a necklace, was in the middle of the floor. He talked like the Orson Welles of the Sandeman ad. 'People have always laughed at things they do not understand,' he told us. I nodded vigorously in agreement. 'I would like to take you on a journey,' he said in that husky and very menacing voice.

The journey began, and we were transported along a road replete with the witches and vampires that had been in the pre-show, and plenty of biting wit. It's just a pity that the vampires hadn't remembered to leave their teeth in. For example, a ghoul told us that he stripped his victims bare and left cuts everywhere. 'You mean like John Moore?' the second ghoul asked – boom, boom. Or alternatively – 'I've come about the job. I've seen your advert in the freaks' weekly.' – 'Oh, you mean, the *Sunday Sport*' – boom, boom.

Another sketch concerned somebody who didn't seem to be a freak at all. 'I've got a nice house, a lovely car, a lawnmower, a job . . .' –

'You've got a job in Sheffield, you're a real freak.' Medusa told us that she had lost her head over Perseus, but the advantage of being 3,000 years old was that when she went for a job interview, she could say that she had lots of experience. There was a sketch about two sorcerers turning each other into frogs – 'You should have *toad* the line.' One was complaining about being turned into a cesspool previously – 'The lazy buggers couldn't be bothered going to the loo, they just used me. I was two stone heavier when I went home.' The other sorcerer said that he had been turned into a smile on Steve Davis's face, but 'that was years ago'.

One of the more original sketches concerned a punk poltergeist, with the disembodied voice trying unsuccessfully for a job – 'I might as well be bleeding' alive,' it said. Then there was a sketch about a man called Mr William Percy Percy who had two willies, being interviewed by the BBC. 'Are you a married man?' the interviewer asked. 'Yes, I am, I'm married to the woman with the two . . . labradors,' came the knock-out reply. 'Which side do you dress?' 'Well, there's one in me trousers and one in me hand. I've got an extra finger.' And on that note, a jet of water shot out of the finger all over the interviewer. A blind professor told us that he could see through his nose, and 'talk through your ass' came the razor sharp retort.

The show finished with the dance of Walpurgis night, the dance to raise the dead, and for a moment we returned to the eeriness of the pre-show, but the dance culminated in 'the birdie song'. The guy beside me looked relieved, he even understood the basic formula – like the old British favourite beginning, 'the woman sat on the graveyard wall,' and ending in, 'Yes, we have no bananas.' I preferred the embarrassment of the pre-show myself, at least it was genuinely different.

In the bar I was joined by Roland Miller, creator of 'The Sheffield Friday Show', and Bill Rodgers, the guest director of that particular show, and coincidentally the actor who played Orson Welles. 'It's meant to be a bit like "That Was The Week That Was",' said Roland. '"Friday Night Live", you mean,' said Bill. 'For God's sake let's get a little bit up to date,' Bill continued. 'Political satire that's both topical and done from an alternative perspective. The theme tonight was a freaks' sideshow, that's why we had so many different sketches.'

The show, I learned, is conceived, written and rehearsed in one week flat, which is really quite impressive given the general level of the performance, if not the script. Few of the actors and actresses that take part in the various shows are professional, some get involved in the hope of acquiring an equity card. Bill, with appearances in 'All Creatures Great and Small' and 'Emmerdale Farm' was the only professional in the Walpurgis night show. 'People just come along off the streets,' he told me. 'We have completely open access. Most of the people who take part are unemployed, and we pay them all their expenses for a week, including any child-minding expenses. It's their chance to make some kind of statement and get some acting experience that might help them get a job eventually.'

Roland's background is in performance art – so I could see where the pre-show came from. But the only example of his art that really stuck in my mind was a toilet scene with confetti falling down the side of his bare backside to represent the fall-out from Chernobyl. He did, however, also tell me that he did some performance art in Krakow, in Poland, representing the miners' struggle in this country. But apparently it didn't go down too well, because the workers in Poland all apparently believe that Arthur Scargill is in the pay of Colonel Gadaffi!

'The problem with "The Sheffield Friday Show",' explained Roland, returning to the present for the moment, 'is that the performance and all the clearing-up have to be finished before the disco starts. The disco really makes a big financial contribution to the running of the Leadmill, and we're under strict instructions not to disturb the disco audience. Ideally, the Friday show should start at midnight, but all things strange and alternative unfortunately have to finish well before the witching hour. At five to ten to be precise. It's a very limited sort of weirdness really.'

I said that I could see that, as the witches and ghouls headed off for a dance to some sweet soul music, while Roland toyed at the bar with a menacing looking pick that he had, for some reason, been carrying about with him all evening.

It must be the weekend

The working men's club

It wasn't unlike an aircraft hangar – huge, cavernous and dark. It had bare floors, and was eerily quiet, despite being full of people. Couples and family groups were gathered around the bare tables with the single Carling Black Label ashtray sitting in the middle, by way of decoration. The couples didn't talk much, the family groups even less. The men drank pints of Stones or Tennent's Lager, the women drank halves of lager. All except one that is – one thirty-year-old woman in a tight off-the-shoulder black dress, with a big bust and a big everything else, who sat alone just by the door, was drinking gin and tonic, but out of a half-pint glass. The glass seemed to be full of slices of lemon. The woman was festooned with gold chains. There was a general air of expectancy as everyone waited for the first act to appear. The older men wore cardigans, one wore a V-necked pullover without a shirt under it. The younger men just wore shirts, or T-shirts. All were casually dressed, except for the committee men that is. Down in the club, they've got the power, and they were all suitably attired in suits or sports jackets. I recognized some of them from their photographs by the entrance. They all knew the woman with the gold chains. The club was very dark, and it wasn't yet 8.00.

Suddenly, the stage some distance off was bathed in light and there was the first act – a lady in a blue velour dress, belting out some old favourite, the title of which eluded me. I wasn't alone, I heard my neighbour asking her husband what it was called. 'Good evening, everybody,' said the singer in a Sheffield accent, when she'd eventually finished the song. Very few people bothered to reply. 'You were a lot friendlier last time. Let's try again – *Good evening everybody.*' This time a few more answered. 'That's better,' said the lady in the velour dress. 'You know,' she said in an accent that had suddenly become vaguely American, 'all the best songs came out of the late fifties and the early sixties. Now, isn't that right?' The woman next to me, who looked as if she was in her early forties, nodded vigorously. She would have been about twelve in the late fifties. 'Just think what it will be like in thirty years time when your grandchildren ask you lot what the top of the charts was in your day. What will you be able to tell them? The grannies will be able to sing, "like a virgin, I've been touched for the eighty-fifth time." There was almost no laughter. The loudest laughter came from four yobs in the corner eating chips and laughing at a private joke. Some committee men glanced their way, and they made their way out – noisily.

The lady in the blue velour dress continued, 'I borrowed the next song treatment from that special Scottish lady, Barbara Dickson – it's a version of an old fifties hit . . . And now for another classic from the early sixties – "My Guy", it was on every teenager's lips at the time.' The woman in her early forties beside me was singing along with the tune that she had narrowly missed having on her lips the first time around. 'It's now time to love you and leave ya,' (the Sheffield and American accents were now being combined in the same sentence). 'There aren't many songs that come out these days that are going to stay on the scene. But one of the best things to happen to showbiz for a very long time is that coloured lady from the United States – Whitney Houston, with "The Greatest Love of All" . . . I believe that children are the future.'

I hadn't noticed up until then that there were quite a few children in the club. They went with their dads or their mums to fetch the drinks from the bar, or the pies and mushy peas for tea. The boys wore cheap American sweatshirts, and a surprising number had wet look gel in their hair, the girls had their hair in pony tails. These were the children of miners and steel workers, these were the children of the unemployed, these were the future. It was the end of the first act by the lady in the velour dress. Despite an excellent voice, there was little applause. 'Thank you very much,' she yelled, as if she had to yell to be heard above the applause, which embarrassingly hadn't occurred.

Suddenly, one of the committee was on the stage. He sounded sombre. 'Tickets on sale at reception for the tombola – prizes tonight ten pounds or eighteen pounds, there's also a fabulous £100 jackpot.' There was a mass exodus of men, women and children for the tombola tickets. Before they could return it was time for 'the crazy, the fantastic, the fabulous – The Three Discos.' They launched into 'Bridget the Midget', with one of them pretending to be a midget in a mini-stage, with his arms acting as legs. One of the others arrived on the stage in a flasher's mac and proceeded to flash at him. The 'midget' squealed with delight. It reminded me of a real-life midget I once interviewed who told me about some of the obscene approaches that men made to her in nightclubs. Then it was time for more nostalgia – 'They don't write jokes the way they used to, you know.' Everything harked back to the golden age, the age that may never have been. Then we were brought rudely back to the present. 'What's this?' said one of the Three Discos making side-stepping movements across the stage – 'Ian Botham following the elephants.' The audience was warming up. 'It took three committee men to measure them lights.' Tonight the committee men were the butt of all the jokes, we didn't need the Irish, but we did need the good old days. 'Remember the good old days of the radio?' said another one of the Three Discos.

This led incongruously into a joke about farting that went on for nearly fifteen minutes. 'That was absolutely disgusting,' said the straight man in the Three Discos as the funny man appeared to fart. 'I know, it weren't one of my best.' 'You've got to learn to control your body, you've got to squeeze your bum a bit tighter,' said the straight man. 'It works, you know, it saves you getting bubbles all down your stockings, or having to put your trousers down inside your socks.' The funny man meanwhile said that he was dying to go to the toilet, so they carried on a mobile toilet, and he dropped his trousers, and did the business, as they say, to the 'Raspberry Song'. He even appeared to pee over the side of the toilet onto somebody's head. It was the biggest hit of the evening so far. Then one came on in a beret. 'Who are you?' shouted the straight man. 'Eclair' replied the first. Another came on in a beret and a gorilla mask. 'Who are you?' – 'Chocolate Eclair.' 'Hilarious,' said my neighbour. I only spotted one black man in the club as the Three Discos exited to very loud applause.

It was time for the tombola, signalled by what sounded like a school bell. The committee man in a grey suit called the numbers in a very sombre tone – 'six and O–sixty.' No legs eleven, or clickety click here. This was serious stuff – a book of cards cost 25 pence a card, or 5 pence a card for pensioners. However, there was a loud tinkle of glasses every time that 11 was mentioned. 'It's a lucky number,' explained my neighbour, Edna, as yet another school bell went off, signalling a full house to the last game of the night. Edna explained that she had been going to see the Three Discos since before she was married. 'They're a very good family act, they've been going for twenty-nine years. They used to be called the "Four Mimes" but one of them left.' Edna explained that all the unemployment about Sheffield had hit the Working Men's Clubs because people couldn't afford to go out so early, so it was harder for the clubs to build up an atmosphere early on. 'But the young lads still join, on their eighteenth birthday, whether they're unemployed or not,' she added. Club membership at the Dial House Club ('one of the best,' said Edna) is three pounds a year, with no charge on the door. Beer is about eighty pence a pint. 'Great value,' volunteered her husband Keith. 'Much better than stuck in front of the video night in, night out.'

It was time for the singer again, returning for her second spot. Unemployment or no unemployment, the place was properly warmed up now. It was 9.45, and back to the good old days again – 'My Boy Lollipop', 'Lipstick on your Collar'. 'Join in if you want,' shouted the singer, Ann Ryder. And they did, the heads of the women rocked from side to side, the men just supped up. 'Would you like some songs that got Connie Francis to the top? . . . I've put them all into one medley of songs.' She finished to loud applause.

In the interval, I was joined by one of the Three Discos – Bob Crawley, who at forty-five isn't the youngest Three Disco, but looks it. 'I get to do Adam Ant and Boy George because of my apparent youth in our next spot,' he explained. Bob told me that they'd been doing The Dial House Working Men's Club about four times a year for the past twenty-nine years. I asked if the routine ever varied. 'Well we work to a basic formula,' he said, 'but we try to tailor our specific act to the audience. For example, we don't do the farting routine when people are eating.' I said that I appreciated their consideration. I asked how the unemployment situation in the North affected their business. 'Well there was a time when people would go to the clubs, no matter who was on. Now, they're more selective. You're competing with the video, don't forget, so you have to give them something good to get them out. Pubs have gone up-market in a big way now, Working Men's Clubs are lagging quite a bit behind, so the acts have to be top class to compete. Our next act tonight is what we call the contemporary bit of the show. Just see what you make of it.' And on that cue he was away, to get himself ready as one of those 'comedy megastars – The Three fabulous Discos.'

So what did I make of it? Their second act was devoted to miming to contemporary pop songs – or contemporaryish, Adam Ant is after all fairly contemporary in comparison to Connie Francis. The Three Discos parodied all the megastars, whose private lives the audience all obviously knew very well from the soaraway *Sun* and similar periodicals. The act concentrated on the well-known pop gender benders, with the emphasis distinctly on *bender*, with lots of bending over and falsetto voices. When Bob Crawley dressed as Ziggy Stardust and mimed to Bowie singing, 'Here am I sitting in a tin can,' one of the other Three Discos squatted over a tin can ('s-itting in a tin can'), to very loud laughter from the audience. When the Three Discos impersonated any black singers, the gorilla mask went on, with the noticeable exception of Michael Jackson. His plastic surgery has obviously made him neither white nor black.

Near the end of their act, the Three Discos performed to the 'Spitting Image' Chicken Song, wearing 'Spitting Image' masks of Thatcher, Reagan and Prince Charles. They tossed a plastic chicken in the air. Not very original, but the crowd was loving every minute of it. Spectators crowded in from the bar. The lady in the off-the-shoulder black dress, with the half pint of gin and tonic was being crushed, but she seemed not to mind. Even the committee men pushed in. All eyes were now on the stage, where all the great icons of our age – the rich, the famous, the powerful, indeed all the regulars from the great soaraway *Sun*, were having their noses rubbed in it, along with all the blacks and gays. And the crowd was going wild. It was as if for one brief moment the audience could see through all the phoniness and all the hype which surrounds the megastars, and were getting their own back on them, and then on everything else modern and contemporary –homosexuality, immigration, deadly sexual diseases.

But it was a great night for nostalgia – for remembering the way things were. Some of the audience could even remember the better life from way way back, from before all this. Some of the audience could even remember Connie Francis. Or so they said.

*

Staying up on Thursday

It's sometimes hard being a fly on the wall. The other day, for example, I was shooed away twice, and hit with a rolled-up newspaper once. I know that real flies have it a good deal harder than this, but it still wasn't much fun. Nevertheless, every now and then I find myself turning into a fly and heading for the nearest wall. Interviews are the journalist's stock-in-trade, but sometimes it's important to hear what people say to each other as well. And sometimes you just can't help it.

The fly on the wall sometimes even manages to end up in the jam quite by accident. Two nights ago was just such an occasion.

I was interviewing a new entrepreneur with considerable entre-preneurial vision; he was making a few bob out of transforming rubbish into something desirable – furniture, somewhat futuristic furniture. We were sitting in a somewhat futuristic pub, all flashing lights and rotating balls. He had suggested the pub.

There was a group of four to our left: two couples. Thursdays are hen and stag nights in Sheffield and here were two stags accompanied by their faithful does. Strong pair bonds and no mistake, signalled through their body language. He changed position, she did. He leaned forward, she did. He twitched, she nearly did. Synchronicity, but she just a moment behind, like the stag and doe transformed from space to the temporal dimension. He giving the lead through the pastures of time. And boy, were these pastures mucky! I could hear the odd word 'sex', 'aids,' or was it 'sex-aids', or 'AIDS', or was it 'sex aids . . . the digestion', or 'sex, AIDS will see it off'?

I was trying to concentrate on my new entrepreneur. I asked him if it was the case that the contented man was the enemy of progress, why had he always been a malcontent, and what had been wrong with his childhood? We, not surprisingly, weren't showing synchronous body language at this point.

Then came the bombshell from the adjacent conversation: 'frenchie' – 'Frenchie?' – it exploded on to my consciousness.

This word has always been of some importance to me. Since I was about five, in fact, when I was out walking with my older brother and his best friend. I found something on a rubbish tip which made me very excited. It was a toy soldier which had lost its left arm. To this day I can remember my brother's friend sneering, 'You'd think to see him he'd found a Frenchie or something special like that.' 'Special – what's so special about a toy Frenchman?' I thought to myself. I remember putting this to him and he threw me a look of total disgust and said to my brother, 'not very bright your little brat, is he?' My brother looked deeply ashamed by the whole thing, but of me, not him.

But there I was in the pub, being transformed into a fly on the wall by that particular buzz word. I justified listening to the conversation (to myself) because I thought they might be discussing the imminent change in sexual practice predicted by 'Panorama', Mary Whitehouse, and American Aids Research Agencies. But change was not what they represented, as it turned out. They were getting louder. My new entrepreneur was listening in as well now. When one of the girls mentioned paras and sex – paras meaning paraplegics, not para-troopers (as I found out three sentences later) I was caught in their web.

One of the girls then told the story of how she had contracted vaginal warts. (I know I shouldn't have been listening, but it's difficult for us flies.) Her previous boyfriend had apparently declined to wear a condom. 'He told me it was like asking an artist to wear gloves. What can you do? You can't force him, and it was a bit too late to refuse to do it. He said he'd give me a night to remember. He did that all right.'

Everybody round the table registered disgust – myself included. The couples noticed this and we all laughed. The ice was broken. 'What a bastard,' said the entrepreneur, and he and I were now in the pond up to our necks. I introduced myself and my entrepreneur, the expert at looking at old things in new ways. It looked as if I was going to see an old thing in an old way; close up, magnified, warts and all. Warts everywhere.

Lindsay and Pete, and Lisa and Mark introduced themselves. They were two couples and they insisted I put their names in the order given. 'I don't want anybody to think I'm knocking off Lisa,' said Pete. 'You'd be so lucky,' muttered Lisa. Lisa's other half Mark chipped in, just to show what a decent, fun-loving bloke he was. 'If you want a good interview, talk to Lindsay – she's a nurse and you know what they say about nurses.' He was really getting his own back.

'I don't think we deserve that reputation, not really,' said Lindsay. 'It's just one or two nurses that – let's face it – get us all a bad name. We're not half as bad as the patients, anyway. They're always trying to touch me up, it's bloody annoying.'

'It doesn't surprise me, that,' said Mark, 'you love it really, admit it.' Lindsay flashed a coy look that some would take as a sign of admission and they all went back to their drinks. The two men were on pints of lager and the two girls on halves of lager – one lager and lime and one lager and black.

Mark explained to me that it was hen and stag night. 'Packs of wolves and packs of dogs tonight,' said Mark. 'All wolf whistles and girls that are ruff-rough.' Mark told the joke twice on the assumption that I was either deaf or stupid. But I've always believed that it was me who invented this particular joke, so I didn't laugh.

How come they went out as couples on hen nights then?

'It's like this,' said Pete. 'We're mature. Well nearly. Thursday night, let's face it, is for hen parties. Up in Frankie's, it's "grab a granny" night where all the married crumpet goes for a bit of excitement. Last year me and Mark would be up there in the thick of it, chatting the birds up, listening to all the guff. They go for young guys like us, honest. They'd take us to their cars and then we'd have to do the business, know what I mean?' Mark just smiled knowingly. The two girls just feigned disgust.

'Dirty buggers, men, they're all the same,' said Lindsay. 'Just as well I didn't know you then.'

'Well, it's like this,' said Mark. 'Older birds want a bit of excitement without commitments – they want some good-looking guy to show them a good time, know what I mean?'

My entrepreneur acquaintance nodded confidently. I just nodded.

'No hang-ups, no commitments,' continued Mark. Lisa squeezed his arm, meaningfully.

They all went back to their lager. Lindsay, it turned out, had to get up early in the morning. She started at 7.30 am. 'I like the ward I'm on. I enjoy working with paras and quads (paraplegics and quadriplegics). Most of them can't manage anything, you know, but it's the worst ward I've ever been on for suggestive comments. They're always going on about my bum. You feel really sorry for some of them. There was this patient today and he asked the consultant what were his chances of being able to have sex again. The consultant, who's a little bit too blunt, told him that he'd have just about as much chance of raising it as he would of raising the *Titanic*. Well, his face dropped. Me and this other nurse were on the other side of the curtain and we fell about laughing.

'I felt really sorry for him, but he doesn't half make some suggestive comments. No, not the consultant, Pete, stop messing about, the patient. There's a jab they can give you, you know, and it goes right up. We had this one patient who got the jab and it wouldn't go down. It kept getting bigger and bigger. We all went for a look. He had to go to theatre to get it down in the end. Some patients go back regularly for the jab. It makes them enormous sometimes. What do you mean, you don't like me looking at other men's privates, Pete? It's my job.'

'Look,' said Pete, and he turned to me and my entrepreneur who was starting to look somewhat bewildered, 'write this down. This is how it is. You've got to be able to make a girl respect you, and how do you do that? Do the business, that's how. It's what being a man is all about. Lose that and what have you got left, eh? What have you frigging got left? That's why they get so depressed on spinal injury wards.'

I asked Pete if this wasn't a somewhat restrictive and dangerous view, a none-too-robust philosophy for our knockabout times, even for Thursday nights. He ignored me.

'I just feel sorry for the patients,' said Lindsay, also ignoring me. I felt as if I was turning back into a fly again: an unwanted pest at the Thursday ritual of the Northern hen night. When sex and doing the business was at the back of everyone's mind, and all human life had to be given a position (nudge, nudge) in this grand scheme of things, where everything had to be inserted (nudge, nudge), or fitted (nudge, nudge, nudge) into this greater order.

Lindsay continued, 'To be honest, working with paras and quads, you end up encouraging their suggestive comments. If you don't they sink into a deeper and deeper depression. It keeps them up.

'Metaphorically speaking, of course,' said Lisa. 'Metaphorically speaking, of course.'

And they all laughed.

And I thought to myself, the next sexual revolution might be a long time a-coming, aids, Aids or no Aids. Just call it a fly's sixth sense.

Ducking and Diving

It was the kind of night that's good for business. Not much happening in the nightclub, so the big wheels started talking business, or tried to. The floor show was on – somewhere in the background, but they were all amateurs, and it showed. All brides-to-be prepared to go on stage for the night, all prepared to slide along a greasy pole for a bottle of champagne, or rather for a bottle of sparkling wine posing as champagne. One model from a well-known girlie magazine, who just happened to be in the club, suddenly mounted the stage and showed the amateurs how it was done. She locked her thighs tight around the greasy pole and she was off. She made it to the tip of the pole with one thrust of her pelvis. The VIPs paid attention – for a moment. The rest of the girls on stage were amazed, but not half as amazed as the ordinary punters standing on the floor of the nightclub in front of the stage. They had seen the strength in those thighs from down below. None of the amateurs made it more than a few inches along the pole.

One rather large bride-to-be mounted the pole rather noisily and very unsteadily. She was festooned with inflated durex and pictures cut out of magazines of men's sex organs, with captions cut out of newspapers pinned below – 'What a whopper!' and 'A right Charlie!'. That sort of thing. It must have taken her weeks to find the right captions in the headlines of various newspapers. But on second thoughts, probably not. You could see that they were all from The *Sun*. Her fellow competitors had to help her on to the pole. Suddenly, and without any warning, she gave a great heave. This one heave took her all the way along the pole and then off the other side. There was a loud bang as her head hit the ground. I don't think that she felt a thing. She was presented with her bottle of champagne and led off the stage, looking quite dazed by the whole thing. She looked as if she would have trouble remembering anything the next morning about her once-in-a-lifetime hen-night in the top nightspot.

It was time for the climax to the show. The DJ asked if there were any stag parties in the club that evening. One group in the corner simultaneously raised their hands. 'Then get the lucky man on stage, let's see what he's got,' bawled the DJ. One very thin young man, in his early twenties, bolted for the exit, but he was dragged back and lifted on to the stage. He stood surrounded by the girls in their funny brides-to-be costumes with the inflated durex billowing out behind them. 'That's right girls crowd in on him, don't let him escape,' ordered the DJ. The girls didn't need to be told twice. 'Now, when I give the word, and not before – wait for it! – take all his clothes off. Rape him girls, that's it, go for it,' screamed the DJ. Three pairs of hands grabbed at his shirt, five pairs grabbed at his trousers. The bloke didn't really resist, there wasn't much point, he just ducked and dived as best he could to prevent the *audience* seeing everything. Hands were being thrust inside underpants. 'He's got bloody holes in his Y-fronts,' screeched the DJ. 'Is that going to be your wedding night surprise? I think we've seen enough of that now, get the curtains closed quickly, *quickly*.'

And the thick velvety brown curtains closed swiftly around the scene. But you could still see bumps in the curtains, with the bumps moving rapidly one way then another. The bridegroom-to-be was obviously continuing to bob and weave and duck and dive for his modesty's sake, even with the curtains shut.

Meanwhile up in the VIP bar, a different kind of bobbing and weaving and ducking and diving was going on. The VIPs ignored the brides-to-be show. 'It never changes, does it?' said one man in his late forties with a sixties Jason King hairstyle and moustache. 'Seen one, seen 'em all. My friends call me Jason, you know,' he added somewhat unnecessarily. 'Now about that Corniche,' he said turning to his companion.

To his right, stood a man in his early thirties chatting to one of the bouncers. Suddenly, he seemed to recognize a face in the crowd, and he started to weave his way unsteadily towards him. 'You were the fella looking at that BMW I was selling, isn't that right?' he slurred. 'Have you got fixed up yet? I've still got the car. It's not that I've had trouble selling it, it's just that . . . well I like it so much I can't bear to part with it, honest to God, swear on my mother's grave. I don't like talking business on a Friday when I, and I'm sure you as well, have had far too much to drink, but why waste the opportunity? Answer me that one.'

The bouncer leant across and whispered in his ear that it wasn't Friday, that it was Thursday, that the noise from across the floor wasn't the hullabaloo of the ordinary weekend punter, but the hullabaloo from the statutory Thursday night rape, but to no avail.

The entrepreneur continued regardless. 'I'll be honest with you, I've got one on at the moment, a punter has been in asking about it – dead keen. A nice little tickle, if you ask me. But . . . but,' he repeated the word for emphasis, although it just came out sounding like a drunken stammer, 'he hasn't come up with the readies yet. And that's what life is all about – readies. Now I'm not going to hassle you, but have you got a private number where I can contact you tomorrow, or what? If I was a high-pressure salesman, I'd be ringing first thing tomorrow morning, but I know what a pain it is to get a call first thing on a Saturday morning, when you've got a hangover and all the rest of it. I hate doing business at the weekend but this is different. This isn't business, we're doing each other a favour. Just helping each other out.'

You could see the unfortunate victim of this sales pitch contemplating whether to tell the persistent car dealer that tomorrow morning was Friday, and not Saturday, but he couldn't think of a way of introducing it at this late stage. It would discredit everything the car dealer had said up to that point. And after all, they had been just helping each other out. So the weekend it was.

But this willingness to cooperate had all kinds of unforeseen consequences. 'Are you going to watch Wednesday, tomorrow,' asked the car dealer leaning right into his unfortunate victim. 'Eh, surely you wouldn't miss Wednesday playing Nottingham Forest at home.' And he exhaled another load of beery fumes right into the face of the perplexed punter.

You could see the poor unfortunate genuinely stuck for something to say, caught in a classic double bind. Should he tell the car dealer that he wasn't going to watch Wednesday play tomorrow (because the team wouldn't in fact be playing tomorrow, since tomorrow was Friday, not Saturday)? But if he did this, then wouldn't he leave this ardent Wednesday supporter, and car dealer, with the impression that here was a man that didn't care one way or the other about the town's glorious home side. Or, alternatively, should he reply that he was going to watch Wednesday play tomorrow, thereby tacitly agreeing that tomorrow was indeed Saturday, and that this indeed was the weekend? But surely this route led ultimately to fantasy, delusion and madness?

You could see him thinking to himself – 'oh, what the heck.' 'Er, I'm going to watch Wednesday play tomorrow,' he stammered back.

'See you there, then,' said the car dealer, 'and don't forget your bundle of readies. We could sort the deal out after the game in the director's suite. Only the best after all.'

And on that note he wandered off through the ordinary punters in search of a toilet.

Other deals were being struck, and other bright ideas tested and marketed. One wide boy with receding hair was swapping stories about money-making schemes. 'I had a friend who put an advert in the local paper advertising a guaranteed safe and 100 per cent foolproof method for killing rodents and other vermin. Only £9.95, the advert said. You know what – for a tenner he sent the punters two bricks and a set of instructions saying "place the rat midway between the two bricks and bring the bricks rapidly together on the rat's head." Nothing dishonest about that, now is there? Hundreds of mugs replied as well. Just shows what a rat-infested hole we live in. But that one's only if you're desperate. I'm into leather jackets now, and the other sort as well. There's a sign at the front of my store that says "genuine leather jackets", then there's jackets at the back of my store for forty five quid. How can they be leather at that price? When it says "genuine leather" at the front of the shop, it doesn't mean that all of the jackets in the store are leather, now does it? But some punters have tried taking the forty-five quid jackets back because they're not leather. The nerve of some people. That's what it's about, you know – ducking and diving, keeping one step ahead of the ordinary punter.' And all his merry band nodded in agreement.

Meanwhile the large lady from the brides-to-be show had made it as far as the steps of the VIP bar, clutching the remains of her sparkling champagne. But all the fizz had long since gone. She clambered wearily up the steps. But, when eventually she made it to the final step, the bouncer standing there to keep the ordinary punter and the VIP apart, stepped in and turned her away. The wide boy and his cronies had, however, started to attend to the spectacle, designed to make them feel special. It seemed to work.

'That's going to be my next little scheme,' said the wide boy, 'mass-produced brides-to-be costumes complete with floating Frenchies, and Y-fronts that don't go into holes too easily.'

And his entourage guffawed with laughter, as the bride-to-be sat herself wearily down on the bottom step leading to the VIP bar, and started to cry, ever so gently.

Legless in Rotherham

Right in the middle of Rotherham in South Yorkshire, there was, I had been reliably informed, a nightclub where beer and lager were sold for twenty pence a pint. Halves were ten pence, shorts twenty-nine pence. 'So,' explained Dave Chandler, one of the owners of the club, whom I eventually tracked down in his video shop in Sheffield, 'you can go to Peppermint Park on a Wednesday night and get pissed for a quid, and legless for two quid. How's that for value for money! And, don't forget,' he added, 'it's only two pounds fifty to get in. The unemployed love us.'

Dave and his partner Steve's 'philanthropy' has not, however, been without its critics. Last November, judge Michael Walton said at Sheffield Crown Court that the policy of having beer at 20p a pint was 'disgraceful' and 'an anti-social act' when he sentenced two youths to nine months at a young offenders' institution for robbing a taxi driver. Both youths had drunk between eight and twelve pints at the club before the robbery (and at that price I suppose it is rather difficult to remember how many you've had. An error factor of four would seem quite reasonable in the circumstances). The judge also said: 'We take the view that those who for profit ply young people with drink should be standing in the dock with you.'

Dave was not, however, impressed. He tossed his long, blond, football-player-style locks petulantly. 'We should be in the dock? What do judges know, eh?' His partner, Steve Walton, who had just joined us, echoed this sentiment by tossing his long, dark football-player-style hair, but even more forcefully. 'As I said at the time,' said Steven, 'a judge doesn't have to go and count his pennies on his night out. Not everyone is on a judge's salary and we get a lot of unemployed in our club. Our low prices mean that they can go out for the evening instead of having to stay at home. I was quite willing to stand in the dock any time and answer any of the judge's questions about this. We cater for the over-twenty-fives, not for kids. I wanted the judge to come down and see for himself, we've nothing to hide.'

I asked if I might do instead of the judge, and so one evening several weeks later I made my way gingerly through Rotherham town centre, listening out for the sounds of bacchanalia on the cheap. Unfortunately, I didn't hear them. I did, however, pass an un-nervingly quiet Jobcentre, and right beside it was the very club that I had been searching for. It was 11.30 pm, but the bar was really rather slack. 'It's not giro week,' explained one of the bouncers. One group of decidedly over-twenty-fives, nevertheless, seemed to be welded to their seats in one corner of the bar. The group consisted of four males, who looked as if they had already consumed about six pounds worth of beer between them. Some of the beer was starting to find its way down their chins. I could see that it was fast approaching *that* stage of the evening, for them at least. The females, who walked past them repeatedly, looked under twenty-five, considerably under twenty-five, in fact. One of these, can we say, younger members of the club explained that one club in Rotherham catered for what she called 'down-and-outs', and another for 'yuppies'. 'The Pep', as Karen called it, was for those in between – 'not slags or not right stuck-up, just ordinary girls like me. I want to be a model, you know.'

'And ordinary fellows?' I asked, gesturing towards the group of men who continued to down their beer regardless, with quite a lot of it now missing their mouths. 'Ordinary fellahs as well,' she said. 'After all, TV's really boring on a Wednesday. The Pep helps to break the week up. Sometimes it's really bunged, especially on giro week, but not tonight.' And on that note, she made her way back to the bar for her sixth Malibu and pineapple.

I was joined at the bar by Dave. He was wearing a Mistral shirt with 'Too Much' written on the back. Steve subsequently came up wearing an identical shirt. They had similar hair styles, and both had gold bracelets. I noticed that Steve's spelt out 'Steve', reasonably enough I suppose. 'I call him Wally,' said Dave, sipping a cocktail. 'Wally Walton, you know from the Waltons, the TV show, eh?' Wally turned towards me. 'What do you think of the place?' he asked in that slightly accusing style that some people have even for the most innocuous of questions.

'Well, er . . . um not bad, I expected quite a lot more drunkenness . . . not bad really,' I replied.

'Not bad, not flipping bad! Is that what you said?' Steve looked around the bar as if searching for words. Eventually he found a sentence. 'Did you hear what he said, Dave? Not bad.' There was an even longer pause, time enough for me to reflect on my faux pas, and on Steve's hairstyle, and time enough for Steve to take a large drink of his exotic-looking cocktail. Steve took a sharp intake of breath – 'I think this place is bloody embarrassing.'

'Eh?' I naturally assumed that I was hearing things. Steve continued, 'I'm embarrassed to be here, aren't you?'

'Er, um, no, not really,' I said, desperately trying to work out what exactly was going on.

'We're going to close this place in a few weeks. We're going out in a blaze of publicity. We've got Freddie from *Nightmare on Elm Street* coming along for the closing. Our line is going to be "Nightmare on Ship Hill finally ends".'

Naively, I asked if Freddie was from England, and, if not, what was he doing coming over from the States just to witness the closing of the Peppermint Park?

'Not *the* Freddie. Just a Freddie, he's a Freddie impersonator really I suppose. He's a big hit in the clubs around here. But he'll do the trick for us. Our closing is nothing to do with the judge's remarks. We're going up-market, way up-market. We may even have cheap drinks when we re-open, we haven't decided that yet. It's under review as they say. But not so much cheap beer as cheap cocktails. You see we're going to bring Ibiza to the centre of Rotherham. Dave has worked as a DJ in clubs in Ibiza for ten years, as well DJ-ing for Peter Stringfellow in Cinderella's in Leeds. We're going to set up an Ibizan-style club right here. We've spent 160 grand buying the club, but we're going to spend 400 grand on a complete refurbishment. It's going to be all white, like the best and most exclusive clubs in Ibiza.'

'Right next to the Jobcentre in Rotherham?' I asked.

'Yes, right next to the Jobcentre in Rotherham. What's the matter with that? This club is going to be different, it's going to be founded on the concept of entertainment,' added Steve. 'Dave is the best natural entertainer I've ever met. He can get anyone to like him within the first five minutes. If you listen carefully you can see that he doesn't really have a clue what he's talking about, but he can chat away alright. I've worked with Dave for ten years in clubs, and I've always been impressed by his special little touches. We were doing this Halloween show once at this club, and I was all dressed up in this monk's outfit. I was standing over this go-go dancer in a coffin. All of a sudden Dave jumped on to the stage and jumped into the coffin with the go-go dancer. It wasn't choreographed, it wasn't even meant to be part of the show or anything. Marvellous. In our new club, the punter will be entertained, they won't know what's going to happen from one moment to the next. In most clubs the owners just wallow with the poseurs, the punters with the cash. We started with nothing, we can mix with the ordinary bloke, we won't just want to wallow with the poseurs.'

The ordinary blokes behind us had now started belching very

loudly and somewhat uncontrollably. Steve didn't look much inclined to wallow with them either.

'We've got the experience you need to run a good club,' continued Steve. 'Dave's background is in entertainment – as a DJ, which is really part of showbiz. I've had some background in entertainment, as a male stripper, but most of my experience has been in bar management. We ran a club in the Lake District a few years ago. It was only two miles from Windscale. The first night I went there in my white tuxedo, black shirt and black trousers, somebody set fire to me. They'd held a match up to my jacket without me seeing them. I thought, right, if that's the way you want to play it. We did the business, alright. The funniest thing about this club was that you could always tell the guys who worked at Windscale. When we had the ultra-violet lights on in the club, the guys who worked there had hair which used to glow bright green in those lights. We used to ask anyone with green, glowing hair where they worked and we were always right. It was a right dive this place, in the middle of nowhere.'

'Just like *Ice Station Zebra*,' added Dave, who I could see by now liked to think in terms of classic films, or should I say classy videos. 'Our new club "Pacha" is going to be that bit different. Stylish, upmarket. "Style city" is what I like to call it. More "Miami Vice" than *Saturday Night Fever*. We're flying in special cocktails from Ibiza. There would be no point in mixing style cocktails for the punters that we have here at the moment. I'll be standing the punters of this new club on their heads, they won't know what's going to happen next. I'll suddenly stop a record and have some of the punters on stage. Audience participation, that's the name of the game. Competitions with prizes of a week in Ibiza.'

'Or two weeks in Ibiza,' added Steve.

'Yes, even two weeks in Ibiza,' continued Dave. 'We'll be playing commercial pop and Balearic beat. No Acid House. Definitely no Acid House.'

'Acid House' had been said with such deliberation and emphasis that I was sure that I was missing something. What was the sub-text here? Was Acid House too emphemeral? Too passé? Too freaky? What?

'Acid House is not for over-twenty-five year olds, Acid House is for kids, our new club isn't for kids,' interrupted Steve rather forcefully. 'We want the kind of punter that can afford foreign holidays, and wants to take a bit of the exotic lifestyle back to Rotherham with him. We want the kind of punter who wants to drink cocktails in an exclusive setting.'

'We're going to be marketing a lifestyle,' said Dave. 'Even the shirts that we're wearing are part of that lifestyle. All part of an image that we're trying to project.'

I reminded him that his shirt said 'Too Much', but Dave took this as a great compliment. At least the judge will have less to complain about, I thought, even if the transformed club does fill up with solicitors, who I suppose will be able to afford between eight and twelve cocktails on a good night.

★5★
You can run, but you can't hide

Exit the Dragon

We live in violent times. Some don't go out, some want to go out prepared. But what kind of preparation really counts when you're out there on the streets? Judo, as we all know, is primarily a sport, perhaps okay for self defence when you've got someone by the lapels and dancing with him in a circular motion, but otherwise? Karate can be spectacular, but is it any use? Were there any martial arts clubs specifically training people for life on the streets of Britain today? Eventually, I found my man when Andy walked into the room – all five foot five inches, wearing spectacles and carrying an umbrella. Real sand in the face material, but lethal, or so I'd heard. He bowed and uttered something in Japanese. I mumbled back, embarrassed already.

This was the man that they had been talking about, the black belt who was pioneering commando-style fighting in the grim streets of South Yorkshire. Andy placed his umbrella carefully against the wall and started to explain the background to the martial arts style that he has recently created and the club that he now runs to promote it. 'I've got a black belt in jujitsu, and a brown belt in karate, but despite what people think even jujitsu isn't about self-defence, and it doesn't prepare you for trouble in the real world. And karate is too rigid and not practical enough if you're small like me. Some of the kicks are useless in a real fight, so I've developed my own personal style – I call it "Jiko Boei Do" – the self defence way. I take the really effective moves from karata and jujitsu and modify them to make them more effective. I use a more upright stance than in karate, and punch with the thumb up rather than with the knuckles up – like this.' There was a huge rush of air as his hands shot forward. At least I think they shot forward. It was so fast that I missed it. 'You don't damage your wrist with your hand held this way. Jiko Boei Do is more streetwise than either karate or jujitsu with no high kicking or no jumping up in the air. It's more like commando-style fighting – all basic and simple. Look, what's the point in learning all those elaborate round-the-house kicks from karate if someone jumps you in an elevator, eh? You'll never be able to get your leg round.' I nodded in agreement, but silently wondered how frequently people got attacked in elevators. What kind of wild, rough world did Andy inhabit, and why was he suddenly talking American?

'Do you by any chance live in one of those blocks of flats where television sets are constantly thrown out of windows and muggers reside in the dark corners of lifts?' I added helpfully. 'No,' said Andy, 'but that doesn't matter. Self defence is about discipline and always being prepared for the unexpected.' My mind started wandering to Peter Sellars as the indefatigable Inspector Clouseau, and I could easily imagine Andy secreting friends around his home in Rotherham to jump out unexpectedly to attack him, just to keep him on his toes. But I managed to show some discipline here. 'I bet you travel in a lot of lifts, though, in those kinds of flats just waiting for the unexpected,' I added. 'Wrong again,' said Andy. 'I avoid those kinds of places. I always stay well away from trouble.'

'Why the umbrella?' I asked. 'Doesn't it invite trouble, increasing the apparent wimp potential of the person carrying it, at least in the eyes of any potential mugger?' And then it dawned on me – 'I bet that's why you do it. You're saying come and get me – I'm a wimp, and you're just hoping that somebody will.' Andy modestly denied this. 'I don't consider this to be an umbrella, it's a lethal weapon, in the right hands.' I asked him to demonstrate.

'Come at me with an imaginary knife,' he said. 'Will this ruler do?' I asked. 'Perfect. Right, hold it out like you would a knife. Right, come at me.' Andy then went into one of those stances that always makes me want to chuckle. You know Indiana Jones pulling out a gun to shoot the Kung Fu expert. I felt like throwing the ruler at him. 'Right, come at me, nice and slowly.' I did, with my right arm conveniently outstretched. And lo and behold the umbrella came down on top of the arm. 'There – lethal,' said Andy. 'In Jiko Boei Do, I teach the use of a number of practical objects for self defence like umbrellas, sticks and keys, which are very important nowadays with the government trying to tighten up on the availability of offensive weapons like knives and so forth. But keys and umbrellas can be just as deadly. You can jab keys into the neck, the cheeks, the groin, you can block with an umbrella or jab it into the groin. All these objects give you the edge in a fight and that's what's really important.'

I had this image of thousands of kids running around the streets of Sheffield with their little black umbrellas in their hands positively inviting someone, just anybody, to rush at them with a six-inch ruler so that they could go for the groin. But Andy soon corrected this false impression. 'You have to be at least sixteen to be in my club, and most of the members are actually somewhat older, quite a bit older actually.'

I asked which particular moves had he found to be most effective in a real fight. There was a long pause. 'Well to be honest, I haven't been in an actual fight since I left school twelve years ago. But Peter who's a salesman for a security firm had to use Jiko Boei Do once at a racecourse. This bloke wouldn't move away from the barrier so Peter put an arm lock on him and marched him away. That were about it really. But in training we use real knives and everything. It means that you wouldn't freeze if someone came at you with a real knife in the street. At least, I think it does. See this scar here on my cheek – that was done by my friend at the club coming at me with a real knife. A lot of people think that it makes you a superman, but it doesn't, you know.'

Clearly not, I thought, surveying the scar. How did he get in to all of this?

'It all started when I saw *Enter the Dragon*, I'd only seen wrestling on the telly before that and I was really impressed. Bruce Lee was about the same height as me, and I thought if it works for him it will work for me. But the point is the kind of stuff that Bruce Lee did was a bit flash, I try to keep it nice and simple. One of the guys from the club is a fork lift truck salesman and he calls it the "kiss" approach – the "keep it simple, sunshine" approach. Nice and simple, the way commandos do it. Look, come along and watch us train. You'll get a better idea of what we do, and you might even learn something that will come in handy.'

So the following night off I went. It was wet and misty – perfect mugging weather I thought to myself. I made my way to an old tower in Sheffield – a perfect location for the demonstration of unarmed combat. But, when I got there, I discovered that the insides of the tower had been gouged out and the whole thing turned into a squash and leisure club. The 'dojo', the area where the martial arts takes place, was a squash court. The first thing that struck me when Andy's club entered, all four of them, was that the Bruce Lee generation were all now in their thirties and forties. These were the kids who used to leave the Chesterfield ABC chopping the air, getting on for twenty years ago. I talked to one nightclub owner from Chesterfield recently, who told me that in those days he used to scrutinize the local papers to see what Kung Fu film was playing in town in order to work out what kind of behaviour to expect in the club that week. And here they were still chopping men up, still chopping men down, as the song said.

Andy, being a black belt, displayed the famous SAS privilege for the elite to modify basic uniform into something more individualistic altogether. He wore a judo suit in the colours of the American flag, the rest seemed content with plain white. They warmed up for what seemed like forever by moving like crabs across the court, then it was time for the first cross-court forays. Jab, jab, punch, punch, kick, kick, followed by ten press-ups on the knuckles. Real commando stuff. Except that Barry, the member of the club who just happened to be closest to my vantage point on the balcony, couldn't manage the press-ups on his knuckles, so he stayed out of synchrony with the rest and just used the palms of his hands. This rather ruined the effect of this mean machine limbering up. With his huge soft belly, he also couldn't quite manage the press-ups, so he just bobbed his head, rather than his whole body, up and down. It really made a most curious sight with his bottom stuck up in the air, and his head showing these rather determined staccato movements. He was also getting further and further behind the other three. By the eighth dash across the court, he was reduced to a walk and a token swivel of his foot round and round. He was not really kicking any more, more just exercising his ankle. One of the others then slid on the smooth surface of the court and he turned out to be the first and only casualty of the night. Andy shouted something in Japanese, it sounded like 'banzai' – it was time for the set moves, all in perfect slow motion. The testicles were grabbed every few seconds, or not so much grabbed as felt and released. 'We call them "prime targets",' explained Andy afterwards.

A couple of six-year-old kids then wandered along. They'd been watching the squash on the other courts and they asked where the Kung Fu was going to be held. I said that it was here and that this was it. 'Why haven't they started yet, then?' they asked. I told them that they had. There was a very long pause. You could see that they did not quite believe it. Then it was time for freestyle combat down below. Barry nervously advanced towards his opponent, watching his own prime targets very carefully as he did so. His opponent seemed less anxious, because Barry's kicks were not high enough to worry anyone's prime targets. The six-year-olds were looking extremely bored. 'I prefer *Ghost Busters* myself. If I had my *Ghost Busters* gun with me, I could zap any of them. Pow, pow, easy peasy.' I reminded myself that Bruce Lee has been dead for fifteen years, and that there are new heroes today. It turned out that they'd both seen *Raiders of the Lost Ark* over Christmas and yes they did remember the bit where Indiana Jones pulled the gun out and shot the foreign gentleman squaring up for a bit of Kung Fu. You could see that they had been impressed, as impressed perhaps as Andy had been once by Bruce Lee.

Andy was getting the umbrellas out now, but it was too late for the six-year-olds who were heading back to watch the controlled aggression of the average squash game.

Afterwards, I had a chance to meet Barry and the rest. It's always easy to sneer from a distance – from reports of what people do, or even from the balcony of a squash court, but up close you get to see the perspiration and the anxiety, and the fear that gets people to such places on a wet and cold Friday night. I noticed that Barry had several teeth missing. It turned out that he had been beaten up in Sheffield station one night. 'Picked on for no good reason, except that I'm small and an easy target. I was into judo at the time and I thought that it might work. I even managed to get him on to the floor eventually, but he just got up and bashed me. Jiko Boei Do might help me a little bit more if I ever find myself in a similar situation again.'

'As long as you don't walk around thinking you're a superman and go showing off all the time,' said Andy. 'That can always be a bit dangerous.'

But you could just see by Barry's face that there was little chance of that – ever.

Dealing with the heavy mob, and the Muppets

Bob is big time, very big time, in fact. He's worth several million. He sipped his gin and tonic, and my eyes flitted to his gold watch and his gold bracelet. I've seen them all – Rolexes, snide Rolexes that look better than the real thing, Cartiers and snide Cartiers with the paint peeling off. But his watch didn't even make any attempt at the right label. It might have been a Seiko, but I couldn't be sure. Functional rather than ostentatious, used for telling the time rather than for telling others who he was. My eyes stayed on his wrists, and my eye movements moved automatically back up to his starched cuffs. The cuffs were somehow more noticeable than all that gold, or gold paint in the case of the watch. This was a man who liked order. But I didn't think that order was the most important thing in building up a huge nightclub and casino empire, in a world full of sharks all wanting a slice of the action. And what self-respecting shark doesn't want a piece of that action? What has order got to do with any of it?

I wanted to find out. So here we were in a world a million miles away from his world of steak and more steak and steak Tartare and steak Bernaise and Moet and Lanson and Dom Perignon. Here we were in a restaurant where books on croquet lay scattered around the place. I wanted to disorient him. It seemed to be working. 'Every time you take me for a meal, it's to a non-smoking restaurant,' said Bob in a somewhat annoyed tone. He looked around briefly at the women with the scraggy necks in the Laura Ashley dresses, and the men who all seemed to be wearing red ties, and probably Seiko watches – but for a different reason from Bob himself. Then he tucked into the 'pan fried calves liver with sauteed apples served with a crisp stir fry of mange tout.' It wasn't prawn cocktail.

My mind wandered away from the disembowelled calves for a moment. You see I've heard them all – small-time burglars with the social skills of a potted shrimp telling me how they're saving all their readies to invest in a club one day – 'maybe Puerto Banus, maybe Chesterfield, I'm not sure yet.' I've spent hours listening to big-time bullies, who like to saunter around clubs showing their bit-on-the-side exactly who they are, by demonstrating who they know, shaking every hand worth shaking. 'How are you, Sir?' they say as they compress your hand for good measure. It's always 'Sir' by the way, their memory bank never quite matches their aspirations. They've spent years doing this sort of thing, now they've decided that they want to do it for a living. 'I could run a club like this,' they say in an expansive sort of way leaning back as they enunciate every word ever so carefully. They lean back until they look as if they are about to fall over, so that they can look around them, and perhaps check who's behind their back. It's a trick that they've learned, presumably to keep themselves safe in very confined spaces. 'There's nothing to it really,' they say. And for a moment you don't know whether they're talking about this strange bodily posture or running a club. But their philosophy comes pouring out, and you realize that they certainly have not spent much time thinking about any aspect of their behaviour, or the kind of image they project, let alone strange and isolated postures. It's their philosophy they ruminate on.

'You just have to be able to identify the good punters,' they say, 'the really big hitters, and be able to talk to them and that's it basically.' And the bit-on-the-side invariably nods feverishly. 'I know all the big hitters around here, and give me a line up of blokes that I've never met before, and I'll pick out the big hitter for you.' The bit-on-the-side's nods go into overdrive. 'Oh, he knows all the VIPs,' she says, 'and he's even introduced me to some of them. I've met Bob who's got a gold VIP card, who's got that used car lot in Rotherham.' 'And a lot more besides,' adds the big bully. The bit-on-the-side continues, 'And Ken who's got the double glazing firm in Doncaster.' 'And a conservatory business tacked on,' adds grizzle again – 'don't forget the conservatory business – a bit special is that.' 'He knows them all,' she says adoringly, 'and they all drink shampoo – nearly every night.'

'It's true,' he says, 'I do know them all. All the shampoo set. Lead me into a room and I could pick them out for you. I've spent a lifetime meeting the right sort of people.' 'And a lifetime of line-ups by the sound of things,' I say in a rather low voice. But he ignores me. 'I'll sort out the big hitter from the two-bob millionaires. I haven't been selling snide Rolexes for nothing, you know.'

And then my mind returned to the man with the starched cuffs. 'I'm a bit of a disappointment to you,' he said eventually. 'You'd rather I was like Bob Hoskins in the *Long Good Friday* or something like that. That's the kind of image the public have. Either a right heavy, a real bully, or someone very crooked. But it's just not like that. The nightclub and gaming business is run on the same principles as any other business. You're basically selling a product at a fair price. In the case of nightclubs what you're selling is an environment. It's up to the punters what they use the environment for. A successful club has to be busy all the time. You have to get the punters to pack in. What makes them go? In my view, it's the herd instinct. The opera's just the same. You don't go to the opera primarily to hear the music, you go to be bundled together with people similar to yourself, or people that you think you're like. It's the same with nightclubs.'

'But what about the sharks?' I asked. 'How do you deal with them?' 'Well the first thing to remember is that ninety-nine per cent of the people you come into contact with are people whom you don't have to worry about at all. There are few people who are out to cause you any aggravation, who you have to treat that seriously. The rest are just muppets.' Now I've seen club owners in the movies and I've listened to their talk but I've never heard anyone using a word like 'muppet' before. But Bob's world is a world of black and white – muppet and non-muppet. The small time burglars are muppets, the big-time bully boys are muppets, I'm a muppet. In fact, I'm definitely a muppet. I couldn't find the entrance to the restaurant that night for a start, and I spent the first half hour of the evening circling the outside of the building looking for a way in – in full view of all the diners. I am not the kind of person to be treated *seriously* in Bob's jargon.

'But how can you tell muppets from non-muppets?' I asked. Bob looked at me, as if to say only a muppet would ever ask a question like that. 'Put it this way, I was approached a few months ago by a couple of guys in one of my clubs who said that they wanted to see the gaffer. They came straight out with it – they wanted to supply all the spirits for the club – at very reasonable prices. I said that I couldn't fault their prices, but asked what would happen if I didn't pay. They just said "Oh you'll pay, don't worry about that." I said "How many times?" "Oh, just the once." These were guys you had to take seriously.' 'Not muppets,' I added helpfully. 'Definitely not muppets,' said Bob. 'It was their manner that told me they had to be taken seriously. Not all flash and threats. Very quiet, a bit understated.' 'A bit like yourself,' I added. But Bob wasn't sure whether this was a compliment or not. Bob continued regardless. 'But the only way of dealing with that sort of thing is not to get involved at all. Not even a little bit – no matter how tempting it seems.'

It was now time for the fillet of local fallow deer served pink with spiced red cabbage and glazed walnuts. Bob seemed relieved that there was no steak on the menu. He seemed to be loosening up, only tensing slightly when he noticed the no-smoking sign again. 'Two weeks ago we had a couple of so-called businessmen in the club, with their minder and the Roller parked down below. Now, they were muppets. It was very late – after closing time, about 3.00 am, and they came right out with it – "How would you fancy having a quarter of a million quid?" I told them I wasn't interested so it went up to half a million. This guy just said, "I can bring it here first thing in the morning in a carrier bag, and don't be clever by saying that you don't want it." So I said, "Look, I just don't want it," so he tells me not to be so clever. He thought that I was trying to provoke him – "You're just trying to be clever, and that's not too clever in itself, you know."'

I said that I was already starting to get a feel for this conversation, fuelled by too much steak and almost certainly too much shampoo.

Bob continued, 'I told them that they were barred from the club from now on. The secret is not to get involved. There are too many club owners who think that they can play it both ways. Some think that they can steal what the club makes, but it's still thieving, even if it is thieving from yourself – you've still got bills to pay.'

'Of course, incidents like this do put your blood pressure up. And it just so happens that I mentioned to one of my doormen that particular night that I could do with one of those machines to keep a careful check on my blood pressure. So he turned up with one the following day. Don't ask me where he got it from. We had a bit of a play about with it. The only problem was that we nearly had a few fatalities. After a day's work, it was a bit of light relief to use it. There was no shortage of volunteers or helpers. But it can be a bit dangerous if you've had a few drinks, because you keep pumping the thing up and forgetting about it.'

At this stage in the evening I started to sweat. It might have been the stories about businessmen roaming the streets with half a million pounds in carrier bags. It might have been the stories about the blood pressure of inebriate volunteers being measured at 3.00 am in the morning. It might have been the blazing fire in the corner of this very up-market restaurant. I noticed that Bob was not sweating at all. 'You know you could stop that if you'd any self-control,' said Bob, noticing my state. 'Just pull yourself together. Just tell yourself that you're cold.' I did, but nothing happened. Beads of sweat continued to form and drip on to the table. I also noticed that the women with the scraggy necks were all sweating, as were the men in the red ties with the tight collars on their shirts. Bob alone was cool. He seemed to be freezing in fact. The fact that I had so little self-control seemed to be irritating him ever so slightly.

'I've met so-called intelligent people before, you know,' he began in a challenging way, 'and I know a lot of questions that can baffle them.' He was staring right at me. 'Okay, let's start with this one – what's the square root of minus 16?' He leaned back. Bob was used to testing people, indeed his whole life revolved around it. Now it was my turn. Unfortunately, the question seemed to me to be something of a nonsense, as it involved the square root of a minus quantity. But was that the test? – to see how I would handle a bit of academic incompetence? Was he trying to determine if I would correct him? Or, heaven forbid, ridicule him?

I played it straight – instinctively, intuitively, without thinking, like a muppet. 'The square root of minus 16 doesn't exist,' I replied, remembering my school mathematics – 'any number squared gives you a positive number.'

A look of glee swept across Bob's face. He leaned back in his chair ever so slowly. I had certainly failed the test at some level – whatever the test was. It was the first time that night Bob had displayed any real emotion. His eyes sparkled. 'That's where you're wrong, you see. That one always gets you so-called intelligent people. The square root of minus 16 is J4. Don't ask me how it's done, but that's the correct answer. And don't argue with me. It's part of a circle or something. You see, what's important is getting the right answer in the end, even if you don't understand how it's done.'

I replied that the same thing could be said about running a successful club, but Bob was off – back into the night.

Knowing the score

Don has always liked the old boxing adage – 'You can run, but you can't hide.' The ring is a very small place after all, not unlike many of the places where Don himself has worked. 'The only difference is that the "ring" in which I work can be a little bit more violent,' said Don. 'I do count some fairly famous boxers – both past and present – among my friends, by the way. I appreciate what they are called upon to do, and vice versa. Most ordinary people would have trouble imagining what it's like to square up to somebody and not be able to hide. The difference between me and other fifty-year-old men, I suppose, is that I've found myself in a succession of jobs where I couldn't hide. When trouble erupted, I had to be there. After all somebody has to sort it. When trouble occurs, Joe Public disappears into the crowd, even bobbies can mysteriously disappear, but I stand out in my bow tie. Violence is something I've had to face, and I was going to say "get used to" over the years, but you never really get used to it. You daren't let yourself get used to it, as if it's some old familiar friend.'

We were talking in a club somewhere in the Midlands. It was 2.00 am. This is Don's kingdom. All the punters, who are worth knowing, know Don. They all greeted him. He can't remember all their names, so he greeted them generically and politely – 'hello, Sir.' There was a certain rigidness and formality in the greeting, which harked back to a time when greetings were indeed rigid and formal – when everybody knew their place in the social order. In this club they still do. Don belongs to that generation, where position and politeness reigned. I noticed that his shirt cuffs, just visible beyond the end of his jacket, were immaculate. There was something about his bearing – others have noticed it as well. 'Some police officers said to me recently that they could tell that I had been in the Forces, they could tell that I had been an Officer, but I was only a Private in the Air Force, during National Service. I was obviously flattered though,' explained Don.

Don turned to greet some more couples entering the club. The greeting almost never varied – all men were 'Sir', all women 'Madam', except on occasions a 'Sir' could become a 'young Sir'. Punters who knew Don well sometimes reciprocated, and he got 'hello, young Sir' back again. To an outsider it all sounded rather strange, as if some elaborate game was being played, perhaps even a slightly tongue-in-cheek game. Don, after all, is hardly a 'young Sir', without stretching the imagination just a little. But it was no game. A black boxer of national standing approached. He was accompanied by an up-and-coming black boxer, who was clowning about a little in the foyer of the club. Both their faces lit up when they spotted Don. They looked genuinely pleased to see him. 'Hello, young Sir,' said the famous boxer. For the first time that night Don used the person's Christian name in greeting, but 'young Sir' was still reserved for the boxing clown.

'I always give them both the same advice before a big fight,' explained Don, as they passed. 'I tell them that they have to imagine that their opponent has just done something really nasty to their five-year-old daughter, and that they've been given the chance to deal with him alone. I use the same technique myself when it comes to dealing with trouble. It's the best way of getting yourself all fired up inside, and you have to be fired up inside.'

Don has worked on the door of a variety of nightclubs for over a quarter of a century. I asked him how violence had changed over that time.

'The first thing you have to remember is that I've changed over that time as well, and not just the sorts of violence that you're confronted with,' he replied. 'When I was twenty-five, I thought that I was invulnerable. You do at that age. With time you start to feel a little bit more vulnerable. I started to feel very vulnerable a few years ago when my son, who was then eighteen, punched me in the ribs during some play fighting. I had to go into the kitchen to recover and pretend that he hadn't hurt me. Of course, in a real fight when the adrenalin is flowing, you don't actually feel anything. We were only messing about, there was no adrenalin, and that's presumably why it hurt so much. But it still worried me. I used to be a very strong person. I used to work out a lot, and run in weighted boots. I found them in my garage the other day. They're hard enough to lift now, let alone run in. I was always testing myself in those days. I used to hit myself with a hammer during my lunch periods at work. I know it sounds ridiculous, but I needed to know where it hurt most – to see how hard I really was. And you've got to know where it's going to hurt others.'

'The way that I know that I'm not as strong as I used to be is that when I take hold of people these days I have to do it with more pre-planning. The main thing a bouncer has to do is to escort people off the premises. You have to take hold, and do whatever is necessary to remove them. In the old days I didn't give it much thought. I knew that I had the strength to hold them, but now I have to do it with considerable care. I always take hold of them from behind, and pull them backwards towards me. They're off balance and can't break free without strangling themselves – accidentally, of course. Everything you do is accidental in this business. As long as I keep walking they've had it. I could walk them for a mile, if I wanted to. They're falling backwards all the time, and it's one of those holds which really is easier with a bigger chap. The older I get the more I have to rely on safe methods like this one. So this feeling of vulnerability is bound to alter your views on violence.'

'There's nothing sadder, of course, than a bouncer getting past it. I remember working in this club, where there were these six right noisy lumps. I asked them to be quiet, but the leader of the group just called me over and said to me, "You don't know who you're dealing with here, mate.' He then pulled out his driving licence and he showed it to me, and, believe it or not, his name was "James Bond". I think that he asssumed that I was going to be impressed by this. But James Bond and his friends just had to go. I was very keen in those days. After we'd escorted them all out, I spotted this doorman, who I thought was really old at the time – he must have been about my age now. He was spitting on his hands and hitting the wall of the club. I asked him what he was doing and he said, "I'm lining them up boss." I told him that they'd gone about ten minutes ago. I saw him later that night with his hands above his head, asking blokes to punch him in the stomach. I thought to myself that I never wanted to end up like that.

'I didn't. I don't wait for ten minutes before I start getting busy. But I do recognize that I've changed. So, too, has the kinds of violence that you come across in clubs. Twenty-five years ago, it was extremely rare to see anyone being glassed. I remember very clearly the first time that I ever saw anyone hit with a glass. He was a foreman of this group of Irish labourers. One of his workers cut him from his eye right across his cheekbone to the side of his chin. It was a right mess. We got the guy who did it, and then got an ambulance for the foreman. I remember that we took the foreman down the backstairs so that no-one in the club would see him and become alarmed by this awful sight. The other thing I remember about this incident was that the following night the guy who had been glassed turned up at the club again, and tried to gain admission. He had got this huge bandage on his face, and it just looked like a giant white scarf. I just told him that he couldn't come into the club looking like that. It was rare in those days to see this kind of thing, nowadays you just pick up your local paper and everyone's doing it. They're glassing old men, women, anybody who's around, anybody who's in their way.

'Some things, though, aren't so new. Fairly recently there was all this fuss about football hooligans throwing darts at matches. I remember this happening in about 1963 in a mining village where I was working on the door. Perhaps the guys who did it had been in the pub playing darts beforehand, maybe they didn't mean to bring the darts into the club with them. Sort of absent-minded like, but they used them all the same, and that was twenty-six years ago. These things go in fashions. I remember the fashion for flick knives, then the fashion for Stanley knives. Guys used to carry Stanley knives in their breast pockets – they just looked like pens. But they were lethal when they got them out. They're very inventive the people who carry weapons, of course. I know of one club where they've started using metal detectors on the door, so what do these characters do – they carry large splinters of glass with insulating tape wrapped around one end. These days too many people carry something on them. In my experience only about one third of these people will actually use the offensive weapon, the other two thirds are just bloody stupid. The problem, of course, is working out who belongs to that third.'

'Twenty-five years of working on the door has made me more wary of certain people. Out there are some people who are prepared to do whatever is necessary in a fight. Never mind who's hard, and who isn't, it all boils down to what you are prepared to do. I think that I've developed the ability to recognize such individuals. You have to when you work in this business long enough. Lower down the scale of seriousness, you also learn to recognize when someone is going to hit you, and when they're not. And, of course, the only way of dealing with this is to get in there first. But can you imagine trying to persuade a court of this? And as for the real hard men – the men that are prepared to do whatever is necessary – you can tell them by their eyes. There's this one little guy who sometimes comes in here – no-one would ever tackle him. He's got these cold, staring eyes. Of course he's got the reputation to go with it. He is heavy. My heart always stops when you see some kid bump into him, and you think, "Oh God, what's going off." Thankfully, most people who don't know him or his reputation, are put off by those eyes.

'You can always tell someone who knows what he's doing in a fight by where he hits another person. Somebody who doesn't know the score will punch another guy on the nose. What good is that? It just makes the other person angry. And it produces a lot of blood which makes it very difficult for the police to ignore. You can break the nose, of course, that's not difficult to do at all. But that just makes them even angrier. Somebody who knows what he's doing will always try to land a good punch in the stomach, particularly if the other person has been drinking. If they go and complain to the police, the police will just send them packing. There's nothing to be seen, you see. Give them a bloody nose or knock them out and it's harder to ignore. I know of one case where a colleague of mine knocked a punter out and the police desperately tried to ignore it. They ended up going round the block four times, but every time they got back the guy was still lying there – flat out, with a crowd around him. They ended up having to arrest my friend. Now that's no good at all – it's just not very professional. I've knocked guys out – accidentally, of course, they usually just stay out for about five or six seconds. Whenever they've stayed out for longer than that I've always got a bit anxious. But that's often because they've been drinking. Imagine if you let guys into the boxing ring with alcohol in their bodies. It would make boxers a bit wary. We have to tread a very thin line.

'I think that one of the problems with violence today is that the police have their hands tied in dealing with some of these really violent punters. There's always a huge fuss if somebody gets a clip in police custody. But the police know what they're doing. It's not Joe Public that's getting the clip around the ear hole, it's probably some nasty bastard that's getting what's coming to him. The police can tell them apart. We're definitely living in more violent times, and in my view police leniency has got a lot to do with it. There are some right nasty bastards out there, and some of us have to deal with them.'

And as we talked, one man of diminutive stature made his way into the club accompanied by a much younger female who towered above him. 'And that's one there,' whispered Don, as he started to adjust the immaculate cuffs on his shirt. 'Good evening, young Sir,' said Don. 'Good evening Madam. It's nice to see you both again.'

The man of diminutive stature seemed to grunt back and tried to force his mouth into a smile. His eyes, however, which I couldn't help but notice were strikingly cold and staring, stayed exactly as they were. Don just sighed.

Britain's roughest boozer

The Manor Hotel in Sheffield is Britain's roughest boozer, at least according to the *Sun* newspaper. In an article in September 1989, it described how landlord Bob Burns was on his way out after just five weeks in the job. The pub had been nicknamed 'New Faces' because every few months there was a new one behind the bar. In fact it's had thirteen landlords in just over four years. Bob Burns' first day was celebrated by the starting of a fire in the pub. Things, as they say, could only get worse. There were regular fights with pool tables overturned, glasses thrown and tables destroyed. Bob Burns apparently likened it to Dodge City, 'but it's me and the staff who are dodging the flying glasses.' One regular commented at the time that 'Mike Tyson would have a job running the Manor Hotel.'

Well they never got Mike Tyson, 'they got a bit of psychology instead,' said Paddy Maloney, the new landlord, all six foot two and fifteen stone of him. We were talking in a city centre pub where Paddy wanted to prepare me for what to expect. 'I use psychology on them. What's the point in going in heavy? That's what the punters want. You can't beat them in the end. I understand them because I've been through all that. After I left the steelworks in the early seventies, I served my time as a bouncer. It was cash in hand and three quid a night, but boy was it rough. I created a lot of the trouble myself. In those days I'd just say, 'Would you mind leaving?' If they said no, I'd just clip them. It was part of growing up, of proving you're a man in the part of the town where I lived. But you can't spend the rest of your days, acting like this. You get nowhere in the end. I got somewhere – I'm thirty-eight and I've got my own security agency now. That's why the psychology's important. You have to suss people out, without clipping them first. When I was still a bouncer I got a job as a debt collector. I learned early on there that the secret is not to go in as heavy. None of this sleeves rolled up nonsense, you go in with a smart suit on. You try the executive approach, or you send a girl. There's nothing more embarrassing than being asked to cough up by a girl.'

Jenny, his girlfriend, just nodded. 'She's one of the best I know,' said Paddy. 'She used to do all the difficult cases, but she's got a tongue like . . .'

'Like what?' said Jenny. 'Come on, like what?' 'See what I mean,' said Paddy, his considerable stature significantly diminished. You could see that they would make a formidable team. 'Come on a Wednesday, it won't be too crowded and you'll be able to get a feel of the place. Don't bring your car, get a bus,' he advised, 'or you'll spend the whole time seeing if the wheels are still on it. Come about 9 o'clock.' 'Can I bring a camera?' I enquired. Paddy nearly choked on his Britvic 55. 'Only if it fits neatly down your gob,' said Paddy. 'We don't want you to have any trouble swallowing it when someone tries to push it down your throat. But don't worry, everything will be alright as long as you just act naturally,' he added reassuringly.

I prepared for my visit with some trepidation. This was a pub with a reputation to preserve. What high jinx lay in store for me? And what was the best way to avoid them? How, for example, do you dress when you visit the roughest boozer in Britain? Do you try to blend in with the surroundings? Or do you dress in a way that you know will set you apart, like some tourist who's just popped in off the street for a casual drink? I compromised – I wore a street-smart leather jacket, but with a shirt and tie. But it didn't really matter in the end.

The Manor Hotel is a huge building right in the middle of the Manor district of Sheffield. The area is fairly well known as well. The huge pub towers above all the surrounding buildings, which I just happened to notice were all boarded up and in various states of decay. I sauntered in casually past the waifs that filled the doorway. Sauntered is the right word because I was already swaying on my feet. I kept thinking about Dodge City, and I really wanted to follow the sheriff's advice and ride on through, stranger. I had heard that the fights in this pub were so frequent that the regular customers did not even stop to watch. I didn't want to miss a thing, so being a good scoop I kept looking behind me. This gave the overall impression of a terrified executive debt collector. Despite my street-smart leather jacket, I stood out a mile as I was the only male person in the bar without a tattoo. I felt like nipping into the toilet to scribble something in biro on my neck. 'Tremble' was all I could come up with. Well, they might think it was a command rather than a description of my current physical state, I reflected. It was a good time for reflection generally – the barmaid explained that Paddy and Jenny had gone for a meal so I would have some time to wait.

How do you stand in such a bar all alone? It's one of those occasions when it's very important to get your body language exactly right. It mustn't say either 'mug' or 'serious challenge', but something in between. I kept thinking that if my body language said 'executive debt collector', the regulars might leave me well alone. It seemed to be working. Suddenly there was a loud commotion in one corner. Significantly, I was the only person to look around. An old lady beside me was having her jug filled up with draught beer, and despite the noise from the corner, her eyes did not once leave the golden nectar filling the jug. I noticed that she had not got her false teeth in, and the lower part of her face seemed to have collapsed. She had her slippers on. Trogy then came in, he's a well-known Manor character. He collects chimney pots, wood and anything else he can scavenge from houses in the process of demolition. His cart has a number plate 'Trogy 1', donated by the regulars of the pub. He bought a half of bitter, it's all he could afford, and he'd been on the road all day. It is easy to see that the pub's notorious reputation, which all the regulars have some share in, is one of the few things that any of these people possess.

You can always tell when you are being watched, and instinctively my eyes flitted from the jug to this character in his mid-twenties watching me from the corner of the bar. He looked away, giving me a wonderful view of his nose – in profile, which appeared to have been broken quite recently, if I'm any judge. He kept eyeing me surreptitiously, and I kept eyeing the writing on his neck. Everyone had a word or two tattooed on their necks, but he seemed to have enough words tattooed there to make a good-length essay.

I kept trying to read what they said, but he kept catching my eye. Eventually he came over. 'Are you looking for somebody, mate?' he asked menacingly. 'Er, um no,' I replied. 'I've just popped in for a drink on my way home from work, er um I work just around the corner actually.' A look of disbelief slowly formed on his otherwise poker features. 'Oh, so you're not the guy coming to do the story for the *Guardian*,' he said. 'Er, well, as a matter of fact I am. When I say that I just popped in for a drink I meant that I just popped in on the off chance that there might be a story. I was actually doing another story on the Manor,' I said, somewhat unconvincingly.

'It's just that Paddy told me to keep an eye out for you, to look after you until he arrives,' said poker face, clearly enjoying my embarrassment.

'The first thing is don't leave your drink down. If you go to the loo, bring it with you. They play a little game here of spiking people's drinks with LSD. They think that it's a bit of a laugh. There was this bloke last week who had his beer spiked and he ended up kissing the dartboard. We had to pull him off it in the end, he was putting his tongue in the bullseye. He must have thought that the dartboard was some real dolly bird. If you want to avoid having your drink spiked, either bring it with you or another good bet is to play pool. Nobody wants the pool table ruined again by somebody on one of those dope-head trips. So be careful.'

I asked if, despite the spiking of drinks, Paddy and Jenny had managed to tame the notorious Manor Hotel. Poker face lit a cigarette, giving me my first glimpse of the tattoos on his knuckles. 'Well Paddy, as you know, can handle himself, but he's been trying to improve things here with a different method – psychology is what he calls it.'

I asked for an example of this psychology in action. 'Okay,' said my informant, ' but you can't really write this. These are the tricks of the trade, the genuine article. The first rule he uses is that he never pulls pints. It's brilliant, you know.'

'You mean that he only serves shorts,' I asked.

'Don't be thick. You're not Irish are you? I mean that Paddy himself never pulls pints. He stays on the other side of the bar with the punters watching what they're getting up to. That's one of the secrets of running a good pub. You don't distance yourself from the punters that way. You're also mixing with them all the time, and listening in to any little plans being hatched. You can stay one ahead of them that way.'

I asked whether there were any other examples of psychology in action being applied to tame the Manor. I was led into a backroom. This was worlds apart from the spit and sawdust room, without the sawdust, that we'd just come from. Here was a world of gleaming brass and deep mahogany, totally devoid of any customers. 'Paddy had real trouble getting the regulars to drink in here any night. When he first opened it up, the regulars said, "Do you mean that we're allowed in this room.' So Paddy started a disco at weekends to give them something to look forward to, and some reason to get them into these marvellous surroundings. And then he pulled his master-stroke. Do you know what that was?'

I shook my head.

'You know that at the top nightclub in Sheffield they play Frank Sinatra's 'New York, New York' at the end of the night. Well Paddy and Jenny have brought 'New York, New York' to the Manor. The punters love it. You should see them kicking up their legs at the end of the night. It's like New Year's Eve for them every Saturday night. Beforehand, the regulars didn't mind being barred from the pub, they knew they weren't missing anything, now they think that if they're barred that they might miss something. So they're on their best behaviour, at least most of the time. But you can't be too careful here. Paddy always says that if the old psychology doesn't work, then you can still clip them if they get out of line, and they know that.'

Our discussion was brought to a premature end by the arrival of Paddy and Jenny and another couple – Walt and his fiancée. Walt just happened to be the landlord of another pub on the Manor. He and Paddy had been comparing notes. He also happened to be an ex-professional boxer from Brendan Ingle's stable in Sheffield, and he had the features to go with it. His nose was even more battered than the man with the writing on his neck. Walt's grip nearly broke my fingers.

'Have you heard how me and Paddy have been bringing psychology to work on the Manor?' he asked as I tried, somewhat in vain, to rub some life back into my crushed knuckles.

Living in fear

You feel safe living in the very heart of England. In the winter, a touch of snow on the Pennines, but well away from the sea and the storms that wreck the coastline. In the summer, the odd disturbance, but well away from the street violence of the South, or the North, that wrecks our complacency. Nice and safe – everybody knows their place, everybody knows how far they can go. Nice and ordered. Or so I thought.

But this last year seems to have been different. Things seemed to be changing. There's been a certain menace in the air. But don't take my word for it. Just eavesdrop on the casual conversations in the pubs and clubs in the nether regions of the night. Doubt has crept in. Doubt and fear, and, of course, that rather cursory glamour that goes with it. There has to be a positive side to everything. First there were the shootings, and then there were the bombings – or rather the suspect bomb. It seems that urban violence had finally arrived up here. And all in such a short space of time. 'It's like Chicago,' said one wine bar habitué trying to get used to the new ambience of the night –

'or New York.' There was a very long pause as his companion tried to think of something topical and yet relevant to say. Eventually, he thought of it – never mind that it was five seconds too late. 'Or Belfast.' Voice number one ignored him, and turned his back. Voice number two went for new alliances – 'I'm John, by the way, and that's Gary – he used to be a footballer, once – a long time ago. He was famous then, now he's jus a has-been. He's also a right shit-head. He went to the front of the queue tonight and left me standing in the rain. He probably went up to the bouncers at the door and said, "Remember me, the hast-been?" That's the only way he gets anything. But not for much longer – things are changing around here – even for has-been superstars who've been getting their own way for far too long around here. You'd better keep your head down Gary, otherwise it'll be "boom, boom".'

Gary parried with a glancing smile, but he did look momentarily perturbed. He clearly believed that the rules were changing – the rules for survival in that dark hinterland where he had made his home, ever since his footballing skills had begun to slide, ever since the thrill of Saturday afternoon had given way to the greater thrill of Saturday night – with the hangers-on, and the parties and the girls.

John was clearly now enjoying himself. 'Gary's put it about just a little too much, you see. There will be a few husbands still looking for him somewhere out there – somewhere in the night. I don't think that he would have been quite so keen at the time giving the birds all that flannel and the rest if he'd known that he was going to be living in Chicago in the near future. Would you Gary, my old son?'

The has-been, and his one remaining hanger-on, went on contemplating their future in an uncertain world. For them now a very uncertain world. Clearly all this new activity was giving them something to talk about. And not just them.

I had heard the news the minute I stepped into the club. Big L had been shot, and it had all been done in such a cold, calculating way, as well. But Big L did have enemies – everybody knew that, and they had been saying that Big L had been getting his own way for far too long. No bouncer would tackle him. They just didn't fancy it somehow. On the nights at the top clubs, when jackets still had to be worn, Big L would turn up with just a shirt and a life jacket of gold chains glinting off his huge black chest. He seemed to like just wearing shirts, they showed off his muscles better. Some big men in jackets look a little strange – awkward, uncomfortable, compressed. Big L didn't like to feel compressed. He liked the freedom of movement – he liked to strut and swagger, and bend all the rules.

I'd talked to him a fortnight before. He'd confessed to me that he had now made it – he had a one hundred grand house and a ten grand car, and that for the first time in his life he was worried, worried that girls might go after him just for his money. 'How can I be sure now what they really want? I'm scared,' he had said. He may have been scared, but he wasn't expecting this. Shot in some city centre car park some months ago. The local papers had made the most of it – MAN GUNNED DOWN ON STREET, in great eye-catching capitals, before adding that 'his injuries were not serious.' But nevertheless he was 'blasted on the left side of his abdomen,' and the paper added for good measure that 'Last month a 21-year-old West Indian was blasted in the hand by a .22 bullet as he left Pinky's on Spital hill,' lest anyone be in any doubt that there had been an epidemic of shootings, at least among certain sections of Sheffield's population. It was Chicago alright. No-one was being merely shot in this town anymore, everyone was being blasted out of existence. Or at least out of doors.

But we didn't even have a chance to recover from all this blasting that was going on, before the next thing we knew there were suspect car bombs in the street. A few weeks after the blasting, a punter was leaving the local casino at 4.00 am only to find his Audi Quattro some distance from where he had parked it. Now, if this had been me, I might have thought faulty hand brake. I might have even have thought 'bloody delinquents'. With a few seconds hindsight, I might even have concluded that Napoleon brandy is a little too strong for me after all. But not this punter. He immediately thought 'Gaddafi'. Gaddafi?

The police took the threat seriously after checking his identity with Scotland Yard's Special Branch files. The rich Libyan businessman concerned, who had recently moved to Sheffield from London, somehow registered on Special Branch files as being potentially at risk. Here in the very heart of England he had set up a very up-market fashion shop in a converted terraced house. Here in the very heart of England, he now found himself with a suspect bomb in his car at 4.00 in the morning. Everything about the man was improbable to say the least. A wide area around his vehicle on the Ecclesall Road in

Sheffield was immediately cordoned off. The Royal Army Ordnance Corps bomb disposal team then arrived with its remote-controlled 'robot' equipped with a TV search monitor. Now, we've seen these robots on the streets of Belfast, we've even seen these robots on the streets of London, but not on the streets of Sheffield, not in the very heart of England. Three rounds were fired into the car in the search for a bomb, and everyone held their breath in anticipation of the big bang. The big one that never came.

That anyway was the excitement of Friday morning, now it was Saturday night, and here was the hunted man in person. Hunted men have a certain look, and here was the expression for all to see. Even uninterested by-standers were attracted by that look. He had apparently spent the weekend ringing round for some bodyguards, but they just didn't fancy it somehow. So here he was sidling up to the niteclub on his own at 1.00 am, complete with shades. 'Who the fucking hell is that old guy with the shades?' said Gary. 'Is he blind or what?' But his question was immediately answered as the fugitive removed the shades, as he took cover in the fluorescent gloom of the club.

All eyes were now on the blind man who had so miraculously shrugged off his disability. He took up a position that had everyone gasping. It was Big L's corner. What strange quirks of fate were linking their destinies? What was happening? What would Big L do when he heard about this in his hospital bed? The Libyan businessman did not look relaxed. Afterwards he tried to put us all at our ease by saying, 'I want to say sorry to the people of Ecclesall and anyone else who was inconvenienced. The authorities took steps to prevent any possibility of injury to people or their property. But I will not comment on why I think a bomb might have been put in my car. I was not in the casino to gamble or drink, that is against my religion. I am organizing a fashion display there and was discussing business. The police have been fine about what happened and I do not think it will affect my business. This sort of thing could happen to anyone.'

Anyone? Our collective pulses were racing. Despite the deadening effects of all that alcohol, Gary's pulse was sprinting away from him. It was as if his whole life was flashing before him rather like a drowning man, which I suppose he was in a way – drowning in a sea of lager and brandy and maudlin reminiscences. His hanger-on was clearly enjoying himself. 'Just imagine if someone slipped a device under your beautiful white XR3. That's the last thing you'd ever know, Gary. No chance to play at Anfield, now, old son. It would be goodnight world, and hello Bill Shankly.'

Gary's face descended into his brandy. 'Mindless bloody violence,' he said, and it echoed in a strange way around the cavernous glass. Even John looked depressed, as he realized that he had gone just a little too far. It's important to recognize change, it's quite another thing to use it for your own ends. Even he felt a little sorry and a little gloomy as he overheard ex-boyfriends and ex-girlfriends trying to patch up their differences 'because you only live once,' and 'you never know what might happen' and exhorting each other 'to live every day as if it's your last, because one day you'll be right.' Everybody was using the unexpected violence of the past year. Thugs were glorifying in it. Relationships were being repaired or ended because of it. The meek stayed at home and worried, or went to nightclubs to huddle together, as a result of it.

Gary's face sank lower and lower into his glass. But just at that moment a huge black hand descended on his shoulder. A hand of greeting. A hand to steady and calm. The hand passed through Big L's vacant territory and brought momentary peace and tranquillity to that unhappy space. The same hand reached across the throng and touched the rich Libyan businessman on the shoulder and comforted him in passing. The hand seemed to be saying that 'others might not fancy it somehow, but here we do. Here, you're safe in this haven away from the terrors of the street, and the hidden menace of municipal car parks.' It was the hand of friendship, it was the hand of comfort, it was the hand of a huge black bodybuilder who just happens to be a doorman at this particular club.

Gary pulled his face back out of the glass, and felt his old self starting to return. 'I feel like a right good drink tonight,' he said. His friend John had learned his lesson, and he went back to trying to persuade Gary to stop off at a sauna on the way home. 'You can sit at the reception, if you like. I'll not be long. It's alright for you superstar footballers. The rest of us have to get what we can.' Things were definitely looking up – even Gary's stolen status had somehow been returned to him, intact.

Perhaps it was all just a passing fancy – a gloom that had momentarily descended from the bleak Pennine Moors. A chill blowing in on a cold winter's night. But in a quiet moment I slipped across to the man whose job it was to comfort the world with those huge hands, to ask what he thought about all these new threats. His head gave an involuntary twitch backwards – it was more than a shrug, but not quite a guffaw, but it was a sharp enough movement to allow me to see right up his nostrils. 'Sometimes people want to believe that their lives are at risk. It helps them appreciate what they've got. But a couple of shootings and one non-existent bomb – what does that amount to?'

I nodded in agreement as the chill dispersed in the air-conditioned ambience of the club. 'But isn't there anything to be really scared of around here then?' I asked. His head shrugged again. 'Well, I'll tell you what I'm frightened of – do you know that I have to eat twenty-four raw eggs a day to keep my body in shape? Two dozen raw eggs a day, full of God knows what. Now that, believe me, is living with fear.'

I appreciated then that it really had been a very menacing year, it's just that I hadn't realized why.

★ 6 ★
Alone with your thoughts

Security guard

Robert walked across the concrete floor of the huge, cavernous building. His footsteps resounded in the eerily quiet building, on an eerily quiet night. A light summer rain fell gently from the sky. The skylights had been smashed and rain dripped slowly in. The huge shell was a steel factory – once, long ago, before the recession, before these new good times of consumer spending. Line upon line of brand-new motors testified to this new age, their seats still covered in polythene. 'That's what I'm here to do – to keep an eye on these new cars just in,' said Robert. 'We've got about 450 on the site. Some of the cars cost twenty grand – the lads who still work in the steel firm adjacent to this sometimes pop over to have a look at the newest models. Not that they'll ever be able to afford them. There's just a skeleton crew on next door anyway. It used to employ nearly 7,000 men, now there is something nearer 700. They're just hoping that it doesn't go the way of this one – car lot – with a difference. Well, it is a decent place to store cars.'

And my eyes automatically scanned the huge mausoleum and tried to imagine the noise and the bustle and the heat which once must have filled this place. But it was very difficult, the shell was so cold. 'Hard to imagine, isn't it?' said Robert. 'It was empty for years, it's good that they've found a use for it at last.'

I noticed two solitary pieces of graffiti high on one wall – 'Up Yours' and 'Ken is a Kunt'. But neither of them looked like relics of Britain's industrial heritage, I can't say why. 'They've only gone up recently,' said Robert, noticing where I was looking, 'but don't look at me, I'm a better speller than that, honest.'

Robert settled down in the on-site cabin. 'All mod-cons,' he said as he scraped some empty crisp packets off the congealed hydrogen-ated vegetable oil, left on the mock-mahogany top of the kitchen surface. 'If you weren't here, I'd be having a kip about this time to be honest. Well, there's not a lot to do really. It's deadly boring. Twelve-hour shifts from 6.00 pm to 6.00 am. I work every night of the week. You need to, in order to make up the wages – £1.50 an hour, cash in hand. It would have to be cash in hand with those rates of pay. I got the job from the Jobcentre. The guy who gave me the job told me that I'd have to sort out my own tax and national insurance contribution – I knew what that meant without him having to spell it out for me. A nod's as good as a wink. It's just a case of getting the hours in. If you can get your head down for a few hours, it helps. But you get some cars delivered through the night so you can't be too obvious about kipping on the job. I set my alarm for 5.00 am, so that I'm up in good time. They had a Pakistani security guard on before me, and he'd sometimes still be asleep at six when the day security staff came on. A bit bloody stupid if you ask me. They sacked him in the end – he didn't show up one day. Can you believe it? A security guard that just didn't show up and never told anybody that he wasn't coming. I used to be in the army – one of the tank regiments. Can you imagine doing that there? Sorry sarge, but I don't feel like going on sentry duty today. I think I'll stay in bed a bit longer. Civvies make me puke sometimes.'

Robert removed a curious looking object from the drawer in the cabin, and started playing with it. It looked like one of those trendy, tactile toys that are designed for infants to manipulate, and are supposed to accelerate the development of visual perception. The kind of useful toy bought by caring and concerned middle-class parents in arty-crafty ethnic shops. It consisted of two pieces of wood joined by a piece of chain. Robert suddenly snapped the two pieces of wood apart. 'It's a weapon, actually,' he said. I started to pay more attention. He tapped one of the pieces of wood on the mock-mahogany surface. The wood sounded very hard, the mock-mahogany top started to crack. 'I'm a black belt in karate, you know. I carry this for self-defence. You probably know what this is . . . now, don't you?'

I didn't want to mention my theory that it was just a trendy child's toy. I just shook my head instead.

'I'll give you a clue,' said Robert. 'Bruce Lee . . . remember Bruce Lee? Still not got it?' So Robert stood up and started flailing this thing through the air, over his shoulder, across his back, between his legs. I was none the wiser, although I was a little concerned about both his and my safety as the 'toy' rebounded off his back, his shoulders and, most worryingly of all, his groin.

'Haven't you seen any Bruce Lee films? Where have you been all your life? It's a *Nunchaku* – absolutely lethal. I haven't had to use it, but I did catch some kids in here trespassing last week. I heard one of them say – "let's try and pinch a car." There were three of them, all about fifteen. They weren't exactly being very quiet about it – they were laughing and giggling, you could have heard them about a mile away. So I hid and suddenly jumped out at them with my *Nunchaku* in my hand. I'm a great fan of Bruce Lee you see. Well they nearly shitted themselves. They'd obviously seen the Bruce Lee films as well. They were backing away and saying, "Sorry, Mister, we were just cutting through." And I was saying all quiet like, to scare them shitless, "Where were you cutting through to? Scarper," I shouted and they were away like the hammers of hell. I didn't want to apprehend them or anything, because I'm signing on as well as working, you see. I'm working under a false name. The last thing that I wanted to do was get involved with the police. That's the most terrifying part of this job – that something might happen which might involve the police. If any trouble happens, I'll have to sort it myself, without involving the police.'

And once more he menacingly snapped the *Nunchaku* apart.

Robert continued, 'I'm an army man really. But I got discharged from the army on medical grounds – I'm an epileptic, a nocturnal epileptic. I just woke up one night and found four squaddies and a nurse holding me down, and sticking a big needle into my backside. The epilepsy started as suddenly as that. It only ever happens at nights, so it's ironic really that I should end up working nights. But everything's fine as long as I remember to take my tablets. I don't miss the army as such, but I do miss the comradeship. I joined up when I was sixteen. I was trained as a tank driver and gunner in Germany. I was driving a Chieftain tank – all sixty tons of her, before I'd even passed my driving test. A brilliant machine – you've got such power in your hands, it's absolutely magic. Nothing gets in your way. Then I moved on to Scorpions, which are just great fun. They're a lot lighter – about twelve tons in all. Being a driver was great. It's not such fun being just a gunner though – you never get your head out of the hatch for a start. You're stuck in this confined space the whole time, with your head between the commander's legs. The whole tank stinks of cordite, and you're coughing all the bloody time. But when you're driving you can get your head out of the hatch for a breath of fresh air. Bloody marvellous.

'After a year of this, I was sent to Ireland – down on the border. You get used to the routine in Ireland very quickly indeed. It's so monotonous – one day you'd be out on patrol, the next it would be guard duty. With guard duty you'd have two hours of peering through a slot in some tower and four hours off – for the whole twenty four hours. When I say two hours of peering through a slot, you can't actually do it for the whole two hours. It would send you bonkers. You can only do it for about an hour at a time, then you have to walk around the tower. It's so bloody monotonous – good training for this job really. You're daydreaming the whole bloody time. In a permanent dream if you ask me. And the worst thing is that you have to keep on your toes all the time. When I'd been in Ireland for just one month, the IRA sent us this letter saying that they were going to hit us on Christmas Day. So for weeks we were all banged up and absolutely shitting ourselves. There were sixteen in my troop, and nine of us were eighteen. The officer-in-charge couldn't have been more than twenty-two. So we waited and waited, and you know nothing happened. They were just winding us up. And when anything does happen, it always comes out of the blue. My best friend had his brains blown out by the IRA. He wasn't expecting it.'

I asked how soldiers in Northern Ireland coped emotionally with death and this persistent threat of death. 'Same as anywhere else – cigarettes, booze, shagging,' said Robert. 'But the comradeship is very important. In the army I had fifteen close friends – you all share the same stresses and, most of the time, the same women. That's what I miss most about civilian life – you're out on your own, having to fend for yourself. Your mates help you through the difficult times in the army and you can always have a laugh. I remember once this Christmas bringing this trailer full of snow into the centre of this village for a snowball fight with the locals. We'd left our guns behind us. Or this other time going into this ice-cream shop where there were these teenage girls. We always welcomed a bit of female company, because most of the time we'd go around with these bloody great hards on. But these girls were Catholic and weren't particularly pleased to see us. One said, "There's an awful bad smell around here," when we went in. So we went off and made a big sign saying: "AC/DC/RCs" and pinned it to the front of our Land Rover and drove through the village with it. The Catholics were furious. But it was our way of getting even, in a jokey sort of way. We didn't harm anybody. But that's the sort of stuff I miss. But I don't miss the army quarters. There were sixteen of us in this tiny room with four-tier bunks. It was bloody horrible. It stank, because when you're out on patrol you're sweating all the time and then all these guys are passing wind all night. Some of them seemed to think that it's bloody macho to lie there farting all night.

'We have our regimental reunion every year in Barnsley. It's great to see the lads again. About a third of the lads that I knew are still in the army, the rest are doing all sorts of things – insurance salesmen, truck drivers, you name it. I wanted to do something where I could use my army background – something like security work. And, of course, I could make use of my martial arts training, as well. But as I said, I have to be a bit careful with that, I don't want the police around here. Well, to be honest, when you approach somebody in that special, quiet way carrying a *Nunchaku*, it puts most people off, unless they're a complete space cadet.'

'Or, if they've never been to see a Bruce Lee film,' I added tentatively.

'Well, there are not many of them about. And talking about space cadets, I was in this pub last week and this guy started mouthing off about something or other. Now, there was a time when I would like a fight but I've been through all that. I've nothing to prove, I've done my time in Northern Ireland. So I just told him to shut his face. So he threw a punch, which I blocked, and then I swept his legs away with the outside of my foot. You should have seen his face. "How, did I get down here?" I just turned and said, "bye, bye amateur." You see you never know just who you're dealing with. I'm always very, very cautious. Surprise is the name of the game.'

And Robert laughed quietly and then crept off to make his rounds, with his torch in one hand and his curious little toy in the other.

The nightshift in the Potteries

It was 10.30 pm, and the room was very noisy, even though there were only two machines working in the decorating room through the long, long night. John, the foreman, was on his dinner break – he had come on at 6.00 pm, and he was not due off until 6.00 in the morning, so he had an hour for dinner – unpaid, which he could have taken at any time. John settled the night men down – they came on at 10.00 pm – then he took his hour. He read the *Sun* from cover to cover twice, there was no-one to talk to, no music, no laughter, no crack, just the super, soaraway *Sun* for company. 'Come into the office,' he said and he led me to a group of dirty plastic chairs covered in pages from the *Sun* clustered in one corner of the factory. I had to sit on a Page 3 girl.

He was going to explain about the work that is done in Grindley's in Stoke-on-Trent at night, but we couldn't make each other out over the noise of the machines. 'You get used to it,' he said, 'even if you can't ever hear what people are trying to say to you.' We made our way past Kevin and the other machine operator on the way to the other office. Neither of them looked up, as we passed by. 'They're interested in a professional performance,' said John. 'In this business if the goods don't come up to the mark, you don't get paid, it's as simple as that. You have to concentrate on what you're doing, or you can come out at the end of the week with bugger all.'

John works a 59-hour week with five 12-hour nights for a gross pay packet of around £210. 'That's very good money by pottery standards, labourers here who work days earn only £91.28 gross for a 39-hour week. The wages in the pottery industry tend to be a bit behind the times. I don't mind nights, I've no family, I live with my step-father. I get in around 6.30 am, and read the morning papers and watch a few films that my brother has recorded for me the night before. He's got cable TV – I've thought about it myself, but I hear that they're going to phase it out around here. I go to bed at 9.00 am with a couple of good books, mainly science fiction. I used to have my own bookshop, you see, before I started working here four years ago. This job is a bit different to running a bookshop. I get up about one o'clock in the afternoon. There's this little dog that starts yapping about this time every day without fail. I can't sleep through it. The whole thing can get you down sometimes to be honest.

111

'You only get paid for the best ware you send out, you understand, and we're paid on a piece-work basis. So you're always trying to do the best work as quickly as possible. It's great if you're on a good shift, but on some shifts you get some right dozy buggers that are always stopping and starting the machines, or dropping the plates. We have one Pakistani that's always dropping plates, he pretends that he doesn't know what I'm saying to him. They just act daft. When you give them their pay packet, they can tell you where every penny has gone. It's always "me no understand" until you start talking about money. They take advantage of being foreign, if you ask me. By the weekend I'm usually that keyed up that I just can't relax. By Saturday night I'm just unbearable. I'm not myself until Sunday night, then it's time to start the week all over again. For me it's one week of days, followed by a week of nights. I've no social life.

'I started work here four years ago as a labourer, and I've made very good progress. Believe it or not, I've also been made redundant four times during that time as well – but I've always been taken on again. The pottery industry has been going through some very hard times, you see, but Grindley's has got some new owners now, and I think that things have really improved over the past few months. Things are definitely on the up-and-up.' John then returned to his *Sun*. 'I've got ten minutes yet,' he said, so he stayed on the plastic chair in the corner – 'the office' – for a further ten minutes, and got up exactly at the end of the one-hour break.

I wandered off in search of the other workers – bowls were being revolved around and around on one of the machines in the decorating room. Two silicon pads with stamps on them, or the 'bombs' as they are known, plunged down on the plain bowls. The first bomb deposited the fruit part of the decoration in brown, the second bomb deposited the corn and the leaves in a blue/grey colouring. Kevin stood beside the machine lifting the finished bowl off and putting the next plain bowl on. He has to check whether the decoration has been put on properly, and stack the perfect plates with a series of refractory pins between them, because the plates are still wet. A pile of rejects also built up beside him. Kevin works nights from 10.00 pm until 6.00 am, with one break of twenty-two minutes. He gets paid for ten minutes of the break, but not for the other compulsory twelve minutes. Everything is worked out to the last minute and the last penny. It is the foreman's job, John's, to change the silicon pads, and

112

it is his job to add the colour to the machine and to wheel away the trolleys stacked with the 120 dozen plates. Kevin just lifts one plate off, and puts another one on, constantly scrutinizing the fruits of the forest – a million miles away from this place – hour after hour after hour. As the personnel manager later explained, 'It may be boring to you, it may be boring to me, but the incentive is there. They are trained people, specialists in their own field. They know how many plates they have to get through in a night, they know that we don't pay for mistakes. We know how to motivate these people.

'Kevin will get thirty pounds and twenty four pence for tonight's shift, assuming that he manages to do the same number as last night,' said John, as we watched Kevin and the machine in perfect harmony, or almost, as another bowl came off with a band that didn't go all the way round.

'It's the fairest system when there's a bit of night-work thrown in, provided that everybody's prepared to play the game,' said John. 'Everybody should have a crack at night work because the pay is so good – in comparison to the day I mean. They're trying to bring in a system of continental shifts with two day shifts followed by two noon shifts, from 2.00 pm to 10.00 pm, followed by two night shifts. Most people are prepared to go along with this – except one that is. There's always one, isn't there. Here it's Mr Saddique.'

Everywhere I had gone in the factory, I had heard the whispers about Mr Saddique. He refused to change his habits, or conform. He worked permanent nights, every night – five eight-hour shifts, and two twelve-hour shifts at weekends – sixty-eight hours a week – week in, week out, year in, year out. You might think that he would be commended for his hard work and industry, but not here. Saddique was earning at time and a half, double time on Sundays. In a factory where everything is calculated to the last minute and the last penny this creates all sorts of petty and not so petty jealousies. 'His wages must be fantastic,' said John. 'It's the other poor buggers that can't have a crack at night work that are suffering because of him.'

Mr Saddique works with the earthenware going into the kilns. He and his helper, who is also Asian, push the trolleys loaded with the earthenware into the kilns and remove them from the other side. The stacked trolleys are heavy and not easy to push. Mr Saddique and his helper dug their shoes into the dusty floor to get the trolley moving. This went on all night long without any real breaks. The kilns are extremely hot and radiate a good deal of heat into the surrounding area. When the doors of the kilns are open, the heat is quite unbearable. Mr Saddique allowed himself a wry smile as I backed off from the open door of the kiln. If, for whatever reason, the trolleys break down inside the kilns, Mr Saddique and his helper have to enter the kilns to drag the trolleys out. Their only protection is the wet towels they use to cover their heads. You can only bear the heat inside the kiln for a few seconds at a time.

The night I was at the factory, Mr Saddique had come on 55 minutes early to get everything ready for his shift. Some trolleys had been overloaded, and he wanted to unload some of the earthenware so that everything would run smoothly. He did this for no extra pay. You might say that he's a dedicated worker.

Mohammed Saddique came to Britain from Kashmir in 1963. His wife and children still live there. 'If they came here who would look after my elderly parents?' he said. He lives with his brothers in Stoke-on-Trent. His life doesn't so much revolve around the work at the factory in Stoke, his life *is* the work at the factory. He goes to bed each day about 9.00 am, gets up in the afternoon, watches some TV, and gets ready to go back to work again – seven days a week. His 'fantastic' wages come to £246 a week gross. I watched him working in the formidable heat, bending forward until he was nearly parallel with the ground in order to get the trolley moving. He didn't complain – except about his shoes. 'They only last about two months here with all the wear-and-tear they get.' And you couldn't help noticing that although they were covered in a fine dust from the earthenware, they had evidently been recently polished – probably that evening, probably every evening. Virtually all his wages, except the little he needs to live on, and replace his shoes with, goes back to his family in Pakistan.

'I came to England for the work, basically,' he said, 'and I found it. I've never once signed on the dole. England is still a fine country, it gives you such opportunities to better yourself and earn a decent living.'

And on that note he was off into the mouth of the gaping hot kiln once again – for another load of plates and bowls for light, airy kitchens – somewhere far, far away.

The Architect

It was 7.20 pm at Barnsley squash club. Richard hurried up the stairs, he was late, again, the match started at 7 o'clock. Richard was out of breath, he'd come straight from work, and his grey suit was looking distinctly crumpled. His bright red tie had been loosened, and flapped out behind him. Richard eyed up the opposition quickly, as he hurried past. They looked as if they were miners, and Richard nodded a greeting as he hurried down to the changing rooms. His Filofax fell out of his suit pocket as he was getting changed. 'That's a big address book, you've got there lad,' said one of the miners, with a large tattoo on his chest. 'Do you keep that for all the birds' numbers?' 'It's a Filofax actually,' says Richard. 'A file of what?' says the miner. 'Filofax,' repeated Richard with the merest hint of impatience. 'Oh . . . fi . . . low . . . facts,' said the miner, as if saying it that slowly and that deliberately, with separate articulation of each syllable, would somehow make its significance become clearer. 'They're all the rage in London,' added Richard helpfully. 'Oh,' said the miner, 'that explains everything.' And the changing room erupted with laughter.

They went on to the court. Richard lost in straight sets – work had clearly taken its toll.

Later in the bar, Richard's partner fetched him a pint and his after-match 'snap' – pie and mushy peas. One of the opposition turned up in a dark pin-striped suit. Richard's eyes perceptibly lit up, and he made his first tentative move. 'You're obviously not a miner, what line of work are you in? . . . A management consultant, really? You don't, by any chance, have any clients that need some building work doing? I'm an architect, you see.' And on that note, the two professionals formed a collective huddle, from which the miners and steelworkers, squash players or not, were most definitely excluded.

Richard was quite forthright about his direct approaches. 'As an architect, you have to push yourself forward and generate work. If you see an opening, you have to go for it. If I overhear someone saying that they want a building done, I'll go over and introduce myself. You have to be a bit pushy. At squash matches, I'll focus in on the guy most likely to be able to give me work. That's the name of the game today in architecture, I'm afraid.'

It was now 10.30 pm and Richard had just returned to work. The office was all bright primary colours, bright red files jostled for space with the yucca plants and bright green lamps. There was a large bright yellow radio sitting on one set of files. 'Image is everything,' said Richard. The office looked very quiet and just a little empty. Richard sat down to his half-finished drawing, the bright yellow radio played some Chopin very quietly.

Richard is twenty-six and has recently set up his own architectural practice with a former work mate, who is thirty-four. They set up the practice on the strength of a large job that they had been promised by a former client. This one job would have kept them busy for the first four months in their new business, and guaranteed them a reasonably secure financial base for starting off. But after they had resigned from their previous employers, the job fell through.

'This was something that they don't teach you at university,' said Richard – 'how to draw when you're suffering from severe panic, and how to make ends meet when you're starting with no capital and without any reputation. We got through the initial few months by having our design accepted for some engineering association's offices. This was another big gamble – we'd put a lot of work into it, about 156 hours in all. We went to meet the Director General of this particular association, to try the personal touch. The only problem was that my partner forgot his suit, so he had to nip into Marks and Spencers to buy one for the big meeting. He took it back afterwards and said that it didn't fit – the suit that is. Luckily, our design was accepted, so we got paid. It got us going.'

'We seem to spend only about a tenth of our time actually doing designs, the rest of the time is spent promoting ourselves, producing working drawings, or meeting clients. We spend vast amounts of time talking to developers about projects worth perhaps two and a half "mil", which will guarantee us about a hundred "thou", if they come off. We're still waiting for the big one, you see – we've got about forty or fifty schemes in the drawer, all worth about thirty "thou" and above to us. But it's all very speculative, if they don't come off, you don't get any money, and that unfortunately is the current state of things. You need the thirty "thou" in the bank, not as some vague possibility.'

It was hard not to notice at this point all the talk about 'thous' in Richard's speech. There seem to be so many alternative expressions for one thousand pounds today, whose use rarely seem arbitrary.

Academics these days talk about thirty or forty 'k', wide boys still use the old favourite 'grand'. Indeed I once interviewed a very respectable undertaker who kept saying that such and such a funeral would set you back 'two or three grand', until he noticed my ears pricking up every time he used this particular word. He begged me not to use the word in the article and I, after some argument, rather reluctantly agreed. 'It'll make me sound like a right wide boy,' he had said. Richard's favourite expression 'thou', on the other hand, sounded more technical than 'thousand' or 'grand', a mere abbreviation to a man in a hurry, a man going places. It also made 'thousand' sound more familiar, like calling Margaret Thatcher 'Mags' or 'Thatch', as if the speaker was used to a lot of them slipping through his hands – pounds that is.

A hundred 'thou' scheme tomorrow perhaps, but tonight it was back to the reality of life in a depressed town. Richard was working on an extension to a chip shop. 'I didn't really want to do it,' he said, 'but you have to eat.' Carefully he drew the east and west elevation of the potato store in between the outside WC and the existing timber hut. He pencilled in carefully, 'smooth red bricks', and 'stained timber', with the emphasis on 'smooth', and 'stained'. 'This isn't the kind of work that I thought that I would be doing, when I was at university. Like most students I was very idealistic. I did my dissertation on "taste", my basic thesis was that beauty isn't in the eye of the beholder, it's a property of the object itself. But try telling that to some clients! The secret when confronted by the real world is not to lose your idealism, but to keep it and to absorb certain practicalities. You have to learn to apply your idealism to whatever you happen to be working on. You can't make a potato store that's going to be art, but you can design it a little bit better, and choose your colours that much more carefully. That's what I'm trying to do here. Generally speaking, clients have great difficulty anyway in explaining what they want. We always say that there's more hassle in a kitchen extension than in a shopping mall. Most people say something like, 'We want an extension done just the same as our neighbour's,' but you're not doing your job right, if that's all you do. Some other people think that they know what they want, but as an architect you have to be able to create a concept for them. You've got to get to know your client to work out what they want, not what they say they want. They're rarely the same thing, you know.'

This, of course, all sounded terribly elitist, and I felt one of those questions coming on – you know, the kind that you can't avoid asking, but the kind that makes you sound, well, a little naive and unworldly to say the least. 'But surely,' I began, like a student in a first-year philosophy tutorial, 'if taste isn't in the eye of the beholder, then presumably it must be the architect's role to construct buildings in good "taste", regardless of what the client actually thinks of them?' (Hyde Park flats in Sheffield city centre were somewhere at the back, or perhaps the forefront, of my mind.)

'I wouldn't quite put it like that, of course,' said Richard. 'The role of the architect is to edge people closer to good taste, but, of course, it has to be a gradual thing. It would be impossible, for example, to sell Beethoven to the masses overnight, but through time you might affect some change. The point is that it would be criminal for architects not to try to point people in the right direction.'

My eyes flitted again to the smooth red-brick extension to the chip shop, beauty clearly wasn't in the eye of one beholder here. Richard returned immediately to finance. 'This particular job will take about two hours, you see, and I'll get about one hundred and thirty quid in all for this, about sixty quid an hour, which is a very good rate of pay. But this sort of work has to pay for all the speculative work we try, all the presentations and feasibility studies we do, which we don't get anything for, unless they're successful. We've got a few other steady jobs on at the moment. We're designing some filling stations – we got this work by a secretary picking our name out of Yellow Pages, if you can imagine anyone choosing a firm of architects that particular way. Architecture is really just an incredible gamble, you know, just trying your best for the one big development worth nine or ten "mil" that will make you really secure. But for us the gamble seems to be paying off.'

The time was now 12.30 am. It had been a very long day indeed, the bright green ferns were wilting, the yucca was wilting, even the bright yellow radio seemed to be wilting. It was now time for other dreams.

Paradoxical people

I went to meet the recently retired National Chairman of the Monday Club students at the Red lion pub in Westminster, just by the House of Commons – at his insistence. He lives in Chiselhurst in Kent, but he

The routines of the fire brigade.
So much bad taste – Auntie Hilda.

Acid House style merchants – Dom is in the corduroy hat (below).

Heavy Metal fans.

Weirdness at the Deadmill – Bill Rodgers is the one in the middle.

Legless in Rotherham – beer 20p a pint.

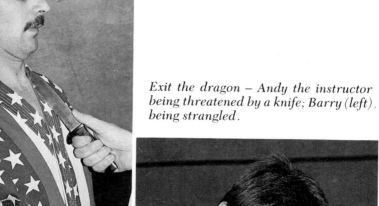

Exit the dragon – Andy the instructor being threatened by a knife; Barry (left) being strangled.

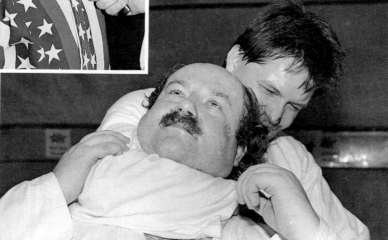

The night shift in the Potteries –
Mr Saddique (left).

Mick ('the Bomb') Mills with
Lurcher, and posing below a picture
of his favourite pit bull 'Eli' (left).

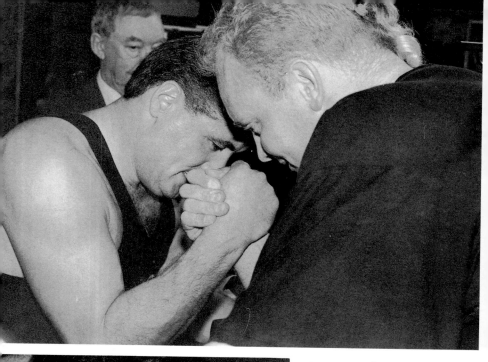

Arm wrestling – Steve Baxendale is on the left (above).

(opposite above) Waiting to go into St Thomas's.

The stage hypnotist – Ken Webster.

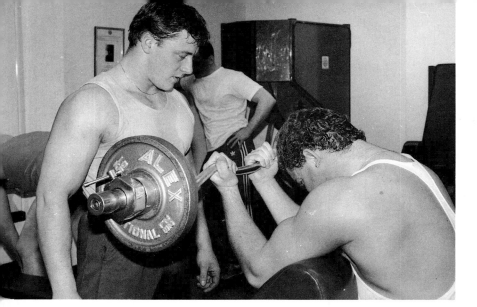

The Country Club.

Alternative medicine – Pam Hampton examines the feet.

Another young hopeful attends for an interview.

thought that the Red Lion would be more appropriate somehow. 'It's where we made some of our most important policy decisions,' he explained. So the Red Lion it was. Winston Churchill stared in that malevolent kind of way, as I made my way into the gloomy pub, looking for the man in the Barbour jacket. 'How frightfully English,' I thought, in my Irish kind of way. The policies hatched in the Red Lion by the Monday Club students included a campaign for the restoration of the death penalty, a desire for broader and more rapid privatization of the public sector, support for the freedom fighters in Afghanistan, and, perhaps most controversially of all, calls for a ban on all further immigration to this country coupled with a policy of voluntary repatriation. I wanted to hear all these from the horse's mouth so to speak, from the society's dynamic ex-chairman, from the man in the Barbour jacket.

Sanwar Ali rose to greet me. Sanwar Ali is twenty-three years old and he described himself as a recent graduate in Electronic Engineering from Hatfield Polytechnic, although interestingly he would not tell me what class of degree he got. 'No comment' is all he would say. Sanwar Ali was born in Bangladesh in 1965, but his family immigrated to this country when Sanwar was one. Sanwar has serious political ambitions. He aims to be an MP in ten years time, and as well as his former position in the Monday Club students, Sanwar was also Chairman of Chiselhurst Young Conservatives. He still is the Secretary of the Monday Club Economic Affairs Committee. He's also currently the director of some company or other, although he said he wasn't at liberty to disclose which company, or indeed whether it was his own company or not. Coincidentally, the first time I spoke to him he did not appear to be in paid employment. This was of particular significance at the time because one of the first tirades he mounted then was against the welfare state 'which is socialist in principle and which discourages people from fending for them-selves.' When I'd asked him originally how he supported himself, I got a 'no comment'. And when I asked him more directly whether he signed on, I got another 'no comment'. I realized, at that time, that I was not dealing with any ordinary interviewee, but in the terms that Sanwar's hero used to describe Russia — 'a riddle wrapped in a mystery inside an enigma.' But now he was a company director things were a lot more straightforward, or were they? I needed to find out. I wanted to ask about the immigration policy of the Monday Club students, when he was chairman, but first he wanted to discuss terrorism, indeed he seemed desperate to bring it up. Perhaps it was my Belfast accent that was doing it.

He was preparing himself. He leaned back and puffed at his cigar, a glass of port in his other hand. Puffed, by the way, is the operative word here, because not only did he not inhale, he took only the slightest of drags before expelling the smoke with a loud noise. I was fascinated. He didn't seem to be getting much sheer enjoyment from this cigar. Indeed, he seemed more interested in the Churchillian gestures with the cigar as prop, than the flavour of the cigar. I had to force myself to stop attending to his mannerisms and to attend to his speech. 'Well basically, we would like to see the death penalty reintroduced for those who orchestrate murder and for terrorists. The reason is quite simple – a bank robber is less likely to go in armed, if there is the possibility of capital punishment. Indeed it is a fact that prior to 1965 bank robbers used to always check each other when they were setting out on their robbery to ensure that none of them were armed. You see if one killed somebody they would all have to pay the penalty.' I asked how Mr Ali knew this, he obviously hadn't witnessed it first hand because he himself had been born in 1965. Had he perhaps talked to some bank robbers about their old habits? 'No, not exactly, I have however spoken to an expert on the subject . . . Teddy Taylor, if you must know, and he explained all this to me.' Sanwar took a quick puff on his cigar, and a quick swig of port, before continuing. 'We need capital punishment for terorrism to show public abhorrence of their crimes. The public in Britain are sick and tired of IRA terrorism.' I thought to myself not half as sick and tired as the public in Northern Ireland, but I kept this to myself and instead aired the familiar objection that capital punishment for terrorism just creates martyrs, and Ireland has got quite enough martyrs, thank you very much. But Sanwar didn't accept the point. 'The hunger strikers made themselves martyrs, even without capital punishment. So there are always going to be martyrs anyway.' I said I kind of understood his point, and in case I didn't he repeated it – 'public abhorrence of terrorism.' 'But isn't one man's freedom fighter just another man's terrorist?' I enquired. What about the freedom fighters in Afghanistan lauded by his own organization. Should they be executed to show the public abhorrence of a different state? He ignored that. I asked whether Bangladesh had continued to use

120

capital punishment as a deterrent. 'I don't really know. I believe that they have a military government there at the moment, but I'm not totally sure. I haven't got time to keep in touch with events in Bangladesh. I have three speaking engagements this week. I haven't much time left over to watch TV, you know.'

Now that Bangladesh had been mentioned, I asked Mr Ali to outline the Monday Club students' views on immigration. I waited for some kind of disclaimer to preface his remarks on the topic, but no, we were straight in. 'Our general policy is a total ban on any further immigration, and a properly funded system of voluntary repatriation.' The word 'voluntary' didn't seem to be particularly stressed, or not stressed as much as I'd expected it to be. Sanwar continued, 'Everyone is happy to have people here who make a useful contribution to British life. A lot of immigrants play an extremely useful role like, for example, the Asian greengrocers open twenty-four hours a day – they play a valuable role in the Thatcherite culture.'

This all seemed a little strange to me. I was perturbed that he didn't display any sympathy at all for those still wishing to emigrate to this country, like his own family twenty odd years ago. And why cite, as an example of immigrants playing a useful role in this country, Asian greengrocers? What about Asian doctors like his own father, for goodness sake?

'We're basically sympathetic to immigrants who participate in the free market culture,' Sanwar continued, 'but the welfare state in this country discourages people from fending for themselves. We would only aim to repatriate immigrants who feel unwelcome here.'

Repatriated back to a country which they'd never known, where there may be capital punishment and where the bank robbers may search each other before they go out on a job. Or not. Sanwar Ali, however, would clearly not be among those being repatriated. 'I personally feel very at home in a free market culture. My immediate intention is to make a lot of money before embarking on a political career. I'm sorry, but I can't reveal what my specific plans are – they're confidential.'

I said that I hoped it wasn't a repatriation business. He laughed loudly, before choking on his cigar that is.

I left in the direction of the Tube, trying to make some sense of Mr Ali. I was looking forward to my journey across London to read again this new novel that I'd got my hands on, *The Men's Room*. Unfortun-

121

ately, it was not a great book to read on the Tube. The words leapt out at me: 'You have a wonderful body,' he said. 'Wonderful. I want to eat it.' Carefully, he opened her legs . . .' It was the kind of book where all the mens' fingers are long and knobbly, and all the women's undies are scarlet. It was the kind of book that is not advisable to read on the Tube. I was starting to shift about rather uncomfortably. Some parts of it reminded me of the kinds of letters that people write to those magazines that are kept on the top shelves of newsagents, giving accounts of incidents that are supposed to have happened to the readers over the past few weeks – the same kind of language and the same kind of fantasies purporting to be reality. I was off to meet the author – not just the Deputy Director of the Thomas Coram Research Institute which is part of the Institute of Education at the University of London, but none other than the well-known feminist writer Ann Oakley, author or editor of some thirteen books, none quite like *The Men's Room*.

I met her in her office at the research institute. Her academic books lined one shelf of her bookcase: *From Here to Maternity*, *The Sociology of Housework* and one of her more popular earlier books *Housewife – High Value and Low Cost*. All very clever stuff. The theme of 'Housewife' was that housewives were analogous to the most alienated workers in industrial societies. Housewives were essentially exploited and used. It was a book that changed people's thinking. So how come an influential feminist like her could write a book like *The Men's Room*?

'It's a book primarily about relationships, and about how men and women relate to each other. Through these relationships, the characters in the book come to learn a good deal about themselves. The central character, Charity Walton, who works in a London University sociology department, has a number of relationships and through time discovers that it is probably easier in the end not to bother with a relationship with a man. It seems to me to be reasonable for a sociologist to write such a novel because the use of the imagination is important in sociology, as in literature. Novels can also illustrate public issues in a way similar to academic works.'

I said that I understood all of this, but was there a peculiarly feminist theme to the book? Presumably, there had to be some-where, because apart from anything else it was published by Virago – the feminist publishing house that gets a very important mention in the book. Indeed, Oakley tells us that 1974 was the year when '. . . Richard Nixon resigned over the Watergate affair . . . and the first successful commercial feminist publishers, Virago, emerged to challenge the male media supremacy (and offend its sensibilities) by choosing such a name.'

'Yes, there is a feminist theme to the book, because it's essentially a novel about gender inequalities, and how society affects the capacity of men and women to relate to each other.' I was dying to ask her about the juicy bits, but wasn't quite sure as to how to introduce them. So rather delicately I said that although I had enjoyed the novel, I found bits of it a little shocking. Dr Oakley threw me a knowing look. I think it was my Irish accent again. 'It's because women aren't supposed to write about these things. People are used to reading books about sex written by men. Women talk about it differently, that's why you found it shocking. You don't like women talking about sex.'

I tried to reassure her that it was no such thing. I found it shocking because I could not understand how her characters, who were so good at talking dirty to each other, couldn't talk about anything else without sounding totally ridiculous, like comic book characters or comic strip sociologists. For example:

She tore him off a strip for this. 'You mean the parameters of the project haven't yet been defined?'
He corrected himself again. 'We've decided to use a stratified sample in inner London and Kent. To get the rural–urban divide, you see.'
'That sounds like a good idea.'

One of the characters called Steve is described as only liking women who are obscure and convoluted, indeed 'he only really got on with those who talked in paragraphs.' In that case he should have got on with everyone in this particular book because they all seem to.

Sorry, Charity. What I meant was that we *are* all surrounded by lies. Your problem is you've got two versions of the truth to sort out, mine and Mark's. But they might both be lies. Gender may make a difference. But understanding the difference gender makes may still not give you the truth.

I asked the author how she would feel if someone only read the steamy bits of the book. The author threw me one of those stern looks that seems to say that there's always one isn't there, and here he is presenting himself in person. 'I would not be very pleased if they were taken out of context,' she warned. But perhaps Dr Oakley has not met enough people like me before. I was genuinely puzzled. How could a leading feminist write this kind of stuff? I could see an argument somewhere – sex is important to relationships, and this was a novel about relationships. The very same author had bemoaned the general repression of female sexuality in our culture in *Housewife*. So it made some sense to put some sex into her novel, as long as it was from a 'feminist' perspective. But why then did it sound so like Jackie Collins, or the very stuff of male fantasies found in 'girlie' mags, sorry 'womanie' mags. She told me during the interview that her daughter had advised her to listen out for conversations on buses to try to get the dialogue right. This clearly had not worked. But where had she been advised to look for the bits and pieces for the steamy scenes?

I couldn't help but think that virtually all the characters in *The Men's Room* were middle class and highly educated. This is clearly the world that Dr Oakley knows best – this is her world. But perhaps she did not consider carefully enough what those from outside this world might get from her novel, where people do not read about sex to understand the basic dynamics of social relationships, but for something more basic altogether.

And on that note I was off, slipping the book into the brown paper bag I just happened to be carrying with me, to talk to Jimmy Reid. Now, Jimmy Reid, you will remember, was the communist shop steward that led the fifteen-month sit-in at the Clydebank Yard of the Upper Clyde Shipbuilders in 1971. One of those names from the past that still resonate very loudly. Even those who have not been watching his recent TV series 'Reid about Russia' know the name. Old press cuttings reveal that in 1971 he came third in the Personality of the Year competition organized by the BBC radio programme 'The World at One'. First was Ted Heath and in second place was Enoch Powell, then still MP for Wolverhampton. So what has become of Jimmy Reid now, apart from guiding a television audience around the Soviet Union of Glasnost and Perestroika? Well, he writes a weekly column for the Scottish edition of the *Sun* newspaper, that's what. Gotcha Mr Reid, communist militant and the workers' champion. So how come?

'Well, it's like this. If I had to find a paper whose policies I agreed with, I'd be silent. It's as simple as that. I still think that the need for one individual to communicate with another is absolutely fundamental. It overrides everything else. The need to communicate is inherent in every human being, it's not peculiar to any group of individuals. It's universal.'

This, of course, was very grand language to describe a column in the *Sun*, a newspaper which some would argue does little for communication at any level, except the most basic of propagating prejudice and stereotypes of the grossest kind. And with a distinctly pro-Thatcherite leaning into the bargain.

But Mr Reid continued, 'They approached me and said if you are opposed to the line of the paper, here is your opportunity to say what you want. I wrote an article attacking Thatcher on the run-up to the last election and they printed that, so I thought to myself that they can't be all bad. And don't forget there are precedents – Nye Bevan wrote for the *News of the World* and Michael Foot was connected with the *Mirror* group.'

This is all very well, but the more usual fare offered by his column is an appreciation of Eddie 'The Eagle' Edwards, musings on Ian Ogilvy's stubble, and an attack (of sorts) on the noble art which Mr Reid would apparently like banned, because 'the professional fight game is controlled by shady characters from America and is squalid and degenerate.' His logic runs on, 'If it is justified then so is cock fighting, badger baiting . . . and what about wife beating?' Although I for one was not aware that any of these other activities were controlled by shady characters from America.

However, you do learn something from his column. In an article on 3 June about Ian Botham, Jimmy Reid tells us that his favourite quote from the Bible is, 'Spew out the lukewarm.' Not one that I myself was familiar with. But Jimmy Reid elaborates. 'My admiration is for those nobler creatures who venture forth in search of new ground, new and better ways of doing things. Sometimes their sense of adventure exposes them to danger and makes them vulnerable.' Jimmy Reid clearly sees himself, like his hero Ian Botham, as not being lukewarm, but on the boil and on the ball – he thinks. He broke new ground alright – a communist and a former shop steward working for the *Sun*, *after* Wapping. But is it at all comprehensible? Jimmy Reid says yes, indeed it is. In order to communicate to a wide audience, it's worth it, no matter what the politics of the paper, and no matter what people think. In fact he said that he didn't really mind what the general public thought of him with respect to this activity, since 'my friends, the ones that really matter, knew that I would never toe the line with the *Sun*, or any other newspaper or any other organization for that matter. One of my main characteristics is that I never toe the line – I'm very much an individualist.' An individualist, perhaps not unlike Eddie 'The Eagle' Edwards who 'showed us how to lose. He did it with style, made a packet *and* kept sport in some kind of perspective' in Jimmy Reid's own words. Change politics for sport and there you have it.

As the conversation drew to a close he remembered to ask me what my article was about. 'Paradoxical people,' I said. 'But I don't see my behaviour as paradoxical,' he replied. But nobody ever does, I told him, and that is the really puzzling thing.

★ 7 ★

Lager louts

Joining the queues at Manchester Airport

He couldn't find the buffet for the complimentary light refreshments. Or rather he couldn't find it on time. By the time he got his companion awake and dragged his friend's considerable hulk over to the appropriate light refreshment counter, it was too late. It was now the turn of the passengers for Monastir. Paul noticed that their flight was only two and a half hours late. Paul was not pleased. 'We had to wait an extra half hour for our free grub, you know, and we missed it.' Paul pretended he was talking to his friend but he was really explaining all this to the mums and the dads and the kids and the assorted grandads and grannies who stampeded past him for the free goodies. Needless to say, none of them were in the slightest bit interested. Even Paul's friend looked bored, until Paul turned on him that is. 'It's all your fault, you fat git. You wouldn't wake up.' His friend tried to look nonchalant, before he realized that Paul must have put some sugar into his ear whilst he had been asleep. He poked and poked, but it only pushed the sugar deeper into the ear. He tried to kick Paul, and some old codger naturally assumed that they were fighting, and got very excited about the whole thing. It seemed to make Paul and his friend feel a little better.

They walked slowly back to their spaces in the departure lounge of Manchester airport, reserved I noticed by one Adidas bag and one copy of the *Sun* newspaper. I somehow wished it had been a copy of the *Independent* marking the seat, because I do not like to peddle easy images, but the *Sun* it was. Paul's friend picked up the paper and started reading. His lips seemed almost to be moving. He was a young man who had several large tattoos, some of which were clearly DIY, set off with considerable bulk. You could imagine people being frightened of him, especially at night, but I noticed that when he walked he waddled. He waddled the way that only fat twelve-year-olds and overfed Labradors can really waddle. It was my guess that Paul's friend could only ever look genuinely threatening when he stood still. From the back his head looked like a huge potato with several large tubers sprouting out of the back of his head – clearly visible through his trendy short back-and-sides haircut. Both he and Paul wore sports gear. Paul's tracksuit looked like he used it for sport at least sometimes. On the other hand, the potato wore what you might call designer sports gear, or more accurately designer-wally sports gear. His track suit bottoms clung to that crevice where his huge belly joined the rest of his body. His sports shirt was never designed to cover that huge mass of stomach so it rode up occasionally exposing a great mass of white hairy belly. I tried to imagine that big slab of meat being roasted on a Majorcan beach. It would be some barbecue. Then it burped, and the whole thing quivered.

For a moment I had to feel a bit sorry for the pair of them. They had, after all, saved for this holiday all year and here they were three hours into the holiday still at Mancheter airport. But worse, they'd been drinking in readiness for a flight leaving Manchester at 9.45 pm, not some time in the early hours. The lager was now wearing off, leaving a kind of sickly metallic taste on the tongue. Paul, for one, certainly did not like that after-taste. His tongue kept rotating around that metallic cage. Some would have read this curious motion as a sign that he was thirsty. I reasoned that he was trying to find a spot to rest his tongue which tasted slightly less metallic.

But you couldn't feel sorry for them for too long, because Paul soon decided to take his destiny into his own hands, as he despatched the potato to buy the Duty Frees – 'we might as well have a big drink as a little drink, I suppose, we might as well have a party.' It was the way that he said 'party' that so alarmed all of his immediate neighbours. This was their cue, the signal that they had been waiting for. They now started to throw each other a whole series of knowing glances as if to say, 'Oi, oi, there's going to be trouble from these two prats in the very near future.' These knowing glances created a nice fine divide between Paul and the potato and everybody else. The looks had redefined the situation. They had christened it – given it a name. It was now 'us' and 'them'. 'Us' – 'normal', 'ordinary', 'decent', and 'them' – 'these two bloody trouble makers', 'these two king-sized prats', 'these two effing lager wallies.' And here we were having to spend the night with them, courtesy of some airline company's technical department or those bloody continental air traffic controllers that are always staging go-slows at critical times. Or something or bleedin' other. Even our private thoughts were starting to swear now because of the frustration of the whole thing.

All eyes were now on Paul, mine immediately started wandering elsewhere. I felt a bit like the sociologist in that well-known old teaser. You know the one – 'How can you tell the sociologist at the strip club? He's the one watching the audience.' Boom boom. It was obvious who the star attraction was here – all eyes were on his little movements. He seemed to like the attention, and like a professional stripper he knew how to tease. He was reaching slowly into his sports bag, what was he going to pull out? A knife? A can of lager? Some Union Jack shorts to change into – in full view of us all, and with all these children present (all of whom were fast asleep, by the way)? I thought that I saw the eyes of these sleeping children being shielded in anticipation of this act of gross indecency. But all Paul extracted from his sports bag was the boarding pass, to check again some details, while he waited for the potato. The potato eventually arrived with a litre bottle of Bacardi and a huge bottle of coke. They mixed their drinks in their empty lager glasses.

An old lady in her sixties sitting opposite the pair of them began to express her profound disapproval of all this new activity. She had glasses and white hair pulled into a beehive, of the kind that small Scottish pop stars might have worn sometime in the mid-Sixties. It all looked a little incongruous, as she was probably too old for this fashion in hair the first time around. I noticed that she was smoking in a no-smoking area, but this slight rule infringement on her part did not deter her from passing judgment – very skilfully and totally silently, I should add, on the two youths. She hated youths drinking in public, but then again Paul hated smoking and he didn't say anything. The thin features of the old lady with the beehive were exaggerated by the way that she sucked the hot smoke into her lungs, and her slit eyes followed the smoke as it was exhaled, as if she was checking that none of the filthy stuff remained inside. Paul and the potato were just a nuisance distracting her from this interesting ritual of hers. She started to tut in disapproval, or rather she tried to tut, but she couldn't make the clicking sound with the cigarette trapped between her teeth. So she extracted it. Or tried to. The wet cigarette had stuck to her top lip. It clung there for what seemed like ages. I had images of it falling on to the floor and igniting the pile of sweet papers and other litter that had built up at her feet. But we were spared this scenario. Just. She finally managed to prise the moist cigarette from her artificially moistened lips and the ash eventually got flicked somewhere just in time, so that a tut of sorts could be made. All this was probably virtually instantaneous – in real time, I suppose – but when the tut finally happened it nevertheless seemed to be contingent not upon one of Paul's expansive swigs of Bacardi and coke, but on one of Paul's more innocuous gestures – a smile at a baby who had just happened to be walking past. The baby was waddling by the way – just like the potato I thought to myself. But nobody else seemed to appreciate the joke.

Paul and the potato continued to drink, everyone else continued to stare. Except, that is, for a middle-aged lady who was stretched out on the seat next to Paul. I had managed to miss her so far, because she had been so lifeless. But dreams were now causing her to utter some very low moans, and motion was being induced in her left foot which now started to twist this way and that. Her body began to move on the seat, until she ended up on her front, and you could just discern some stains on the back of her pink, crimplene slacks. I waited with quiet expectation for this foot, now firmly out of control, to connect with Paul's thigh. The tension was building up in Paul's audience. Would he punch it away? Would he bite the toe? Would the potato smack her in the face? The toe eventually touched Paul, and then it seemed to come back again for more. I wanted to see a real lager lout go nasty in the flesh. The toe now dug in. I held my breath – as Paul disappointed us all by just moving a couple of inches further away, and out of range. It was a dramatic anti-climax, if anti-climaxes can ever be dramatic. Even the old lady with the beehive would probably have flicked some ash on the offending toe. Paul was proving a bit of a let down – to all the spectators.

It was now just after 2.00 am, and the flight was eventually called. It had been a wait of just four hours, not bad for a typical holiday delay. It was now time for the fifth queue of the night, after the queue for the tickets and the queue for the check-in and the queue for the buffet and the queue for the Duty Frees. Paul had, of course, quite sensibly managed to miss some of these queues, quite unlike the rest of us. The queue formed slowly out of the half-awake, bleary-eyed individuals who had been lying all over the place and had somehow managed to get upright. The queue wound its way around the departure hall. But this great winding stream of people was even more stagnant than the rest. Those stranded there survived as best they could – one did a crossword, one read a novel, most looked heavenwards and tried to forget. Or remember. Depending. The old lady with the beehive sucked even harder on a cigarette.

Paul grinned, and for the first time that night I knew that he was not going to let us all down. He stepped out in front of the queue and pretended to collect boarding passes. 'Come along ladies and gentlemen, your plane is waiting.' The potato offered his boarding pass up immediately. The old lady with the beehive was next. 'Boarding passes, please,' said Paul. The old lady sucked even harder on her cigarette, ignoring the little git. 'And would madam kindly extinguish her fucking cigarette before boarding the plane,' he yelled in her face. The old lady gasped and then choked violently on her fag, more or less simultaneously. It was the gasp which set her off. But I suppose that depends on your point of view. Anyway, she was still choking as her husband led her on to the plane.

The holiday had now, quite clearly, finally begun.

An away game

There were six of them. 'Enough for a five-a-side football game and one reserve,' said the largest in the red 'Crafty Cockney' darts shirt. He had short spiky hair and a single earring. There was a picture of a London bobby superimposed on a Union Jack on the back of his shirt. One of his friends had a pair of Union Jack shorts on. 'That one's Little Mo – he's the reserve,' said Crafty Cockney. 'No good in a punch up, not much good in a piss up either.' And they all laughed.

Crafty Cockney went back to his San Miguel. This, after all, was Majorca. All six of them sat by the bar in a long line. It stretched all along one side and right round the corner. Somehow they found that particular configuration comforting. They all drank quietly. The owner, all five foot nothing of him, looked very uneasy, but nevertheless continued to serve them and continued to rake in the pesetas which they dumped on the bar. 'I can't work this toytown money out,' said Crafty Cockney. 'Here, Hosé, six San Miguels, but we want any change back, comprendez, s'il vou plait?'

Crafty Cockney turned from his linguistic endeavours to sketch out the background. 'We came to Majorca out of season, because we wanted to be that bit exclusive,' and the team all laughed again. 'We didn't know where we'd end up. We booked late you see. I've never heard of this place before. In fact, the only places I've heard of in Majorca are Magaluf and Arenal, and we're definitely not there, worse luck. My mum's been there, you see. She filled us in on how good it was in Majorca. But I don't think we're near any of those two places. In fact I don't think we're near anywhere at all. Just two bars that stay open past twelve and one empty disco where the Spanish waiters go when they've finished work. This is the best – the Acid Bar, and there's nothing happening here, as you can see. And I've saved all year for this. But you've got to make the best of it. You've got to create your own fun, your own excitement. Hey, Dave, it's your round.'

Dave got up to go to the bar. He wore a black shirt and black trousers set off with bright yellow braces. His head was completely shaved but was covered by a black cap. The Spanish barmaid looked totally confused by his outfit and by his demeanour. He tried smiling at her but she didn't respond as she popped the tops on the six bottles. Dave took his cap off to show her what was underneath. 'Skinhead . . . skinheado,' he said, trying to raise an inkling of a smile, just on the off chance. But she just stood there, totally expressionless – dead from the neck up – hand outstretched, waiting for the money. He handed her a 100-peseta coin – 'for the lot, keep the change.' And Dave and his friends creased up with laughter. But she showed no emotion. Except perhaps contempt as her lower lip seemed to curl ever so subtly around her momentarily bared teeth. Dave then handed her two 1,000-peseta notes. 'Is this enough then?' he asked, trying to sound insolent, but it came out in such a way as to make him sound uncertain and unsure of himself. She snatched it from him. There was no change. 'Where's your change, Dave?' asked Crafty Cockney. 'That was the biggest tip she's ever had.' Dave tried to look cheerful but he felt cheated and it showed. He sat and sulked. Five minutes later the waitress returned with a 1,000-peseta note and a 100-peseta coin. She dumped them in front of Dave and allowed herself the slightest and briefest of smiles as she did so. She obviously felt she had got her own back.

Crafty Cockney returned to scanning the bar. His eyes settled on the video dispensing a never ending stream of pop videos, with no perceptible gap between them. 'The Spaniards aren't as up with the times as us – they're not even as up with the times as my mother, and she's in her fifties. I used to listen to the Human League when I was a lad. Here, they think it's top of the frigging pops. And that old rapping song with that line, "I've got more clothes than Mohammed Ali" – Jesus, that's a bit behind the times. All Mohammed Ali's got now is that disease that makes you shake all the time. What's it called? My granny's got it as well. The same name as that guy from the TV with the baggy eyes. No, not Barry Norman – Michael Parkinson, Parkinson's disease. I think you get it by being clouted round the head a lot. I think my grandad must have knocked my grandma about a bit. And here we are on holiday, talking about disease. Just shows you what kind of hole we've ended up in.'

Cockney's eyes flitted back to the video. The old song by Desmond Dekker, 'The Israelites', was the music, illustrated, it seems, with some dancing model with gelled hair and bright red lipstick. 'Either I'm more pissed than I thought, or that video is out of synch. Don't these people even know how to work the bleedin' video? What on earth has that girl got to do with the Israelites?'

Cockney tried to scan the bar without looking at the video or the waitress. 'I want to try to stay in a good humour for God's sake – I'm on my holidays.' His eyes settled on two tall Spaniards with long hair and droopy moustaches. 'What on earth do they think they are? Come over here Dave. What do you think of these two?' And Dave came over and pulled his black 'Boy' cap low over his eyes and gave them a good hard look. 'I think they're dressed up as Mexican bandits, for a joke.' 'Or a bet,' added Cockney. The two bandits meanwhile returned their stare. 'We're teamed up tonight, lads. Six of us, two of them. Not much of a match, if you ask me. I think I'll stick to drinking. Six San Miguels please, and never mind the glasses. We're so hard we don't ever need bottle openers, let alone glasses. Oh yeah.' And they all laughed again.

One of the two Mexican bandits made a gesture with his finger rotating to his temple as he stared in their direction. But luckily none of the team spotted it.

'I'm going to get pissed tonight,' said Cockney. 'For a change,' said Dave. 'For a bit of variety,' added Cockney. And they all laughed. Cockney stared morosely at his beer avoiding the contemptuous look of the waitress, avoiding the video pumping out Europap where the sound and vision didn't quite gel, avoiding the two Mexican bandits who wouldn't have been any sport anyway. They drank three San Miguels like this. The humour had all passed.

It was five past twelve. They set off along the seafront, past the shops that sold the buckets and spades and air beds and genuine Majorcan pearls. All shuttered, all boarded up. 'They want your money and then it's piss off,' said Dave. Without warning, Cockney punched the wing mirror off a car and it flew off with a very satisfying thud, the glass shattering all over the roadway. They all laughed. Cockney inspected his hand but it wasn't even marked. A little smirk momentarily lit up his whole face. 'They can use our pesetas to have that repaired,' said Cockney. Two English girls hurried past and commented loud enough to hear that the team were 'troublemakers, just out for bother.' 'That's all you Brummies think about,' retorted Crafty Cockney, 'Holidays, love, we're on our holidays. You can keep your bovver, Brummies. Bovver Brummies, quite poetic eh?' And they all laughed again.

They wandered slowly back to the apartment, meandering all over the road. It wasn't that they were that intoxicated, it just took more time that way. When they finally got there, they discovered that the landing light wasn't working again. This seemed to increase their sense of frustration. They made their way unsteadily up to the third floor. It was Dave's idea to get the duty-free Bacardi out. It was Cockney who decided to climb on to next door's balcony for some small, pink tee-shirt that he said would have looked good on his kid brother. They'd all been eyeing it up every night. Just sitting there, temptingly out of reach. Just a little too far for someone who had been filling the long empty night with bottles of San Miguel and tumblers of duty-free Bacardi.

You could hear the siren of the ambulance all the way back in the Acid Bar and I swear I saw the barmaid give a genuine smile for the first time that whole week.

Pitching hotels

He emerged out of the shadows of the bright midday sun. He was carrying a map and was wearing nothing so much as a bewildered expression. A London boy, you could tell, before he opened his mouth. Spiky hair, an earring and a tattoo located roughly where his bicep should have been. A lager lout on holiday, without his pals. He looked quite lost. Probably looking for the Real London pub or the Crafty Cockney Cafe, or so I thought.

'Excuse me mate, do you know where the Apartments Calypso are?' he enquired with an accent straight from the heart of Peckham. His first day, and here he was lost. 'I'm sorry, I don't,' I replied – 'better try somebody else. I've just got here as well.' There was a long silence during which he slowly drew his rather sharp features into an expression of even greater bewilderment. Then he spoke slowly for maximum effect. 'You don't know where the Apartments Calypso are? The fabulous *time share* Apartments Calypso?'

I couldn't work out what he was getting at here, or what he was trying to tell me, but I didn't like the way he was stressing 'time share'. Were you supposed to be able to recognize these apartments from the fact that they were time share? Were the fifty odd owners succeeding in levelling the place in the space of a year, or something along those lines?

He interrupted my musings rather suddenly. 'Wouldn't you like to know where they are then? Everybody's talking about them and you, you've never even been. Look, I'll show you where they are on my map. I've got a car to take you.' And he started waving his arms in the air and a girl in a white Fiat did a racing U-turn and pulled up just beside me. Not before banging into the car in front that is. 'Just hop in mate and we'll have you there in ten minutes.'

It was my turn to look bewildered now. 'But I thought you were lost,' I stammered. 'Lost, me lost? It's you that's lost mate. Lost out, if you ask me. How much did you pay to come here? Five hundred quid? Payable to Mr Thompson or Mr Cosmos, eh? That's how much you've lost. And what do you have to show for the money you spent on your holiday?' 'Memories,' I suggested. 'A few poxy snaps,' he snapped back, hurriedly drowning out my attempt at a reply. 'But with time share you get your own pad – for ever. Holidays for a lifetime. Leave it to your kids. Hop in the car mate. Do yourself a favour.'

'But I don't want an apartment for life,' I said, rather pathetically. 'All I want is a bit of sun, a brief respite from the British winter.' He looked incredulous. 'Sun? Sun? There's plenty of it here, mate.

Plenty. It'll be here when you get out. I guarantee it. What's more important – sun or lolly? Come with me and you'll be saving yourself real lolly.' He was now starting to nudge me towards the car. His accomplice already had the passenger doors open. 'We call it kidnapping,' she said with a broad smile.

'Look,' said Mr Peckham, 'I'll make it worth your while. I'll give you two tee-shirts before you go and a track-suit. What could be fairer than that?' He started scrambling about in the back of the Fiat to fetch the tee-shirts. He held them up as if he was a market pitcher back in the East End, which is what he was starting to remind me of more and more. It was his spiel, or rather the structure of his spiel. 'We're a responsible company. We're not sponsored by any poxy little company, we're sponsored by the Royal Bank of Scotland.' His patter was straight out of the market, full of contrasts like, 'not twelve grand each, six grand the lot . . . or rather for two weeks.' He went on, 'It's got the name of the bank on the back of the tee-shirt. Just look at this. We're not a cowboy outfit, this proves it. Go on, help us out.' I expected to see him get the pots and pans out next.

The sun had meanwhile momentarily ducked behind a cloud and I felt my general level of anxiety rise as it always does when the sun, as well as the pitchers on the street, start to duck and dive. I said that I'd help him out later. 'Later? How much later? What's your name again? Where are you staying? I'll pick you up. My name's Phil, by the way. See you at your room at half four.'

I'd made it, or so I thought. I'd walked perhaps twenty yards along the road when a blond athletic-looking lad stopped in front of me. 'I saw you talking to Phil. A bit of a bloody nuisance, if you ask me.' I smiled and nodded. He was holding some brochures in his hand. I wasn't that concerned because I assumed he was advertising the local windsurf school. 'Did he sign you up by the way?' asked the windsurfer. 'Sign me up? What do you mean?' 'Did he give you one of these?' enquired the windsurfer. I shook my head. 'Well, in that case, let me give you one. Look, just do me a favour. I need four parties a day and I've had three so far. Go on, give us a break.'

There was a long silence during which I had ample opportunity to scan his long tanned face. He kept trying to make himself look pathetic by shrugging his shoulders and attempting a little boy smile but the whole thing just emerged as a convoluted grimace. I said 'later' and scurried past him vowing not to speak to anyone or indeed catch the eye of anyone else for the rest of that day. Nevertheless, in turn, I was offered a bottle of champagne, a bottle of whisky, and a twin cassette player, just to attend one of the time share 'presentations'. I declined ungraciously. I started to lie. 'I've been to the Calypso,' I told them. 'Well then, go to its sister complex, it's the same company but they'll never know.'

In the end Phil got me in the rain. I needed shelter. Phil's instructions were precise. 'Just listen to the basic fanny for twenty minutes, then leave. There's lots of exits from the Calypso. I don't care if you don't sign up. In fact, I'd prefer it if you didn't. Once they've filled up all the appointments, I'm out of a job, you see. I get my basic commission for just getting the punters over the threshold. When the salesman goes to put the video on, nip off if you want to. And make up a name if you don't want to give your real one.' Meanwhile, his girlfriend was stuffing tee-shirts and tracksuits into my beach bag. 'See you later,' said Phil as his girlfriend led me into the foyer of the Club Calypso.

'Hi, I'm Nick,' said the voice from the corner. This was a different category of salesman. This one had been trained, you could tell, right from his correct level of eye contact down to his basic foot position. 'Sit right down and make yourself comfortable. Just there, if you don't mind. Now what do you know about time share?' 'Only that it's a con,' I replied, and Nick laughed uproariously. Or at least, his vocal organs did. The rest of his body, especially his eyes, made no movement at all. 'Now that's not quite true, as you know. Now time share basically . . .'

And as he talked I felt myself drift off. It was as if my astral body was starting to float over the swimming pool and the carefully manicured lawn; over the show apartment and over the other customers with their Nicks. Incredibly, cheques were changing hands. One man at the next table offered his Nick a cigarette. 'You've done me and the missus a real favour. I never realized how stupid I'd been all these years, signing out my cheques to Mr Thompson. And what have I got to show for the money that I've spent on my holidays all these years.'

I wanted to shout out, 'A few poxy snaps,' but my Nick was engaging in various subtle and not-so-subtle body language ploys to regain my attention. 'Geoff, you're a doctor – you make important decisions every day. In a little while I'll be giving you the opportunity to make one important decision which will change your life.' I hadn't got the heart to tell Nick that I was a psychologist, personally capable of few decisions. If I could make decisions what would I have been doing letting myself be press-ganged into a meeting with Nick in the first place?

But now it was time for the video. I remembered Phil's advice about nipping out at this point, but Nick hadn't just been trained to send out the right body language signals, he could read the signals of others. He read my retreat preparatory signals very well indeed. He put his hand on my shoulder and led me to the show apartment for the video.

'By Frank Bough, no less,' said Nick, 'still the housewife's favourite. Still Mr Clean despite his little (feigned sneeze) problem. Too much of the real thing if you ask me. But still very popular.'

Frank Bough then tried to persuade me of the value of time-share. But the figures spoke for themselves. £6,000 for two weeks for a tiny apartment. That means that they're selling these apartments for £150,000 each. Somebody, somewhere is making an awful lot of money – enough for a beach full of tee-shirts and complimentary cassette players.

Nick was now nudging me and reminding me that it was decision time. 'You're a man that can make decisions. Make one now. I can take a cheque or you can use your credit card if you prefer. It's time for your decision, make it now . . .'

I escaped in the end. I'd made it through virtually unscathed. So when a few days later some black guy, also from London, offered me £50 'in my hand' for attending another presentation, I cautiously accepted. 'Put it in your sock,' he said, 'here,' as he handed the money over. So I stuffed it into my sock and I was off to a new site where only the show apartments had been completed. On the journey I asked how he could afford to pay me this. 'I'm on a big bonus, mate,' he replied. 'Not as much as the guy you'll meet when we get there – he's on 10 per cent. If you buy even one of the small apartments, he'll get £800 – not bad for an hour's work. And you'd be surprised how many of the punters do buy.' My next salesman reeked of drink but still managed to get to 'decision time', and again I was told to 'make it now!'

I did.

And what was this momentous decision? Well, put it like this –

what will I have to show for the money that I spend on my holidays next year?

A few poxy snaps, that's what.

In search of the real lager louts

All year I've been fascinated by lager louts. They've been mooning at me from almost every tabloid newspaper that I've picked up. They've been up North, some have said that they were at Hillsborough on that fateful day. They've been down South, they've been spotted disturbing rural tranquillity, fighting on the village greens. According to some reports they've even been at Stonehenge. The regular travelling people have, it seems, been complaining about the presence of a distinctly different set of revellers, who show little interest in weed and the remnants of peace and love. 'They've come down here for the aggro,' said one travelling person. 'They keep asking when the pitched battles are likely to start. We call them "the brew crew".'

The pieces I've read about the lager louts have, however, left a lot to be desired. I could discern that violence was part of their culture, and beer, but what was the symbolic significance of 'mooning'? Why did they do it? What did it mean? And what were lager louts in previous incarnations? Punks? Yuppies? Skinheads? Young Conservatives? I needed to find some lager louts to answer just some of these questions. Now that, as they say, is easier said than done. I started in the way that I usually do – I asked my friends and acquaintances. Now, some of my acquaintances are not averse to the odd spot of violence, some of them are rather loud, some have mooned – inadvertently, of course. Some of them even drink lager, before it became *de rigueur* – 'just a half of lager, Sir, that's marvellous,' is how they order their lager. I wasn't quite sure whether real lager louts used a similar technique. But none of my acquaintances admitted to being a lager lout. I tried them with the dictionary definition of 'lout' and the binding logic to go with it. 'Look, if you can be considered "a coarse, ill-mannered fellow" – by anyone mind – and you drink lager, you're a lager lout.' But they could see through this argument a mile off. 'I may be a lout,' said one, 'but not a lager lout. I'm more a lager-drinking lout, or a lout with a fondness for strong beer, including continental lager. Lager louts are more your contemporary figure like yuppies or bimbos, aren't they? I've got a girlfriend who's blond and a bit thick, but she's not a bimbo because she's a bit old fashioned, in fact she seems a bit of a rum-and-blackcurrant lout if you ask me. If birds count that is.'

I said that they might have to, and that I'd be in touch. But I had one card in reserve up my sleeve. I went out looking for George.

Now, George is rather special. I found him, predictably enough, at 2.00 am in a nightclub, with his customary pint of lager in his hand. What George doesn't know about lager, or the people who drink it, quite frankly isn't worth knowing. I told him about my quest. 'Lager louts? You're looking for lager louts about here in Sheffield's top nightspot? What's the matter with you? Get yourself off down to Rotherham or try Westminster. There are only VIPs here at this time of night and the top birds.' A tall girl with a slightly vacant expression and an ill-fitting blouse greeted him. George showed great lager-lout ingenuity. 'Look,' he said, 'my mate and I are shooting a documentary about lager louts. We need a top bird to present the programme. We're looking for a bird a bit like Angela Rippon but without any clothes on. You'd do, just, are you game?' She stared at me with an unconcealed look of disgust. 'Have you put George up to this?' she asked. She glanced at the half of lager in my hand. 'Men are all the same.'

George got down to business. 'Look, let's start with the basics. Where do lager louts like to find themselves after a good night on the piss?' 'The toilet?' I suggested helpfully. George looked at me in a way not dissimilar to the girl with the vacant expression. 'Look, I'll make it easier for you. After ten pints of lager, what do you really need?' He looked at me very expectantly. My eyes lifted heavenwards. George nudged me – 'Come on, think. What do you think that they really want?' 'Well, it's not a toilet,' I said. George nodded. I assumed that George was playing some kind of sophisticated game. 'A catheter,' I suggested at last. George swore very loudly. 'I can understand why some of these lager louts stick the nut on people sometimes. No, not a bloody catheter – a nice fat kebab, a big juicy curry. Haven't you ever been out before? Haven't you lived? It just so happens that I know this bird who used to work in a curry house. She had to leave in the end because she was getting a bit of stick. She's Chinese, you see, and the blokes ribbed her a bit because of it. You'd probably call these blokes lager louts today, because they'd had a skinful before they went for their curry. She used to tell me about these blokes pissing under the table, when she was serving them. They sound just up your street.'

'Indeed they do,' I said as I got my notebook out. 'Urinated under the table, did they? Was there any mooning to go with it? Was there any symbolic display attached to the urinating, or was it purely functional?' George ignored me, but borrowed a lipstick from the girl with the vacant expression and drew the number of the Chinese girl on the back of a VIP pass. 'Give her a ring. Tell her that you're a friend of George, and don't ask her any daft questions. Tell her you're doing a survey of restaurants for that free paper they stick through the doors. She'll talk to you then.'

I rang her number the following morning. Or rather I rang several numbers. The number written with the mulberry lipstick had got rather smudged in my pocket, and each '7' could have been a '2'. With some imagination, it could even have been a question mark. Unfortunately, there were three 7's in the number. I had to go through my opening routine several times. 'Hello, are you a friend of George?' 'George who?' 'Well, I don't actually know his second name. He's the one with all the chat. The one who describes all girls as 'top birds'. The one who likes curries.' 'What kind of curries?' they asked. 'Big juicy ones.' Several people quite sensibly hung up on me at this point in the conversation.

Eventually a rather meek sounding voice answered the phone. I knew it was the girl that I was looking for. I felt that I couldn't lie to such a trusting voice. I explained the real purpose of why I wanted to interview her. It may have been my imagination, but the gaps between the 'mm-hmm's' and the 'yeahs' seemed to be getting longer and longer, after I'd explained this to her. I told her that I would ring her the following day to arrange the exact time of the interview. I was over the moon. This was going to be real hard-nosed journalism. I was going to carry out a first-hand analysis of lager louts in action. Lager louts would be given the chance to speak back. I could see the headlines in my mind's eye – 'The intimate secrets of a mooner!' 'Lager lust turned me into a mad mooner!' The headlines were getting larger and shorter. Eventually I settled for 'Mooning mania! An exclusive on lager louts.' This was going to be hard-hitting journalism, this was going to be journalism with an awful lot of exclamation marks.

I slept soundly. The next day was Friday. I decided to get into the mood by spending the night in a bar, ordering pint after pint of the amber nectar. I tried to put myself in their shoes, you see, I wanted to see things from their perspective. I seemed to be succeeding. I almost accidentally mooned, when I emerged from the toilet without properly fastening my jeans. I rang Susie when I got home. It was only 11.45 pm, but Susie appeared to have been asleep. See what having to deal with those people all the time can do to you, I thought to myself. 'Now, about tomorrow night, Susie, let's run through a few things. What's it really like to be called "Chinkie" to your face? What's it like to have urine splashing all over your feet? What do you actually say to someone who moons at you from a few feet away? This is going to be really great stuff. I'm really going to nail these guys. You know, I'm really on your side.' Susie hung up on me.

I rang the following morning. Susie unfortunately had changed her mind about the interview. 'They were horrible times. I don't want to talk about it.' 'But,' I protested 'you can't do this. How are we ever going to understand these lager louts, if we don't get information about them?' 'Don't worry,' said Susie, 'I already understand them. I just want to forget about them.' 'But what about the headlines?' My pleading was bubbling to the surface as poorly concealed anger. I realized that I was shouting. Susie hung up on me again. My head slumped forwards, observers might have described this as me headbutting the wall in frustration. I rang George.

'Don't panic,' said George. 'She'll change her mind in a few days. In the meantime, you and I could take a little trip to try to find some of these lager louts. I feel like a break. You decide where you want to go and I'll be your guide – for expenses, for the beer and that.'

I pulled a map of Great Britain out of the drawer, and a pin. The pin, like the glass on a Ouija board floated across Liverpool and Manchester – no football at the moment – it then drifted somewhat mysteriously out to the North Sea. It seemed to hover off the coast. I could hear a strangely familiar voice in my head. It was just the odd fragment. Where was I going to find men 'as hard as shite?' Familiar pictures filled my mind. Where was I going to find men with T-shirts who could talk like this without laughing? Some people would say that Harry Enfield has a lot to answer for. The pin moved mysteriously back to dry land again, and landed smack bang in the middle of Newcastle. George set his can of lager down right in the centre of the map, leaving a damp ring. 'Just the job,' said George.

The train journey was uneventful, or as uneventful as a day out with George could ever be. He insisted on offering his opinions on the contents of other people's newspapers to the people who were reading them. I was tired before we even got there. We spent the night ambulance chasing in Newcastle – on foot! Our informants, when we eventually caught up with them, were not that forthcoming – 'We're only trying to have a good time, man.' George insisted on putting the questions to them, and then threatened to stick his nut on to one informant who he felt was not cooperative enough. We got the train back to Sheffield early. George insisted on one last quick bevy when we got back. It was nearly time for last orders and we pushed our way towards the front of the bar. We made it as far as the beer garden at the back clutching our valuable prizes. A gang of mates, huddled in one corner of the beer garden, were running through their repertoire of stories about last year's football season. Their companions were in a huddle some distance off – engaged in girl talk. I couldn't help noticing that all the girls wore white stilettoes. George said that it was good to be home – 'the birds in Newcastle are classy, but not as classy as the birds from around here.' The group of men were getting louder and louder. Some of the more expansive gestures now became little playful shoves. One little playful shove caused a lot of beer to be spilt. George was brightening up. 'I think we may see some action around here before the night is out.' This group now started singing. The landlord asked them to quieten down, and I thought I saw the first tentative approximation to a moon, in that one of the gang stuck his bottom out. The girls in their white stilettoes seemed to be egging the prospective mooner on.

George told me to get my notebook out. Suddenly he grew agitated. George, it seems, had spotted somebody right in the middle of the group of females – a girl with distinctly Chinese features who appeared to be swapping dirty stories. 'It's Susie, from the curry house.' He started dragging me over towards her. Susie appeared to be fleeing. George refused to believe that she had seen us, and dragged me after her. We pushed through the packed beer garden in hot pursuit. Rather unfortunately, one of Susie's white stilettoes got caught in a grate. But so desperate was she to get away from us that she kept on retreating with the grate attached to one shoe. She was now virtually running, with the grate clanking along behind her. The rest of the clientele of the beer garden scattered at this strange sight. George, still apparently believing that she had not seen us, was shouting after her. He dragged me by my lapel. All I could think of was that most of my lager was tipping out of my glass and splashing all over my shoes. Susie was running for the refuge of the Ladies toilet. She made it. But George is not the kind of guy who is that easily discouraged, and he started banging on the toilet door. He nudged me, and I had to plead for her to come out. What emerged instead was a fifty-year-old woman with a face somewhat reddened with anger.

'Bloody lager louts,' she bellowed in my face.

★ 8 ★
A fair fight

Still game in the Pit of Hell

The setting was a barn just outside Scunthorpe. The venue had been kept secret, known only to the select few, until the very last minute. And even then you had to be in the know to get sensible directions to this barn in the middle of nowhere. The entrance fee was a fiver. It was 1.00 am, and it was very wet and miserable, but they didn't seem to feel it. There were about fifty of them all gathered around the twenty-foot-square 'ring'. This was the one that they had all been looking forward to. The big one. This was Sledge, the local hero, and his big chance against a champion called Peace. You could tell that Peace was a champion just by looking at him – he had one eye and one ear. Most American Pit Bull champions are missing some important part of their anatomy. Peace's missing parts were plain to see. The stitches looked very crude indeed. 'Well, you can hardly take them to a vet,' explained one of the ringside buffs.

The two American Pit Bull terriers were being displayed – not so much like race horses, more like boxers. Or gladiators. This was going to be a real display of guts, in every sense, and the crowd knew it, and loved it. Peace was being carefully scrutinized. 'Awesome', said one regular. 'Awesome,' said another. It was already obvious that the specialized vocabulary of the American Pit Bull Terrior fraternity was somewhat limited. Their world, I couldn't help think, must be just as limited, limited and very, very mean.

Peace was led our way. 'Peace has been through the wars, you know,' said one of the regulars pointing at the awesome creature in front of us. A dog with the most incongruous name imaginable, as well as the most incongruous teeth. The teeth, which were really fangs, dwarfed its stocky little head. 'Peace isn't technically a champion, which would mean that it's a three-time winner,' said my informant seeking to clarify things. 'Peace is what you call a "two-time winner", but that's still pretty good.'

I could see already that if three victories made a dog a 'champion' then the fighting life of these dogs was really rather short. I was already thinking to myself that they must er um 'retire' rather early.

My new acquaintance interrupted my musings. 'But old Peace has got a lot of fight left in him yet. He may be half blind, but he's still as game as hell. That dog likes fighting more than fucking. All good Pit Bulls do, you know. I owned one Pit Bull who was up this bitch, and just after it had finished the business it was trying to bite the bitch's head off. But that's Pit Bulls for you. They're great dogs, and great companions, they're all very game. See Rottweilers, they're useless. As soon as you injure them, that's it – they're off with their tails between their legs, if they could get them between their legs that it. It's exactly the same with Alsatians and Dobermans. They're good guard dogs, don't get me wrong, they're good at biting people, but they can't fight. My Pit Bull killed an Alsatian in the street a few weeks ago, and the Alsatian was a right big brute as well. I kept my Pit Bull in a pen at the bottom of the garden, and it got out somehow. A friend of mine saw it run across the road after this Alsatian. But the Alsatian had no chance against my dog. My dog topped it in a few minutes. My dog was a big 'un, mind you. It stood 23 inches and weighed 60 pounds. It had a 21-inch neck as well. It were right solid, really awesome. It would have tackled anything.'

My informant leaned back, relishing every minute of the tale, basking in the pride that emanated from this great breed. 'Pit Bulls never give up, they're one of the few breeds that will fight to the death. They're dead game and I've heard that old Peace is especially game. They're bred for gameness. But even some Pit Bulls quit after they've given everything that they've got. But I've heard that Peace never quits. It just keeps going and going. I've got great respect for that dog, and I've spent all my life with dogs so I should know. Pit Bull fighting does come in for some criticism, but the way that I look at it is that the dogs love it. These dogs have been bred for it. And when you watch them fighting, the first thing that you'll notice is that their little tails are going all the time. They love it.'

This ringside aficionado was getting into his stride. He was drinking neat vodka out of a bottle. This may have helped. He continued, 'Pit Bull fighting is just like boxing really. It's like two trained, fit men fighting. It's all run in a very professional way with a referee, a time keeper and judges. There are some idiots who own Pit Bulls, but there are idiots in all walks of life. I know of one guy who had a pair of dogs and he set them at each other when he came in from the pub one night. He had them fighting right in his front room. They wrecked the place, the ornaments were all over the place. There was such a hell of a commotion with all the breaking glass and yelping that his neighbours actually rang the police. He panicked when they told him. He couldn't get the Pit Bulls separated so he ended up having to drag the dogs outside and having to stab one of the dogs, to get them apart. Idiots like that shouldn't be allowed to own any dogs, let alone Pit Bulls. They're also the guys who get away with fighting Pit Bulls. Those that organize proper fights get prosecuted. You see the way that I look at it is that it's like the difference between a scrap in the street and a professional boxing match. There's rules here. The main rule is that when one dog turns away from its opponent it's taken to its own corner. The other dog is held in its corner. The dog that has turned is then given ten seconds to go after the other dog and cross that line there, or it has lost. It's a way of seeing that the dog is still game, that it wants to get stuck in there one more time. Of course, if the owner of the dog touches it during a contest, then that dog has lost. That's really like throwing in the towel, you see.'

At this point in the proceedings, I noticed that the dogs were being scrubbed. My informant noticed my perplexed expression. 'That's to make sure that their owners haven't put any stuff on the dogs to stop the other dog biting it. Before big contests, the owners always swap dogs and wash them to make sure that they haven't been coated in anything. Just look at the shape that Peace is in – it's awesome. Greyhounds are bred for running, Pit Bulls like Peace are bred for fighting. Just look at the neck on Peace. It's a bit like Mike Tyson. Of course, like boxers, Pit Bulls fight in different weight divisions. This particular pair of dogs have been matched at fifty-five pounds. Peace has come in overweight tonight so its owner has had to pay a £200 forfeit. It's not his night, let's just hope that it will be Peace's night.'

It was time for the fight to begin. 'Face your dogs,' shouted the referee. 'How long is a round?' I asked – naively as it turned out. 'There's no rounds, they just fight to the end,' said my new acquaintance. But the end was a long time coming. One hour forty-five minutes to be exact. At that point Peace was picked up by his owner. Not before time – its bottom jaw was hanging right off. But the contest was not stopped on humanitarian grounds or whatever the equivalent is for canines, as my informant pointed out. 'It's gone,' he explained. 'With a jaw like that it can't bite properly. There's no point in letting the fight go on, it's useless now.' Sledge's owner picked up the £600 prize money.

But the 'entertainment' wasn't over for the evening. The consensus around the ring was that Peace was still dead game, so it was decided to give it a courtesy scratch. Its owner held it in the ring to see if it was still game to fight. It stood there motionless half blind and half deaf, with its lip hanging off like some freshly cut liver on a butcher's slab, and with its lower jaw resting at a very odd angle. It stood there trembling with anger and determination. And presumably pain. There were all these people hanging over the ring egging it on. Its owner's eyes seemed momentarily to fill with tears – of pride rather than sorrow. Peace bolted forward – blindly, obediently, instinctively – beyond sensation, indeed beyond sense. Sledge, still held firmly by its owner, seemed to brace itself for round two. The seconds should have been out, as Peace tried to bare its heroic fangs which could not grip or bite or even meet any longer. Sledge rolled its muscular shoulders bracing itself for the impact – that never came. Peace was dragged up and out of the ring. 'Game to the last, what a dog. What a scrapper. They'll be talking about this fight for years. Your dog is a hero, mate.'

The hero, which couldn't even eat after going the distance that night, was kept for one week after the event, and then shot. I remembered what I had been told about not being able to take such dogs in that condition to the vets. 'It was good for nowt,' said his owner afterwards – 'perhaps I should have dragged it out of the ring sooner, but there was Peace's pride to consider.'

That was a wet windy night outside Scunthorpe, now it was a bright winter's afternoon in Dalton, outside Rotherham. I'm sitting in the front room of Mick 'The Bomb' Mills, an ex-professional boxer of some considerable repute, and a dog lover. His Lurcher sat on his knee, licking Mick's face affectionately. Drawings of his favourite Pit Bull, Eli, occupied pride of place in his living room. Mick saw me looking at the drawings. 'I had to get rid of it, because of all the bad publicity that Pit Bulls were getting. If you've got a Pit Bull everyone expects you to fight it. I got fed up with all the hassle. A lot of people were asking me when they were going to see it in action. It would make a change, they said, from watching all the druggies around here topping themselves.'

Despite all the hassle that he'd had, Mick had agreed to try to explain to me not so much the thrill of Pit Bull fighting – because he considered me too soft – as the inevitability of the sport. 'Pit Bulls need to fight. It's like some people. They're bred for it. It's best to put them in against something that can fight back. It's just like professional boxing, and like boxing, the sport is well regulated.' I felt that I had heard all this before, but from a boxer it sounded different – not necessarily more convincing, just different. Mick continued, 'In America, it's an even bigger sport, but the Yanks always do everything in a big way. I went up to Newcastle a while ago to see one of the all-time greats from America. This Pit Bull was valued at ten grand, the stud fee alone for that dog was a grand. The dog was truly incredible. It had the biggest teeth I've ever seen on a Pit Bull, they were 2½-inches long. This dog was a real champion – a three-times winner. In its first two fights it had killed both its opponents in half an hour each. In its third fight it was put up against another champion. Now that, believe me, is a real test of the character of a dog. But this particular animal managed to break the other dog's pelvis in forty-two minutes.'

I flinched. I didn't like to think about broken pelvises, I didn't even like to hear about them. I mentioned Peace's broken jaw. Mick knew all about this classic fight. He reached for the video-recorder in the corner of the room. I assumed that he was going to re-run the fight in Scunthorpe – all one hour forty-five minutes of it, in all its glory, but no, this ring was different. This ring was round, and I could make out Mick's stocky form laying punch after punch into another boxer called John Ridgman. Mick was tearing at him, wearing him down, snarling around the heels of the taller boxer. In the second round Mick floored him. Whilst the viewers watched the re-run of Mick's bomb landing, Mick explained that something happened at that point in the fight. 'That's when he broke my jaw,' explained Mick. 'He broke my jaw and dislocated it and split it right down the middle.' And sure enough when the camera eventually returned to the action, you could see that Mick's jaw was now resting at that improbable angle. I had only seen a jaw at that angle once before, and that was on a dog.

'I had to retire at that point in the fight,' explained Mick, 'in front of my home crowd at Bramall Lane, but I'm not finished yet – I've had two fights since. They say that I've made more comebacks than Frank Sinatra. And don't worry, I've broken a few jaws myself – six to be exact, and only one of them in the ring. I broke my first jaw when I was sixteen in the car-park of the pub at the bottom of the hill, and that's the only one that I've ever been prosecuted for. I'm thirty-two now, but I still keep on training. Did you know that the referee Harry Gibbs described me as having the hardest punch since Randolph Turpin. When you've got a punch like mine, there's always a place for you in boxing. Perhaps one day I'll be back. I'm still very game, you know – very game indeed.'

'As game as old Peace,' I added, 'and used probably just as much.' But my half-hearted comment was drowned out by noise of the video-recorder and the crowd at Bramall Lane baying for blood. It was almost funny.

Championship boxing

It had been a wet day, so I turned up at the Sheffield City Hall to watch Herol (Bomber) Graham fight James Cook for the vacant British middle-weight championship, carrying an umbrella. Now this might not seem to be a problem but I was going to watch the fight with a bouncer, his girlfriend, and her dad, an ex-boxer of some repute. All were, coincidentally, ardent Bomber Graham fans. The last thing they expected was a man carrying an umbrella. 'Did you get that free with Aramis?' asked the girlfriend helpfully. 'Are you carrying it for some bird?' asked the bouncer. Harry 'Boy', the ex-boxer, just shook his head.

The steward who looked at our tickets was wearing a dark suit and hob-nailed boots. He spoke with a peculiarly middle-class accent. 'Look at the state of him for goodness sake,' said Patrick the bouncer. 'Are you expecting a bit of trouble then?' The steward told him that he was wearing the boots just in case there was a stampede to get near Bomber Graham at the end of the fight. 'Not very professional, is it?' said Patrick. We made our way to the balcony of the City Hall. We were right above the ring which had been placed right up against the stage of the hall. It was 8 pm, but the hall was virtually empty. The balcony was emptier still, except for three kids – one black girl of about twelve and two white waifs, from Brendan Ingle's gym, where Graham trains and dreams are nurtured. 'If they mess about bring them downstairs,' said one steward in his shirtsleeves to the steward with the hob-nailed boots, who was now starting to look a little perplexed. Patrick just grunted, 'He hasn't got a clue, has he?'

We went off to the bar, passing the waifs on the way in. Patrick recognized them immediately. Lisa Bailey, the twelve-year girl coaches down in Brendan's gym – 'I help with the pads and things, I do proper coaching with the young boys down there.' The two thin waifs nodded vigorously. I asked what Brendan Ingle's gym was like. 'Magic,' said Lisa. We eventually got into the bar, past the waifs and the steward in the hob-nailed boots. The bouncer, all six foot four of him, was on coke. I was still carrying my umbrella. The fight fans made way to let us through. The talk in the bar wasn't about boxing at all. It was about pubs and the sizes of lunchtime crowds and reminiscences about the days when certain pubs were so busy at lunchtimes that you had to bring your own glass with you. One customer, who was obviously a pub landlord, was telling his friend that he knew a pub down his way where they used to get so desperate at lunchtimes they had to use jam jars to serve the beer in. He was also moaning about the fact that there were no cigarettes on sale in the City Hall. Ice cream was on sale in the auditorium, but no cigarettes. Perhaps the organizers knew all about the fight fans from Brendan Ingle's gym, like Lisa.

It was time to get back to the balcony where the first two supporting fighters were making their way into the ring. I had only seen boxing on the telly before and I'd grown to expect the grand entrance – the theme from the film *Rocky*, the corridor of stewards, the silk dressing gowns, the audience response. You don't expect two fighters with towelling dressing gowns to amble towards the ring, admittedly from different directions, climb in, do the business and amble off again, in a hall only one quarter full. The boxers were substitutes as well, not even on the official programme. There was more response to the female who was carrying the card around the ring informing the audience of the number of the forthcoming round, than to the boxers themselves. Even if the boxers did put on a good show. In between rounds the girl who carried the card sat motionless with her legs crossed and her hands placed on her knee. Amateur psychologists would probably describe this as a very closed posture. She was registering no discernible emotion. At the opposite end of the stage there was a man in a wheelchair, lying right back, with his elderly grey-haired mother acting as commentator on the fight for him. I could have done with her help. I was getting slightly lost without Harry Carpenter, who I could see sitting directly below me, to guide me through the action. So Harry, the ex-boxer beside me, sensing my confusion stepped in to deliver some form of commentary into one ear – 'that was a slip, not a knock-down,' 'he hit him when he was down, disallow that punch,' 'he's holding too much.' The fighting looked a lot messier than I expected, and a lot noisier. Perhaps it looked messy because I was watching it from above. I could see the clinches from every angle – simultaneously.

The crowd was very subdued, in fact so subdued that at one point when the referee shouted 'break' very loudly, a largish section of the crowd could be seen to jump quite noticeably in their seats. Patrick was looking bored and went in search of the steward in the hob-nailed boots. 'What did I tell you?' he said when he returned. 'Talk about professionalism. The stewards are from a local rugby club. Someone just rang them up. They don't even know what money they're on, until the end of the night. They've just been promised a meal.'

Patrick then started to work his way through the personnel gathered around the ring, filling me in on some personal details. 'That's Brian Anderson, the ex-British Middleweight Champion, he's training to be a referee at the moment. He used to be my apprentice when I worked at Brown Baileys. And that little black guy on the stage with the steward's badge, standing just beside the ring, I got him a job doing some security work in shops. He was no good, he was always walking around the shop shadow boxing. He didn't exactly blend into the surroundings. He also asked the manager of one shop whether he'd got a receipt for his cigarettes. All the stewards near the ringside are boxers from Brendan Ingle's gym, not like the clowns up here from the local rugby club.'

My attention started to slip to the fight that had been continuing in the meantime. Whilst we had been chatting away, the two boxers had been slugging it out for the full eight three-minute rounds. The referee awarded the fight to a short, stocky white kid whose name hadn't appeared on the programme. Harry 'Boy' stood up and shouted, 'No, never. There was nowt in it, but the coloured kid just had it.' There was little applause for the winner, but the audience suddenly came to life to applaud the loser. They clearly agreed with Harry 'Boy'. The black boxer told the MC that he had taken the fight at very short notice – at 12 o'clock that day to be exact. For that he got even more applause.

The next fight on the bill was between Rambo Loughran of Ballymena and Tony Britland of Cardiff. Rambo was from Barney Eastwood's stable, and it showed – silk dressing gown, spotlight, with his Seconds leading him in. His opponent walked across the floor to the ring, with nobody taking a blind bit of notice of him. The kid who looked as if he had just wandered in off the bus was stopped in one minutes twenty seconds of the first round. The third fight was also stopped. This time the crowd voiced their disapproval, with shouts of 'give him a chance ref' and 'rubbish'. There was a slight gap in the boos from the audience, during which one punter from the balcony decided to articulate the views of the crowd, 'You're a tosser, ref,' to considerable applause.

The fourth contest had one local lad appearing for the first time, and you could see the atmosphere of the place suddenly changing. Nigel Bradley from Sheffield gave a sterling performance, with Brendan Ingle in the corner ducking and weaving every punch for him. The referee warned Ingle twice for shouting instructions into the ring. There were chants of 'easy' when Nigel's victory was announced, but it was anything but easy, he won by 59½ points to 57½.

Then it was time for a long intermission, occasioned by the fact that the fight was being broadcast live. You could see Harry Carpenter drumming with his pen to while away the minutes, as they grew and grew. The hall was filling up, as assorted characters from the Sheffield underworld entered to take their seats. One was wearing a steward's badge. 'He never pays for anything,' said Patrick. 'The last time I saw him at a fight, a steward asked him for his ticket and he just knocked the steward aside. I suppose it's easier to give him a badge and let him get on with it.' When I spotted the kids from Brendan Ingle's gym move into position near the ring, I knew that the waiting was nearly over. A huge barrage of boos greeted James Cook as he made his way out to the stage, only eclipsed in volume by the cheers that greeted Bomber Graham. Sheffield's adopted son had come home. As Harry Carpenter said in his commentary, 'I don't think that Peckham would have turned out in quite the same force for James Cook.' Or he might

have added – sung with quite the same force – 'We love you Bomber/
Oh yes we do/We love you Bomber/Oh yes we do.' Lisa had now
climbed on to the stage right beside the ring, and was chanting
loudly.

The fight started ferociously, but now I was beginning to adapt to
the ferocity of boxing close up. The crowd started chanting, 'Are you
watching, Nigel Benn?' after each of Bomber Graham's assaults
(Nigel Benn being the great new British Middleweight hope).
Suddenly someone from the balcony shouted that he'd spotted Nigel
Benn in the audience. 'There he is, down there.' All eyes were
rivetted on this black man in the main body of the hall with a partially
shaved head and a green tie. 'The bastard with the green tie, that's
him down there.' Patrick, however, was looking quite sceptical –
'That's not Nigel Benn, that's Slugger O'Toole, the black Irishman. I
should know, I've got him a job on the door of a pub this week.' But it
was no good, everyone was trying to spot that bastard Benn with the
green tie. Some of the audience seemed more intent on eye-balling
Benn than watching the fight.

But Graham gave them all what they wanted – a characteristic
show of brilliance, and much, much more – the return of a hero.
Despite the fact that Harry 'Boy' had told me not to blink in the fifth
round, I somehow did manage to miss the final punch, as Cook
crumpled and the crowd went wild. Even the girl who carries the
card around the ring was jumping in the air. Brian Anderson had
forgotten all about his refereeing practice and was on his feet
cheering for his pal. But I'd seen enough. I left the City Hall, as the
kids from Brendan Ingle's gym tried valiantly to scramble into the
ring to stand beside Bomber Graham, their hero, back in the
spotlight again. The middle-class chaps from the rugby club, who had
been acting as stewards, were meanwhile trying desperately to keep
them out. Without much success.

Arm wrestling

They arrived in a pink XR3. 'Who are your friends, ducky?' said one
passer-by as the car drew up beside me outside the town hall. He
hastily made his exit as the four huge hulks hauled themselves out of
the tiny car. It was, of course, a normal-sized car, it just looked tiny

with these four emerging from it. This was Steve Baxendale, thirty-eight, and three friends. Steve is a professional arm wrestler, 'and a professional fist fighter,' he added later – 'the bare knuckle job, none of this messing about with gloves. I'm a fighter not a boxer. Most boxers can't fight – Mike Tyson might just be the exception.' Steve, as they say in Belfast and I'm sure in parts of Yorkshire as well, is a hard man.

Tonight he had promised to introduce me to the world of professional arm wrestling. We were leaving the west side of Sheffield for something more primitive altogether – a pub beyond the east side, in one of the myriad mining villages, which still survive out there somehow. 'An ordinary pub,' explained Steve, 'where I happen to know that the locals go in for a bit of arm wrestling. We'll see if we can make a few bob tonight.' The hulks all chuckled.

So we set off across Sheffield in his pink XR3. The first mistake that I made that evening was that I commented on the colour of the car. 'It's not pink,' interrupted Steve, 'it's purple. Don't mention this car unless you also say that I've got a white Porsche Carrera as well. It's just that we couldn't all get into that one – unless we were all your size.' The hulks chuckled again. I sat in the back of the *pink* car squashed by two of the huge shapes – I couldn't quite see their faces. That would have required a periscope. Steve was busy giving the instructions. 'When we get to the pub, just act casual,' said Steve. 'Just look as if we're nipping in for a quiet drink on our way out for the night.' The hulks all nodded. We pulled up outside a very ordinary looking pub situated in a very bleak, urban landscape. It was raining heavily. It did not, I thought, look very promising.

The hulks all shuffled into the bar. I had to shuffle in behind them, because I had now lost all feeling in my legs from being squashed up that much. One of the hulks was Steve's son, Stephen Jnr., only eighteen but quickly transmogrifying into Steve's basic mesomorphic shape. 'He may only be young,' said Steve, 'but he'll take on and beat nearly all the arm wrestlers in Sheffield, including big Mick there. Just look at Big Mick, who would fancy my lad against him? Mick's six foot six and twenty-one stone, and fit with it. But the problem with some of these weightlifters is that they blow up like balloons and really they're as weak as piss. I'm naturally strong, so is my son. You've either got natural strength or you haven't. There's no point in trying to acquire it through training. The only training that I do is advanced aerobics – it's a kind of circuit training, used by professional footballers.'

Even at this stage in the evening I didn't fancy making any jokes about a man who drove a pink car and practised advanced aerobics. I still didn't know a lot about Steve, but I do know something about the concept of respect as practised in certain sections of society. And respect was what Steve was getting in great dollops – from big Mick and everybody else who surrounded him.

We drank quietly at the bar. Steve drank ginger ale, the rest drank orange. I felt like a degenerate with my half pint of lager. Miners sat in little knots and supped their ale and did very little else. Occasionally, they glanced our way, more often they did not. There were a lot of big fit men about the place – four more, and a hanger-on, were neither here nor there. Eventually, an arm wrestling contest started up in one corner of the room. Steve watched from a distance before dispatching his son to say that one of the group fancied his chances against the winner of the contest. The miners stared back in disbelief. 'What, with that big, fucking cunt there?' said one of the incredulous miners pointing at big Mick – 'fuck that for a laugh.' 'No, not him, it's me who fancies a go,' said Steve, stepping forward. The miner turned momentarily to his companions and a collective smile started to form. They had brightened up. It was not hard to see why. Steve's six foot one inch, fifteen-stone frame, seemed puny in comparison to big Mick's. He seemed more like a boy than a man – beside big Mick that is. 'Okay, lad, step this way. Let's be having you,' said the miner who had won the arm wrestling contest.

It was now time for the sting. 'But what about a little side bet?' said Steve. 'My mates fancy my chances. They know that I've been trying to do a little practice at this here arm wrestling. What about a tenner a head from all your pals? We'll cover the bet. We'll let the landlord hold the money.' The miner just needed one more look at Steve standing beside big Mick to convince him that he was on to a winner here tonight, and after all it was Thursday night – pay night. One of his friends was given the job of collecting the nice crisp tenners, and then they cleared the table of all the pints of bitter. I almost felt sorry for them.

I had asked Steve to talk me through the contest and this was what he tried to do – discreetly, of course, that is – out of the side of his mouth. I knew something about Steve's previous form – I had seen photographs of him arm-wrestling Geoff Capes. Earlier this year Steve was also involved in an arm wrestling contest with Jamie Reeves, officially 'the World's Strongest Man', who just happens to live in Sheffield, and who used to be a blacksmith at a local coal mine. Steve had drawn with him. Last year Steve was also runner-up in the British Arm-Wrestling Championship. He lost to Beefy Trevor Lloyd in the final. "Beefy Trevor Lloyd is only five feet tall, but he's twenty-two stone,' said Steve. He's so short that he has to sit on an orange box to arm wrestle in the British way, which is seated. The Americans arm wrestle standing up. The American style is all about body weight – it involves strength, speed and power. The British style just involves the sheer power of the forearm. Trevor's got a brilliant technique – he's been trained in the American style. But Yorkshire people like to sit down and do it. You might look at somebody like Beefy Trevor Lloyd and think to yourself that surely someone that size couldn't be much good. But the first thing that you have to remember in arm wrestling is that you must never underestimate your opponent, no matter how small or how big a sucker you think that he might be. Someone like you, for example, might pose a problem, whereas some of these big, weightlifting types are as weak as water. As soon as you apply any pressure to them, their tendons snap.'

'Tonight, in this pub, you can tell that these guys are probably suckers, but nevertheless they might be good. The guy that I'm about to compete with might be just like me and have real natural strength, and don't forget that some of these miners are as hard as nails. A lot of miners are good arm wrestlers. The other Mick that I'm with tonight – Mick Walker – used to be a miner at Brookhouse Colliery in Beighton. He used to do the tunnelling – they call them the 'rippers'. But he was made redundant, and now he's a binman. But that keeps you fit, shifting 1,300 bins a day. He's ranked in the top ten of British arm wrestlers. But you must never underestimate your opponent. You can never tell how strong they are until you take hold of them,' said Steve, gripping his opponent's hand – 'then you know.'

And at that precise moment Steve's lips started to curl into something resembling a smile, as he took hold of his opponent.

'You can always tell a professional arm wrestler because they often use the 'over-the-top' technique,' said Steve, still talking out of the side of his mouth, 'that is manipulating their opponent's fingers, in order to go over their opponent's hand to bend it backwards – that way they can weaken your opponent's arm. You've got to climb over your opponent's hand so that you're pushing forward all the time rather than backwards. Of course, if both arm wrestlers know this particular technique then you can get a stalemate situation. So what they then do in competitions is they strap the thumbs together so that you can't break the grip. The technique was made famous in the Sylvester Stallone film *Over the Top*. I took part in a competition to appear in that film. I got through to the finals and came third, if I'd won I'd be a Hollywood star now. Stallone took the arm-wrestling very seriously apparently, and now he's meant to be one of the best arm wrestlers about.'

Unlike Sylvester Stallone, the miner whom Steve was now gripping was not one of the best arm wrestlers about. Steve made a bit of a show of the first contest, but after that Steve made it all look very easy, which undoubtedly it was. 'The secret now is to pick up the money and leave before there's any come back,' said Steve. 'Of course, it's handy having a few friends with me tonight, so that we can handle any come back. I try to arm wrestle like this about once a fortnight – you need a bit of a break to recuperate. But to be honest, tonight's contest wasn't very taxing. In the past, I've picked up £800 for a night's work – £500 prize money and £300 in side bets. But tonight's takings of £100 is about average. Not great money, but nice and steady.'

'But what about "come-backs"?' I asked. 'Don't you ever worry about trouble that may arise from these contests, when disgruntled punters realize that they've been set-up to a certain extent?'

Steve shrugged, his friends guffawed with laughter. 'Don't forget I'm a professional fist fighter as well. I've been fighting all my life. I can handle myself. All of my brothers are professional fighters – one is a fifth Dan at karate, another was a professional boxer. I've done hundreds of fist fights with gypsies. It's not like boxing – the fights only last three to four minutes. Basically, I can't resist a challenge.

'And talking about challenges, there's a guy called Lennie McLean, who's been in the *Daily Star*, described as the King of the Gypsies and billed as the best street fighter in the world. They're planning to make a film about his career. I've thrown him a challenge to fight in a club in Rotherham. If he doesn't agree to the fight, then we'll expose him as a "bottle dropper". Bare knuckle fighting is illegal, but the idea is that we'll go into the ring with gloves on, then we'll have the gloves cut off. By the time that the police manage to get into the ring, the fight will be all over. These fights never last too long anyway. You hear about these professional street fighters biting each other's tongues off, putting the boot in during fights and that sort of thing. It does happen, but when I fight professionally I let my opponent try whatever he wants, and then I do the same back, only harder and worse. I don't lose these fights. With this show in Rotherham, we're planning to sell 500 tickets at £40 ahead. This would be twenty grand, split two ways, for a night's work. Perhaps after that I'll retire to France or wherever. You can't go on forever in this game, but I've got a few years left. Isn't that right boys? So far we've not had any firm commitment from McLean's people, but how can he refuse? How can the best street fighter in the world just bottle out?'

We walked out of the pub in the middle of the industrial wastelands of South Yorkshire, and across the wind-swept car park, covered in empty lager cans and wet chip papers. The pink car, which now seemed to be positively glowing in the moonlight, seemed like some kind of strange mirage. I wanted to comment on it, but I realized that it might be diplomatic and safer to keep my mouth well and truly shut for once.

Sheffield shares

He was a socialist alright. You could tell by his Scottish accent, and his tie. It may have been a conservative blue colour with an elegant stripe down the middle of it, but it was still all skew-whiff. And then there were his eyes. They were burning with a fervour, an intensity, as if he had his prey in his sights. Hadn't he already described himself as 'a political animal' – 'and with nineteen pounds fifty attendance money a day as a Sheffield councillor, on which I'm dependent by the way, I'd need to be a political animal.' And here he was with his eyes burning bright. 'Tiger, tiger, burning bright.' The lines stayed with me. And as I looked at Jimmy Boyce, ex-industrial tiler, ex-foundry worker, ex-redundant foundry worker, I realized that it really was the law of the jungle here tonight. The jungle of the night.

My eyes flitted around the table. Here they all were – business, commerce, the big banks. The political animal's eyes were burning again. 'I want the Midland bank.' It seemed outrageous. Nationalize the banks. Poppycock! But he didn't want to nationalize them, he just wanted them – for himself. There was a long gap. His neighbour cleared his throat. His neighbour worked for the Midland Bank. In fact, he was the Sales Manager of the Midland Bank in Sheffield. He looked at Jimmy Boyce, or rather he looked at his tie – all red and blue, almost patriotic, and yet the tie still hung at that curious angle. It reminded him of shop stewards with their sleeves rolled up in those endless conferences when it was said that the country was being held to ransom. It reminded him of the big shots in the Trade Union movement having sandwiches at Number 10 all those years ago. Number 10 indeed! Images of that magnitude never fade – 'never', the distant memories were starting to surface. 'Never!' he repeated as his mind returned to the present. He cleared his throat again. This time it was done differently, it wasn't so much a reflex action, an attempt to remove something nasty somewhere down his windpipe, as a deliberate social signal – even if it was almost subvocal. It seemed to be saying, 'Really, you and who else?' or 'Do you think that you're really big enough?' and many similar things, more or less at the same time. It acted as both a challenge and a rebuff. It did its job.

Jimmy paused momentarily, and then he started to speak. 'But I don't want to overstretch myself.' The man from the Midland Bank looked rather pleased with himself. His throat had stopped tickling, but then again perhaps it never had.

But this was no place for the faint hearted, and Jimmy knew it. 'What the hell. It's for the people. I'll go for it. I've been through it all. I was made redundant less than a year after I became a Sheffield City Councillor, and I've never believed in those sorts of coincidences. You have to fight and fight again.' Now it wasn't just the man from the Midland Bank who was clearing his throat. Everyone in the boardroom was either clearing his throat, or shifting position in his seat, or doing both at the same time, which is actually rather difficult. Except Jimmy Boyce that is. Jimmy's audacious move was making everyone feel uncomfortable, except himself. He had finally settled to his fate – socialist entrepreneur of the grand scale. 'It's early days yet,' said Colin Appleby from the

Midland, 'early days.' He seemed to be saying it as much to convince himself as to convince all the rest present. They were all still busy with their ticklish coughs.

But it was now Colin Appleby's move. Fate had got him as far as a leading Sheffield Estate Agents – Blundells. Colin gave that certain smile – that smile of familiarity, that smile of superiority, that certain smile that says it all – 'Ah, Mike's place. Yes I am interested in that. I think that I will purchase it.' It was like a red rag to a big, black bull. Or, given that we were in a quasi-political domain (and not the bull-ring or the jungle – despite all the emotion and fear that was flying about the place) – a big, black flag to a red bull.

'I want to buy up all of the city,' said Jimmy in reply. But the outrageous statement startled no-one. 'I'll be happy with Mike's place for the moment,' said Colin, again just rubbing in that he happened to know a thing or two about some of Sheffield's leading businesses, and that there really is no substitute for that kind of detailed and expert and intimate knowledge.

But now it was time for some wheeling and dealing. Shares in the Sheffield Development Corporation were up for sale. Richard Holmes, the Sales and Marketing Officer of the YMCA in Sheffield had somehow managed to get his hands on some. He needed to raise some capital fast. The man from the Midland Bank said that he hadn't got the kind of money required. He would have liked to help him out, but . . . All eyes were now on Jimmy Boyce. He had the capital, but did he have the inclination to buy into yet another business in order to help one of the managers out? The minimum bid was established. Richard assumed that it would be doubled. 'It would be a bargain at twice that price.' Nobody doubted him, or failed to recognize his temporary financial embarrassment. It's just that they were not inclined to help him out. 'If you can't stand the heat. Richard, old boy,' an anonymous voice said. Jimmy, however, did show some interest – 'I'm always in search of a bargain, sonny . . . for the people, you understand,' he added after yet another one of those pauses that suggested it might have been an after-thought. He eventually offered Richard ten pounds more than the asking price. 'Typical socialist,' someone muttered. Jimmy heard the jibe. 'I'm a Scot, after all. Never forget that, sonny. And I'm not the one with all the money – just look at the pile that Colin Appleby's got. A typical bloody banker, if you ask me. Not a bit of wonder the country's in the state that it's in.'

161

For those readers who are already familiar with the trans-mogrification of Sheffield from the Socialist Republic of South Yorkshire to something altogether more 'pragmatic', you could be forgiven for believing that the drama that was unfolding around the boardroom table was just one more step along the route in this particular transformation, with committed socialists playing the stock market, and buying and selling shares in companies with the best of them. But this was just a game, and before some interested individual points out that the stock market is itself just a game – for somewhat privileged people – I should point out that this was just a family game being marketed in Sheffield in the lead up to Christmas. It was called 'Sheffield Shares', and it was like a form of Monopoly for the late Eighties. It was local companies that were now being bought and sold, and the involvement and interest that the game generated, as I discovered, was really quite intense.

Richard Holmes, the Sales and Marketing Officer of the Sheffield YMCA (and the man who had earlier that night been desperate to raise some quick finance from the sale of shares in the Sheffield Development Corporation – only in the game, you understand) told me a little about the background to the game. The basic idea was that Sheffield companies would pay for the privilege of being squares on the game – for the obvious advertising benefits – with the Midland Bank, as the major sponsor, paying £20,000 for the privilege of being two corners in the game, and having their name and logo on all the notes used in the game. This sponsorship money, with thirty squares and the £20,000 from the Midland Bank, which amounted to £150,000 in total, paid all the production and advertising costs for the game. All subsequent profits from sales of the game, which retailed at £13.99, then would go directly to the YMCA for their work in the community in Sheffield. Several other British towns and cities were already committed to developing their own version of this game, with all profits going to the local YMCA.

Keith Wells, the General Secretary of the Sheffield YMCA, and the fourth player that night, outlined some of the projects that the profits of the game would be used to finance. These included a number of projects in the inner city, including one preparing those young people, just past the teenage years who have never had a job, for a working life, as well as the more familiar work of the YMCA in youth clubs and schools. The idea for the game, Keith explained, originated

in Norway, where an extraordinary total of ninety-five towns beginning with Bergen, had produced the game to finance their local YMCA.
In the United Kingdon, Derry/Londonderry was the first town to
produce the game, but the game was called there 'The Maiden City',
presumably in order not to alienate the half of the community that did
not approve of either the name 'Derry' or 'Londonderry'. Keith Wells
also pointed out that the title 'Sheffield Shares' is itself deliberately
ambiguous – 'Sheffield Shares' can be taken to mean Sheffield's shares,
as in 'shares' which are up for grabs by keen or greedy speculators (my
interpretation), but it can also mean 'Sheffield shares' as in 'shares its
wealth' – 'and that's basically what we are trying to initiate here. We're
trying to get big, local companies to plough some of their profits back
into the community through the work of the YMCA. We're extremely
optimistic about the potential of the game, and so are all of the
companies that have been involved with it as sponsors.'

So what kind of advertising do the companies get for their money?
On the share cards used in the game, it is not only the name of the
company which is printed, but some succinct message about the firm.
Such messages could (at a push) be used by those playing the game to
help them promote the value of the shares in that company in the
interminable rounds of wheeling and dealing. As in, 'How would you
like to buy some shares in Stocksbridge Engineering Works –"Manu-
facturers of high integrity alloy, stainless and re-melted steels for the
aerospace, energy, bearing and automotive industries? The Strength
Behind Engineering Progress".' Or the more punchy, 'How would you
like to buy some shares in Gibbs Building Contractors –"Don't pick
your contractor/By throwing a dice/Bring GIBBS into the game/Ask
us for a price"?' And even if the message is not read out in the endless
rounds of buying and selling shares, then the message, passive though
it might be, should still find its way into the living rooms of a high
proportion of homes in the Sheffield region. The plan was, in fact, to
sell 20,000 copies of the game in Sheffield over the Christmas period –
that is one in twenty homes. There were already 4,000 advance orders.
A lot of families in the Sheffield region, it was hoped, were going to be
hearing or reading about Stocksbridge Engineering Works, Gibbs
Building Contractors, and a few other Sheffield firms this Christmas.

Colin Appleby, the Sales Manager of the Midland Bank in Sheffield,
whom we last encountered communicating via coughing during his
negotiations with Jimmy Boyce, was extremely pleased with how the

game had turned out. He pointed out that as well as being the major sponsor of the game, the Midland Bank is the largest private-sector employer in Sheffield, and for them the game provided another opportunity for the bank to demonstrate that it was prepared to invest in the city.

But what sort of person would make a good player at Sheffield Shares? I had already noted the very different styles of play of the four who had assembled. It would have taken a blind man, or a very naive one, not to spot some connection between their style of play in the game and the kinds of responsibilities and decisions that they had to make in the outside world. I asked Colin Appleby first. 'I liked Jimmy Boyce's style of play for his very quick decisions. Richard Holmes was something of an expert at the game, but he ended up as a down-and-out by the end of it. I think the main ingredient for success in this game is that you have to have a good sense of timing. There is nothing wrong with being a bit conservative and building up financial resources, and not just jumping straight in. Jimmy had a lot of flair but it didn't help him win.' Indeed it did not, Colin's conservativism and steady timing had won him second place. Richard Holmes was next to offer his opinion. He thought that 'the best man usually wins,' despite the fact that he was last. Jimmy Boyce, on the other hand, thought that it was nearly all down to luck – 'with negotiation skills being very important.' Jimmy said that he really enjoyed playing the game, but that his only slight worry about it was that at £13.99 it might prove a little expensive for the unemployed. But what did the winner of the game actually think – Keith Wells, the man who had brought the game to England, and a man coincidentally who had never actually played the game before?

There was a long pause, the kind of pause that winners always display as they create a little time to savour the taste of their victory. 'It's basically a fine balance between being a good steward of what you have already acquired, and being something of a visionary. Rather like running the YMCA in fact, although I'd never thought of it like that before. It was all jolly good fun as well, of course.'

Having watched the game in action, I would say that it should do very well, and I think that some Sheffield socialists could be in for quite a bit of excitement this Christmas.

★ 9 ★
Altered states

Dead ordinary people

'Mr Smith' from the Stretford end of Manchester is reputed to be one of the best mediums in Britain today. Mr Smith is not his real name, but it could be. He seems very ordinary. He is very well known in spiritualist circles, but he didn't want to be exposed to the great British public. At least not yet. So Mr Smith he remains. I went to visit him with as open a mind as possible, which was difficult given what I had heard about him. Mr Smith greeted me at the door with a firm handshake. It was a wet and bitterly cold day. 'Not a great day to be out and about,' I said. 'Not a great day for the spirit people either,' said Mr Smith. 'You mean that the weather can affect them?' I asked. 'Of course it does. The spirit people have told me so themselves.' I realized then that this was going to be a day with very few laughs.

Mr Smith had been recommended to me by someone who had spent the best part of forty years investigating the claims of mediums, and exposing the charlatans in their midst. However, according to this one expert, 'interesting' things were said to happen in Mr Smith's seances. 'Like what?' I had asked. 'Oh the usual – talking ectoplasm, ectoplasmic voice boxes – that sort of thing. Just the normal stuff really, but the materialization of spirits still isn't at a very advanced stage yet.' I was already starting to wonder how I would cope when faced with an ectoplasmic voice box. I was also starting to wonder how I would cope when confronted by any skeletons from my past. You see I had also recently talked to a lorry driver who had been to one of Mr Smith's seances, and had one old and particularly nasty skeleton dragged out of its cupboard. It seems that the experience wasn't very pleasant. The lorry driver in question had attended one of Mr Smith's seances, in his own words, 'for a bit of a laugh and to give me something to talk to my mates about down the pub.' He gained access to the group because his mother was a regular member. But the joke backfired. 'During the seance, this child's voice said "Hello, Dad" right to me. I thought to myself that they hadn't done their homework very well. You see I had a daughter, but no son. But anyway, this child's voice started telling me all sorts of things about my daughter, about watching her in her playground at school and it all started to feel a little eerie. Eventually, I asked the voice how old it was and what was its name. It said, "I'm thirteen, and my name is Terry." I was dumbstruck. You see, what nobody at that seance knew, was that thirteen years previously, my wife had had an abortion. Before we decided on the abortion we'd decided that we were going to call the baby "Terry". Nobody at that seance could have known anything about this. I locked myself in the toilet after the seance for three hours and wouldn't come out. When I eventually came out my mother and I had a row about the abortion. But now I know there's nothing to be afraid of, and I regularly talk to Terry.'

I was trying to prepare myself for a few surprises as I was led into Mr Smith's drawing room. I noticed the thick velvet curtains, and the smell of a pet dog. Mr Smith eyed me suspiciously. 'You know some people come here rather sceptically. Some so-called intellectuals think that there's no such things as spirits and that contact with the spirit world is all in the mind. I think that some of these people should see a psychiatrist,' he said – preempting a view which some people might hold about certain mediums. It had been decided that I would not yet be allowed to attend an actual seance, instead I was to be allowed to hear some tape-recordings of spirits talking. I settled myself back in the chair for my first experience of the spirit world. Then the little pet dog of the house, of some unclassifiable breed, wandered in. I reached out my hand to stroke it. 'Don't touch it,' yelled Mr Smith, 'it bites.' I had already jumped into the air and we hadn't even started yet. The little dog wandered out again. 'The evidence of the spirit world is plain for all to see,' said Mr Smith. 'Now you're going to hear some of that evidence. You'd have to be a fool not to believe it.' He continued to look straight at me. He pressed the play button. An eerie sound emanated from the machine. I nodded knowingly. 'That's not the spirit people. That's just us singing "Let me call you sweetheart",' explained Mr Smith – 'we always start with some good old-fashioned songs.' Then the singing slowly died away. Suddenly a child's voice spoke, 'I enjoy the singing, you know.' Mr Smith stared at me – 'there was no child present at the seance.'

166

Goose bumps formed on my arm, and a chuckle was initiated somewhere deep in my throat, more or less simultaneously. 'Just listen,' said Mr Smith.

Woman's voice: 'Is it Terry?' [the lorry driver's aborted foetus apparently thriving in the spirit world].

'Hello Auntie Rose.'

'Hello my love. Where's my kiss?'

This was followed by a kissing noise. After Terry came a whole series of spirits recorded from different sessions. The first thing that struck me about them was how well spoken they were. Indeed, Mr Smith had pointed out that some of these spirits were 'better spoken than the Queen.' But, as I listened to the tapes, I discovered that the spirits that frequent Stretford are not just well spoken, they're fairly outspoken as well. Stretford spirits do not mince their words. Referring to practising Christians, one spirit, a Mr Powell, referred to them as 'misguided'. He continued, 'They are ignorant peasants. They are compensating, so do not worry.' Mr Powell had apparently delivered this message in a darkened room through an ectoplasmic voice box, although he was hoping to deliver this and similar messages in person later, as he himself explained. 'We were hoping that we could have shown ourselves before now, but at least you can hear us speaking to you for the time being.'

Whilst listening to the tapes, I was relieved to discover that spirits retain their sense of humour. One spirit was holding a conversation with a scientist called Ronald. The spirit began by insulting him. 'Your theories are not quite right. You're only scratching the surface. You think you're an egghead and clever, but you wait until you learn about our world.' The spirit then told him his name. Ronald, the scientist, misheard it – 'Crook?' The spirit corrected him – 'Cooke! Just think of your dinner,' he said. It wasn't much of a wisecrack, but at least it was something.

Mr Smith just nodded – 'marvellous these spirits. There's nothing they don't know.' He then played me a section of tape where he discussed my impending visit with one of his spirit guides.

Mr Smith: 'God Bless you – Just a second, Mr Powell, we've got a Gerald Beattie coming to talk to me tomorrow.'

Spirit: 'Oh yes, you have many people coming here, he'll be one of many who will come – he will go away with his own ideas.'

Mr Smith: 'Yes.'

Spirit: 'But I think you will give him a lot to think about.'

Mr Smith: 'That is good.'

Spirit: 'A *lot* to think about – you could open a whole new world to this gentleman.'

Mr Smith: 'Yes.'

Spirit: 'If he cares to learn, but he has to learn the truth and to be well-read on the subject. You carry on, my friend, telling him to read – because there are books we value very much.'

I wanted to point out that there were clearly some things that these spirits did not know. My name was Geoffrey for a start, or as these spirits would probably put it – 'Geoffrey! As in just think of that sheepish Deputy Prime Minister.' But I left it. I asked instead when did Mr Smith first realize that he had psychic powers? He said that it first dawned on him when he was about four. His father had gone to the races and left him and his mother alone on their farm in Cheshire. 'This particular night mother said that the two of us would sleep in the guest room of the farm. I woke up in the middle of the night and mother was shouting at something to go away and stop it. I said, "What is it mother?" She replied, "I think it's Alice Healey." Alice Healey had been dead for some years. I could see these unseen hands pulling at the bottom of the bed, so I dived under the bed clothes. Mother told everybody that the spare room was haunted and that I had psychic powers. All the neighbours heard about my psychic gifts after this.

'One other incident convinced me of my psychic powers. during the war, I was stationed in India. In 1944 I had to take a special message to divisional headquarters. I passed this signal operator in a trench. He asked me to take over for a few moments, while he relieved himself. A message came through for one particular soldier to report to Bombay for repatriation to the U K on special leave. That soldier was me! There were about 150,000 troops in that area, and just by chance I received the radio message. When we were two days out of Bombay, we heard that a 30,000-strong Japanese army invaded the area that I'd just left. Most of my friends were wiped out. The Japs even bayonetted the patients in the field hospitals. I realized there and then that there must be something I had to do in my life – that I'd been chosen for something.

'When I got back home to the farm in Cheshire, my father hardly recognized me. He hadn't seen me for six years, and he was shocked by my appearance. I'd gone down from fourteen stone to nine stone. He said, "By God, they've taken their toll on you alright." When I was demobbed in 1946, the vicar came round to say that he hoped to see me in church on Sunday. I told him that church was the furthest thing from my mind after what I'd seen in the war – ministers blessing guns for killing people with. And I didn't believe in the stories either – Noah's Ark and all that tripe. If it were true just tell me how the Kangaroo came to be in Australia, eh? I was more interested in gambling than church to tell the truth. Whilst I'd been away mother, who had 2,000 poultry on the farm, had been saving the egg money for me. There was a bank book with £140 in it, waiting for me when I got home. I said to her, "Mother, what a delightful person you are." We used to go to these steeplechase meetings, and one day I backed horses in eight races and had eight winners. I must have been psychic, or so mother said. About that time mother became a spiritualist. It was about the only thing we ever argued about. I said, "Don't bother me with that tripe." In 1952 I decided to give it a try. We sat in what's called a development circle with a red light above the circle. It was so dark that you couldn't recognize the person sitting opposite you. I saw this light on the wall of the church, but I was sitting there real arrogant. I was thinking to myself that I bet there's a hole in the curtain and all these mugs are taken in by this. Suddenly something happened to me. I could feel my eyes pulling out, and my face being contorted. I thought to myself, what the hells's this? There's some bugger here sitting with me – their legs in mine, their face in mine. Then this man from across the room shouted at me, "Young man let that spirit doctor come through." I was panicking. That was my first experience. Later I found myself talking like a Scotch man in that church. The Scotch man's name was Jock McCullough. Jock McCullough entered my body. Shortly after this experience I became a spiritualist.'

Shortly after this, Mr Smith's mother encouraged him to go to a very well known medium where materialization was common. 'We all had to pray at the start of the seance, but because I wasn't used to going to church anymore, I wasn't sure what to say. So I just said, "Dear God, I've come here by invitation.' You have to pray, by the way, so that you don't contact lower evolutionary forms of life, such as the lower ape man. We've had cases of dogs materializing, and little dogs sitting on people's knees. So we always pray. After the prayer, as we were singing, this bright light, the size of a sixpence but brilliant like a diamond, went round the room and stopped in front of me. Suddenly there was this huge noise like a "whoooosh" and it materialized as an angel. She walked up to me and said, "God bless you in the name of Jesus." She told me her name was Sister Helen. She was the most gorgeous figure I'd ever seen and had this beautiful face. She told me that we had been brought there for a special reason. "Do not believe the priests," she said. 'You do not lie in the grave until some far off day of judgment, when the great trumpets sound. I am proof of that."

'One man at this particular seance had a wife who was dying of cancer. Sister Helen told him that if he did what she told him, that she would get up off her sickbed in three weeks' time. Sister Helen told him to go to the chemists and buy these Dutch drops – capsules with cod liver oil in them. She told him to give her two in the morning and two at night. She also told him to take her to hospital in three weeks to have her inspected. Up until then she had this huge cancer as big as a coconut – doctors could feel her cancer by poking about up through her rectum. But now it had gone. The doctors were baffled. Sister Helen was lovely. She told my mother that she would be there to meet her when it was her turn to pass into the next world. She had a lovely voice – very soothing, and far more educated sounding than you or I. In fact she also spoke in a way superior to the queen.'

At that point, I nearly put my foot in it. It had already been explained to me that your spirit body can transfrom after death. Terry was after all now thirteen, and not a foetus any longer. Were voices also transformed? Did you lose your accent in the afterlife? Would my mother be pleased that I had lost my Belfast accent after all? Unfortunately, I blurted this question out. Mr Smith looked at me as if I had just spewed up some ectoplasm on to his lap. 'Of course not. Sister Helen was educated in this life, Mr Beattie, unlike some people.'

Mr Smith's mother passed away three years ago. She was ninety-two. In a seance shortly afterwards she explained that Sister Helen was there to meet her on the other side, along with her sister Winnie. Mr Smith continued his account. 'Nobody except me at that seance knew about Sister Helen's promise thirty-five years previously. My mother stayed in the astral plane for fourteen days before being led to the spirit world. For fourteen days you could smell her perfume all over the house and then it was gone. It was the same with Jesus –

that's why his disciples reported seeing him. Jesus was a great medium. He never said he was God. It's the same with all religions. All the great religious leaders were mediums. The problem is that ordinary people want to turn these great mediums into gods. The astral plane is a world of our own mental making, the spirit world is a world of anti-matter. When some people die, they think they're in a nightmare. Others are brainwashed into thinking that they will sleep until the trumpet sounds. So they do sleep because they've been hypnotized. But a belief in the spirit world would change the way that people live. How could one person kill another knowing that they would have to come face-to-face with him again one day?'

'Or indeed abort your unborn foetus,' I added, thinking again of the poor lorry driver, as I made my way out on to the cold streets of Stretford. It may indeed have been my imagination but the temperature seemed to have dropped again sharply in Manchester that day. I consoled myself by remembering that these know-all spirits didn't even get my name right, confusing my first name with that of an ex-President of the United States who was reputed not to be able to walk and chew gum at the same time. I remembered all this, as I stumbled into my taxi, my Wrigleys Spearmint falling out of my mouth and on to the icy pavement.

Stuck with the unchurched

The first thing that hit me was the noise. The noise of expectation, the noise of nervous excitement, the noise of bodies squirming in anticipation. Like the noise of a childrens' party, before it all gets going. A few outsiders, here to spectate for the night, laughed nervously and looked around expectantly. But they were squirming as well, in a different kind of way, though, from the regulars. One of the outsiders held his hands up high in a parody of the faithful in prayer, and the whole group giggled. They had come for a good laugh. That was what they thought.

It was hot and sticky, the way that clubs always get when they're packed, and when there are all those bodies anxiously waiting for the band to appear. The 'event' had been postponed for ten minutes, I wasn't sure why. So there was plenty of time for the punks and the Goths and the Acid House Freaks, ekeing out the dying embers of that particular cult, to extinguish their cigarettes and make their way in. It was already full inside and more came tumbling in. The girl sitting immediately in front of me, somewhat incongruous in her Sunday frock and therefore presumably another outsider, had her feet up on the pew in front. But even the balcony was so full now that there was little room for expansive body language. She had to pull her feet back in, withdraw them close to her body, to make way for two Goths. She had started to look a little uncomfortable. I felt cramped as well, and it hadn't even started yet.

The music suddenly began. It sounded a little like House music – some would have described it as bland and meaningless. I wouldn't have dismissed it quite so lightly. It was highly persistent, insistent, uncomfortable. What's bland and meaningless about that kind of build up of excitement? The effects the music was producing reminded me of David Byrne's and Brian Eno's 'The Jezebel Spirit' from the album 'My Life in the Bush of Ghosts'. I was feeling unexpectedly anxious. It was the music that was doing it, I suppose. Iggy Pop concerts have always had the same effect on me. No-one was squirming now, at least not in the way that they had been. Even the little group of outsiders had stopped smirking. The audience was starting to get into synchrony with the insistent beat of the music, and with their neighbours. In real life we sometimes get into synchrony with those with whom we feel rapport. We do this by moving in time to the fundamental rhythm of their speech, or so it has been claimed. It's a complex and delicate process. It's easy to fall out of synchrony. Music can by-pass all that. It can short circuit the process, short circuit the brain. That's part of the power of music. Who could get out of synchrony with a beat like that? I was even squeezing my biro in time to it.

One guy at the front of the balcony in a grey-and-white sweatshirt, with the top of his hair dyed blond and the lower regions black, started dancing in that exaggerated Acid House Style. I had once heard it described as resembling someone squeezing an orange box. But here the box was higher, as if it had been reached down from above, and somehow got stuck about chest level. Occasionally he glanced around, and then it was back to the music, back to that insistent rhythm. I could just about discern the huge message projected on the wall at the front. It seemed to say: 'EAT GOD'. I wasn't sure if I'd read it correctly. Suddenly the background changed

172

and the message got clearer. I had read it correctly, now I just wasn't sure what it meant. The vicar, Canon Robert Warren, of St Thomas's in Sheffield, where all this was taking place, has described the use of the nine slide projectors to cover the walls with such graphic images as an 'electronic-age form of stained-glass windows.' But stained-glass windows never had messages like these. I could see the crowds down below, all dancing. I alone seemed to be rigid, frozen in a mixture of embarrassment and inexplicable anxiety.

Suddenly someone in jeans and a pony tail appeared in the middle of the floor down below. He had that kind of hip laid-back speaking style. 'This is our first normal service for ages,' he began. He didn't look at all like Canon Warren. He pointed out that the first service in the month was a Communion Service, the third in the month was the 'Club' Service, where the service was held in a local nightclub. Alcoholic beverages were not, however, sold. The man with the pony tail had suddenly finished speaking, without displaying any perceptible cues, in his intonation or elsewhere, to warn us of this. The band started up. They performed among their speakers, to the side of the church. 'If they were on the platform in the middle of the church, it would be as if we were worshipping them,' explained one regular. 'Look around and touch the new age,' the first song said. The chorus 'We have a victory' had the congregation singing with a level of exuberance and volume (not to say a message) that would have been the envy of the Kop. It was hypnotic. I had heard, however, that as a result of complaints from neighbours, the environmental health officer had been called on several occasions to check the noise levels outside the church.

I stared at the 'EAT GOD' image on the wall. It appeared to be moving! But the apparent motion of the message may have just been an illusion caused by the changing backgrounds being projected on to the white wall. It was still quite eerie, despite my conscious search for a rational explanation. The next song from the band began with the words 'You give me love'. The crescendo here was, 'I want you, I need you, I love you.' 'You' here was God. The music was louder, everyone was now dancing. And when I say 'dancing' I don't mean swaying, or tapping their toes, or nodding along in time to the music, I mean dancing. I wasn't dancing, I felt that I stood out a mile.

These were the NOS people. Those who attend the Nine o'clock service held at St Thomas's – there are two other services for the more normal church-goer. NOS was a service especially designed for the 'unchurched', as one member had explained – 'those who had never been to church before.' NOS has now been going for three years, although no publicity material has ever been produced for the service. Its popularity is spread by word of mouth alone, and approximately 400 young people attend every Sunday evening, and the number is growing. St Thomas's is an Anglican church, which is also part of the Charismatic movement, the neo-Pentecostal movement which emphasizes the importance of the Holy Spirit in the Christian faith, or, perhaps more importantly, the experience of the Holy Spirit. Indeed in the Charismatic movement there is a very great emphasis on demonstrable gifts from the Holy Spirit, including prophecy, healing and 'tongues'. The General Synod of the Church of England, which has published a report on the Charismatic movement within that church, has described this latter gift of 'tongues' as 'the central recognition symbol for Charismatics. And for the Charismatic who is visiting a new church or fellowship, the sound of tongues will . . . make him feel instantly at home.'

I had been told that 'tongues' was a common feature of NOS. But not just 'tongues'. Many at NOS had been 'slain by the Holy Spirit,' which apparently means that the Holy Spirit had entered their body and 'they shake and fall down and laugh hysterically for ages and ages, or they just freeze,' as one who had experienced this personally, subsequently explained to me. I asked in my usual naive fashion whether this was a pleasant or an unpleasant experience. 'Brilliant' was how my informant had described it – 'absolutely brill.' But then she had gone on to tell me immediately about the power of radiators. The Holy Spirit, she claimed, often liked to travel down cold metal. Her best friend, as a consequence, had on one occasion found herself stuck to a radiator for hours when the Holy Spirit entered her. 'She couldn't move, she was obviously quite frightened. Her eyes wouldn't open, and there she was stuck fast to a radiator.' Her friend, I later discovered, was generally a somewhat 'emotional' character – 'but nothing quite like that had ever happened to her before.' 'The thing that worries me,' confided my informant, towards the end of our discussion 'is that if nothing so dramatic happens again to her in the very near future, she may get a bit disillusioned with the Holy Spirit, and stop believing in it. That's always the danger when you have such a dramatic conversion to Christianity in the first place.'

I talked to two other NOS people about their experiences, and about their own conversions. Gail was a twenty-year-old student. She had been brought up rather conventionally in the church, and at fourteen she had become a Sunday School teacher. A conventional Sunday School teacher. Then adolescence intervened. Today she wears Doc Martens and tie-dye leggings, and a shirt with tassles. She also has a ring through her nose. Cliff Richard was never like this. Her conversion happened quite suddenly eighteen months ago. 'I was going out with a guy who was a Christian, but he didn't look like it. Like everyone else I had certain stereotypes of how Christians looked. I went to NOS with him, I'd heard how trendy it was. And, of course, I thought it was a bit of a laugh when I got there. I then went on a Christian holiday with my boyfriend, but I was determined not to become a Christian. They were all talking about God non-stop. I was stuck there for a week in this caravan with them in the middle of nowhere. There were these punks there and that really surprised me, but there were also these schoolteacher-types. I just thought to myself, how can they make such fools of themselves behaving like this? You know, waving their hands about all the time and singing "hallelujah". Then it happened. Don't ask me how, I don't know.'

Her friend, Caroline, aged nineteen, got converted at NOS itself. 'Don't ask me how it happened either. How are we supposed to understand someone who made us?' Today both help with NOS. Gail is the roadie for the band, Caroline is a member of the 'visuals team'. 'We make up the slides and videos. We might have a picture of Jesus in fluorescent colours or a blue Jesus or Jesus with a spiral behind him. We flash messages up, things like, "Do you know what time it is?" They have an effect alright. We believe that the Holy Spirit is with us at NOS, and we have to fight the devil using whatever resources we have at our disposal.'

'What about the devil?' I asked. 'How do you envisage him?' 'Well put it like this,' said Caroline – 'the devil's a complete bastard.' 'A complete and utter bastard,' echoed Gail. I was somewhat taken aback by the language, and it must have showed. 'Oh, we don't mind swearing, you know. What's the harm in it?' said Gail reassuringly. I then asked them how they conceived Hell. The Reverend Ian Paisley had rather dwelt on this, during one of my last visits to his church. I was still somewhat worried. The NOS people

175

selected less arcane language to describe it. 'Oh Hell is going to be really bad, really crap,' said Caroline. 'Shit, in fact,' echoed Gail.

It turned out that Gail and Caroline were both members of the 'seventy-two', the discipleship groups run by St Thomas's. They both felt that they had been called to do God's work 'using whatever means and whatever resources that are available to do God's work and fight the devil.' 'Put it this way,' said Gail. 'If God asked me to walk around with a sandwich board, I'd do it, even if I felt a total dickhead. Luckily, he hasn't.' 'So far,' laughed Caroline. 'I've been called to help with the band,' said Gail – 'I'm pretty lucky really.'

And back in St Thomas's the band kept belting out, 'I want you, I need you, I love you.' The audience were as one, singing and dancing. A series of shots of nature appeared on the video monitors in synchrony with the song – a pebble dropping into a pond, the ripples moving outwards, a flower opening in the rain, a waterfall. This was, as they say, a total experience, and again it seemed to be producing some sort of emotional reaction in me. I had heard the word 'brainwashing' used several times about the experience, before I attended the service. I was taking no chances. I kept myself distracted by considering the incongruity of a skinhead with his hands raised in exultation during the song, producing pelvic thrusts in time with the bass. For a moment I felt that I could have been anywhere, and not necessarily in a place of worship. More so when the couple in front started touching each other. But then it was time for prayers, and they stopped touching each other – for the moment. The House music continued in the background during the prayers. When the music stopped, I realized that it was time for the sermon. We were asked to turn to page 47 of the Bible, but it was pitch dark, and no-one could read it. The preacher, who looked just like any other member of the audience, attempted to explain why Christ employed parables in his teachings – 'anyone could hear them, only some would understand. Only those spiritually prepared to listen to the messages,' he emphasized. I was wondering aloud whether this whole service was good spiritual preparation for anything. I did learn something, however. 'Messiahs at the time of Christ,' we were told with some assurance, 'were popping out of the woodwork all the time. That's why Christ called himself "The Son of Man".' The preacher was not spell-binding, indeed he trailed off so badly at the ends of sentences that I felt I was missing the most important bits of the message.

The service ended quietly and abruptly. I felt it ended somewhat prematurely. After the emotional build-up, I felt vaguely let down. Perhaps that was the point. Perhaps I'd return for more. Those wanting to pray or be prayed for, were asked to stay behind. The church apparently stays open to around 12.30 am on occasion, and I noticed as I left that groups of punks and Goths and bikers were hanging around outside, lighting up as soon as they were out of the church.

I hurried off, but with some determination I kept well away from all radiators for the rest of the night.

Spaced out on the Tour de Sponsors

Paul Watson is a professional cyclist with a formidable pedigree – he has ridden in the Tour de France, he was third in the Milk Race in 1985 and fourteenth in the World Championship that same season, where he won the climber's jersey. Today, he's resting. Or unemployed – depending upon how you look at it.

'Put it this way, I'm between sponsors at the moment. I've got a few groups interested, but basically I'm looking for one big sponsor that can come up with fifty grand for the coming season for me to get a team together.' So here he was, desperately trying to make the connection that would guarantee his future. It was 3.00 am, and he was in a nightclub. As the owner of the club talked the last reluctant punters out through the door, Paul hung about purposefully. 'Well, you never know. He must be worth a few bob. The one thing that I've learned is that a cold call never works, I've got a £500 quarterly phone bill this week to prove it. You have to have connections.' So here he was desperately trying to connect, desperately trying to meet the main man.

I met him the next day complete with his promotional video, prepared by the Professional Cycling Association. The arguments presented in the video seemed compelling enough. The statistics alone persuaded me. There are fifteen million regular cyclists in the United Kingdom, and cycling has now equalled jogging as a leisure activity in this country. Two and a half million new bikes were sold here in 1989. In Europe it is even more popular, and is the number two sport after football. In 1989, forty million viewers watched cycling on the thirty-eight hours of television devoted to cycling, which coincidentally represents a 100% increase in the amount of air time in one year. Four million people even came out of their houses to watch the major races in this country. Then there is the excitement, glamour and ecologically sound (and all-weather) nature of cycling, and last but by no means least there is the branding. As the video says, 'riders are fully branded.' And somewhere among the exciting and glamorous and ecologically sound and heavily branded riders in the video is Paul, still searching for his main man.

But still in vain. 'Part of the problem,' he explained, 'is that I just don't look the part of the professional cyclist. It's because of my pony tail and earring. Team managers find it hard to accept me because of my appearance, they're all from the old school. It's just like in tennis – when John McEnroe came along he blew their minds. He just didn't fit in. It was as if he had beamed himself down from another planet, they just couldn't understand him. I feel that I'm a bit like that. They take one look at my hair and my earring, and they think "oh, no". I've never got on with any team manager.'

But I looked at the hair and the ring in his ear, and I somehow couldn't help thinking that these were not the problem. I couldn't quite put my finger on it. I asked him how he got into professional cycling, and he quoted some lines by a group that he identified as 'Talk, Talk'. 'You may find yourself in another part of the world in a beautiful home. And you might ask yourself "how did I get here?" I pointed out that the group was 'Talking Heads', and then I realized that he hadn't got the lines quite right. All this passed between us, before I wondered at the relevance of the answer. He could sense my puzzlement. He continued, 'I always think that it's just like life. I just found myself on a bike.' Then I realized that it was Paul's air that confused me, his manner – more than unconventional, a bit distant, a bit too distant.

His introduction to racing wasn't that conventional either. He first made his name in cycling when he won the National Junior Cyclo-Cross title in 1977, aged seventeen. He said that he was obsessed with cycling, and that he never wanted to do anything else. When he was nineteen he decided that he wanted to break into the European circuit. He had already ridden a race in France for Great Britain, and he thought that he might just have a chance of racing in Europe, because someone had sent him a good write-up in a local paper in

Lille in Northern France. So he got the ferry and the train to Lille one weekend, and simply marched into the nearest bike shop, armed with the cutting. '"This is me here," I said. "I want to join a bike club." Of course, I didn't speak a word of French. The guy in the shop just didn't want to know, so he kicked me out. But I thought to myself that guy just doesn't know the score, so I then made my way to a proper racing shop.'

Paul still didn't speak any French, but he made himself understood somehow, and was put into contact with La Redoubte team. 'Here I was set up in a flat, with bikes supplied and a car to run around in – that was the season 1982–83, and I was in my element. In 1984 I got a contract to ride in the South Pacific in New Caledonia. That's when the uprising started.'

I wasn't sure what uprising he was talking about, but I encouraged him to tell me about an uprising – any uprising – as seen from the saddle of a bike. 'The uprising started with our race. It was unbelievable – we were caught on the north of the island and all these natives were making a protest. It all started with the bike race. I was getting to see the world through my cycling.'

And perhaps even making history by starting uprisings, I wanted to add. But Paul continued, 'In 1985 I was the British Amateur Champion, and fourteenth in the World Amateur Championship. Then I turned pro, and that's when things all started to go wrong.' I didn't want to point out that things didn't seem to have been going all that well up to that point, what with irate French bike shop owners and uprisings in the South Pacific. But I kept my mouth shut.

Paul sighed audibly. 'As an amateur I was still looking at the glossy pictures, you see. I was still taken in by the image of cycling. As a pro you get to see behind it. It must be the same with all other professional sports. That's when you start questioning everything. The other thing is that it is so bloody hard in the professional world. You ride yourself into the ground – quite literally. The other thing was that as a pro I was making less than I was as an amateur. As an amateur in France I was picking up between £300 and £500 a week. I was struggling to make that kind of money when I turned pro, and it was so much harder.'

As an amateur in 1985 Paul came third in the Milk Race, a race which involves both professional riders and amateurs, as a professional in 1986 he crashed in the same race, losing sixteen minutes in the process. The pressure was clearly getting to him. In 1987 he signed with ANC, the first British sponsored team to go to Europe. Things started to improve. Paul was sixth in a race in Fleche Wallone in Belgium, and at one point the team lay sixth overall in the World Cup series. But the pressure was increasing. 'I was the only one doing well for the team, the team was pushing me all the time. You can't ride 145-mile races every week. My body just couldn't take it, in what was really my first year. It was being pushed too much. We were travelling so much with ANC, getting home at 3.00 am, it was all proving too much for me. For two months I was never at home for more than a couple of days. Then we went into the Tour de France. This had been my ultimate ambition since I was a boy. I lasted six days and then I was out of it. I never recovered.'

Paul shrugged – 'my body just couldn't take it. They were pushing me too hard.' I couldn't help thinking at this stage that Paul was really talking about more than psychological pressure bearing down on him. An obvious question was forming. 'Being pushed, did you find yourself being pushed to take any substances as well?' Paul gestured defensively. 'I don't know what I was given.' He repeated this assertion several times for good measure. 'You have to remember at that time it was like being on a campaign crusade. A tour is like being in prison. Everything takes on different values – you're constantly with the same group all the time and you're never allowed out. A routine check-up before the Tour de France started revealed that I had an irregular heart beat and really low blood pressure. I was advised to consult my team's doctor, which was a bit of a laugh because we didn't have one. Everything was being run on a shoe string, you see. I rode for six days in the Tour and then I had to withdraw.'

I asked what the Tour de France had been like, and Paul's face contorted. I thought that he might scream. 'You just can't imagine it. I wish I could take somebody like yourself and put you in my body for a day, to experience the pain. I'm sure that nobody has ever experienced pain like that before. It never eases. On the Tour de France it was from the gun – whooooosh up the road, whooooosh down the road for seven hours. I couldn't believe it, nobody could believe it. Up this bloody mountain – whooooosh. Whooooosh down round the corners.' Paul seemed really quite traumatized by having to relive all this. His legs were now pumping furiously, and I half-expected his chair to circle the room. The memories were being rekindled with a vengeance. 'There's so much tackle that goes down – so many are charged to bloody Armageddon. There are all these doctors doing dope tests, but you hear all these stories about ways of beating the tests. Sometimes they say that you don't even have to beat the tests – doctors from some teams also do the tests. But I've heard of powder that you can put under your foreskin, and when you piss it mucks the test up. Then you can take this tablet for gout that masks all the steroids. I've heard of riders having urine flushed through their penises, so that when you're providing a sample, you're not providing your own urine. In the days when you didn't have to strip off to provide a sample, one bloke even had a bag of urine strapped under his arm. He was squeezing the bag and it looked as if he was doing the business. He wouldn't have got caught except the bag burst. I've even heard of guys with cigar tubes of urine up their backside.'

I wanted to bring this account back to Paul's own experiences, so I had to ask him again. Did he himself ever take anything? Again, Paul went on the defensive. 'I don't know what I took. But there was so much pressure. The short-cut always is charge – steroids, cortisone, amphetamines. You get them from what they call "the *soigneur*" – basically bent doctors. All my *soigneur* had was two cases full of stuff that he knew about. Every professional rider walks around with an attaché case. What do you think they keep in them? Not their bleedin' sandwiches, that's for sure. They sit there. "Have you had this one?" "No, what's that one then?" "This one makes you go really well." This is their conversation, honestly. It buggers up your mind as well as your body. In one of the teams I rode for it was like the Mad Hatter's Tea Party. Either you'd all be on some sort of high, with everyone laughing and screaming and joking, or it would be a real downer, with everyone wanting to punch each other's lights out. You had to judge what sort of level things were at before you sat down for tea. The races were hilarious. You'd get your profile of the race, and you'd look at the map and go, "Jesus Christ." You can't take your amphets before the start, you only get about three hours on them. So you want to take them just before the biggest hill. But, of course, other riders want to take them there as well. So on the race at the start of this hill, you can suddenly feel the speed go whoooooosh. It's like going up a gear. Then suddenly you see all this silver foil coming fluttering between the bikes. Then all of a sudden all these animal noises start up – all this screaming and laughing. You think to yourself, What's going on here? It's like you're in some nut-house. All this hysterical laughter, with riders having fits of giggles. Guys will just ride up to you and shout, "Yabadababadoooooooooooo." It's quite funny at the time. But then again it's not very funny when you see the speedometer climb up and up. So you're charged up all day then you need sleepers at night. Everybody's at it. There was one rider who was so charged up that I was afraid of sleeping in the same room as him, in case he grew an extra head. His attaché case would have registered on a Geiger counter. I used to panic whenever he shook the case. You hear these guys saying, "Are you taking any vitamins?" And I'd say, "Yeah, I'm taking C, D and E." And then they'd say, "Not those, I'm talking about real vitamins, dummy. Show Paul the vitamins." They they'd get all this gear out. But despite the pressure, some riders still manage to stay clean.

'But look where it gets you. Everybody knows about the really famous riders who've won the Tour de France, who have then died prematurely, but how many further down the pecking order have slipped off somewhere and died quietly, without anyone being any the wiser? Where are all those riders now?'

In 1988 Paul decided to get away from it all, so he headed East – to India for three months, to get his head and his body together. 'I was interested in Eastern philosophy, but it was shit out there basically, the food was terrible.' However, a few months after his return he entered the Grundig World Cup series race at Crystal Palace in May of 1989, and there he produced the fastest qualifying time. His luck seemed to be changing – temporarily. He was leading the world-class field on the second day when he came off his bike, badly bruising a rib. He hasn't ridden competitively for the past seven months. He is now without a team and without a major sponsor.

'But I've got my enthusiasm back, and now I feel like I'm eighteen again. I survived the Tour de France in the end, and perhaps that's the main thing. I know that I can get a very successful team together if I can just find a major sponsor,' said Paul as he left, gripping his attaché case full of glossy promotional material and videos. For once.

The stage hypnotist

Dr Michael Heap was moving uneasily from foot to foot by the time I got there. We had a date – we were off to see a show at the City Hall in Sheffield. No ordinary show either – Ken Webster, an up-and-coming stage hypnotist was appearing. Dr Heap is the Secretary of the British Society of Experimental and Clinical Hypnosis, and interested in the more serious applications of hypnosis. Many in his society, but not Dr Heap himself, want to see a total ban on stage hypnosis. So I'd asked him to come along and talk me through the performance. He looked me up and down. 'I just hope you're not susceptible,' he said. 'Unfortunately, you look as if you might be.' And on that note we made our way into the half-empty hall.

We had a few minutes before the start of the performance so I asked Dr Heap to run through some of the problems with stage hypnosis from his point of view. 'The first problem isn't really to do with hypnosis at all,' he said. 'A number of those that end up on the stage won't be properly hypnotized. They will be merely role playing, acting how they think that they should behave under hypnosis. This creates problems when people turn up to a clinic which uses hypnosis for therapeutic reasons. They arrive with totally the wrong conception, they think that this is all that hypnosis is. But the biggest problem with stage hypnosis *per se* is that the hypnotist practises on people that he doesn't know and this can be problematic. I went to one performance where a patient of mine who was an alcoholic took part in an act where the hypnotist suggested to the people on the stage that they were drunk. Luckily my patient wasn't in that particular sketch, or the consequences could have been very severe. Some hypnotists regress people. What happens if people are regressed to an age where they had particular psychological problems? And a lot of hypnotists use the infamous Grand National routine – what happens if these people are phobic about horses? The problems are endless. There's also lots of circumstantial evidence of the specific dangers, reported recently by the psychiatrist David Waxman. For example, a young couple who attended a performance at a club were found the next morning asphyxiated in their car in the garage, with the radio on. The suggestion had been made by the hypnotist that they would go into a trance every time they heard a particular tune.'

I was just about to ask if there was any evidence that the particular tune had, in fact, been played, when an eerie and disembodied voice told us 'to make ourselves comfortable, for a journey inside our minds.' The couple in the row in front were in the meantime in the middle of a journey inside their mouths – they were stuffing crisps into them. Suddenly, there was a loud bang and smoke poured from the stage. The female immediately in front dropped her crisps, her companion munched on regardless. I could see that some people were going to be more open to suggestion that others (I had dropped my pen, Dr Heap hadn't flinched). 'Ladies and gentlemen, please welcome Ken Webster,' said the voice. There was little applause.

Ken Webster beat his way through the smoke to the front of the stage, looking not at all how I imagined a hypnotist to look. Indeed, he looked much more like a Northern comic, with streaked blond hair and an earring. I always assumed that hypnotists would have piercing eyes, not pierced ears. 'Some people like to watch, some like to participate,' he told us. Dr Heap looked at me warily. 'There are three types of people that I prefer not to hypnotize – drunks, mental delinquents . . . so that's you lot ruled out. No seriously folks – drunks, delinquents and those people who just come up here to challenge me. I can assure you that we will have lots of fun – no ladies will be taking their clothes off, sorry fellas, but that's not to say that some blokes won't be stripping. So ladies stay awake. Now hypnotism is the second best thing in your life. What's the first? I'll tell you what,' and he started to make a hand-jerking movement. The evening was warming up alright.

Dr Heap clearly hadn't expected hypnotism compared with this, but no matter, it was time for the suggestibility exercise. 'What I'd like everybody to do is to clasp their hands together like so, index fingers together. Concentrate on your hands getting tighter, *tighter*. Now separate your index fingers and feel them moving together.' No matter how much I willed mine one way or the other, they didn't respond – to him or to me. They just reached for my notepad, as the rest of the hall stared at their index fingers doing nothing in particular. Nevertheless, this exercise did uncover twelve volunteers – all about twenty years old. All looked like the sort of people that would be game for a laugh – the kind who play charades at parties, the kind who as adolescents acted drunk, or hypnotized. I noticed that there were more than twelve seats on the stage.

The hypnotist asked them if they had ever been hypnotized before. One put up his hand. It turned out that he had been hypnotized to stop him smoking, but it had not worked. 'Sssh, don't let the audience hear you,' said the hypnotist. Then it was time for, 'Your eyes are getting heavier and heavier and heavier . . . Nothing bothers, nothing disturbs, nothing can bother, nothing can disturb. Your mind and your body are in perfect balance.'

I had tried this routine a hundred times myself as a child, but it had never worked for me. So I was more than a little sceptical. I was so desperate as a boy to believe in the powers of hypnosis that I once devoured a whole raw onion to show that I was under the influence. However, I did balk at the bar of Fairy soap that my best friend offered me next to eat. It wasn't the soap that I was really worried about, I was more concerned that if I ate the soap, I'd be given something even more disgusting to eat next. We were performing on my door step at the time, and I had noticed my friend eyeing some dog pooh on the street. So I mysteriously awakened from my trance as he was unwrapping the soap. The conditions, of course, were not exactly conducive to putting you at your ease, but nevertheless they had left me with a very healthy scepticism about the powers of hypnosis.

Ken was having more success. 'Imagine you're on a beach,' he said. 'Push your feet forward as if you're in the sun. Feel the sun beating down.' And sure enough some looked as if they were really on a beach – they were sweating and shifting about uncomfortably in their seats. But so would I probably, if I had been on that stage, in front of all those people. One guy at the end of the line just looked as if he had fallen asleep, which really took some doing in the circumstances. 'Rub on the sun tan oil,' shouted Ken. Never mind the sun tan oil, I thought to myself, bring on the dog pooh. On the basis of the sun tan oil exercise Ken selected six subjects – five male, one female 'as the ones he would work best with.' The other six, looking very downcast, left the stage.

He brought the best six back to the beach again, this time it was ten times hotter, and this time they had to rub the sun tan oil all over their bodies. They were definitely the sort that would play charades. Then it was time for the infamous Grand National. 'I just hope that none of them are horse phobics,' whispered Dr Heap in my ear. That didn't seem to be the problem. 'Imagine that in front of you is a very large horse. Get your leg over it,' said Ken. Four swung their legs, and two stood bolt upright. 'The winner of the horse race will get £30,000, the loser will spend three weeks in a cellar with Ted Rodgers. Go!' The four rode frantically, the other two just stood in the middle of the stage looking increasingly embarrassed by the whole thing. 'These four are the comedians, ladies and gentlemen, give them a big hand,' said Ken. One of the two that had declined to ride in the National was kept on stage as the straight man. 'Imagine that he has made a really strong smell, imagine that he really stinks,' said Ken, whilst at the same time making a loud farting noise. And sure enough the four Horsemen of the Apocalypse recoiled in horror from the stench of the man that had only gone so far, the man who had gone to all the trouble of having his fingers welded together by the power of suggestion, but had chickened out at the last minute.

Then the four were regressed – 'imagine you're all back at school.' 'Role playing rather than true regression,' whispered Dr Heap. And the straight man at the end became 'the school swot – Cecil, the man who everybody hates.' Hypnotists have real power alright. I wouldn't have fancied having to be Cecil beside those four, up in front of an audience. Next, they had to watch 'a very, very naughty film. You've never seen anything like this one before. You're really excited . . . then your father walks in.' The lone female then had to kiss the most beautiful man in the world. 'You will not push your tongue into his mouth, I repeat, you will not push your tongue into his mouth,' instructed Ken. Suddenly, the person she was kissing became 'the grubbiest old man you've ever seen in your life.' 'Disgusting sod,' said the girl, just before she was told that she was a chicken trying to lay very large, square eggs. She turned bright red with the effort. One of the four called Steve was then instructed to be a stage hypnotist. 'It's getting hard, it's getting tighter, tighter, the blood is rushing through it,' he shouted during his own version of the suggestibility exercise. It was time for the interval, but not before they were given a post-hypnotic suggestion to make sure that the four returned for the second half of the show.

Steve's wife was waiting for him when he got off the stage. 'You're not going back for the second half, do you understand me?' Steve nodded obediently – he was clearly very suggestible. Steve was out for the night with his in-laws. 'He's the quietest person in the family, he's the last person that I expected to get up on the stage,' said the father-in-law – 'I'm gob-struck frankly.' Steve said that he remembered very little about what had occurred on the stage. 'Amnesia is common,' said Dr Heap, 'but, of course, it's not confined to hypnosis.' I said that I realized that, indeed every time I make an ass of myself, I seem to suffer from certain lapses of memory.

So after the interval, the four were invited back 'to come and join the party,' and there was literally no holding Steve, although his wife did try. In the second half Steve and the rest of them devoured a few raw onions ('lovely juicy peaches,' said Ken). Steve was selected to be a drag artist, another was selected to be a ballet dancer. This all led up to the men performing as 'the world's greatest strippers'. 'You will not take anything out of your underpants, you will not dangle anything in the ladies' faces. If you are not wearing underpants, you will keep your trousers on at all times,' instructed Ken. 'Steve hasn't got any skid marks in his underpants, by any chance, has he?' asked Ken of Steve's wife.

The funniest bit of the evening, however, and it was impossible for either Dr Heap or myself to keep a straight face during the second half of the show, was Steve acting as the Martian translator for the other three. He had to ask them questions in Martian and then translate their replies. Steve's Martian had a sing-song quality about it, and it sounded for all the world like one of those songs from an obscure Scandinavian group in the Eurovision Song Contest. The Martian national anthem, as sung by the four of them, probably would have won the contest.

A very confused Steve was eventually led away by his in-laws, with another post-hypnotic suggestion still ringing in his head. The suggestion was that he would have an irresistible urge to buy the hypnotist a pint of beer in the bar the next time he saw him. His in-laws were taking no chances, they marched him straight out of the building, past the bar, at double speed.

Alternative medicine

I picked the therapy more or less at random. I liked how it sounded – 'Electro-Crystal Therapy'. Its name had a vaguely scientific ring to it, with the prefix 'electro'. It reminded me of electrodes, electro-magnetic radiation and O-level physics. But this therapy went beyond the mere confines of the laboratory. It managed to get a little bit of mysticism in as well with the word 'crystal'. Its flexibility was also appealing. The advert explained to me that this was a 'Safe, effective and simple therapy for a wide range of illnesses from simple headaches, colds and energy loss, to eczema, menstrual problems and on to more serious conditions such as arthritis and other degenerative diseases.' I wasn't sure about degenerative diseases, but I needed my energy loss worked on. And just imagine calling in to your local GP to get him or her to treat your energy loss. No, it was Electro-Crystal Therapy or nothing.

My friends were sceptical to say the least. Only one had claimed to have heard of it, and he said that he only knew it from its acronym – ECT! Even when I pointed out that ECT was electro*convulsive* therapy, and that to the best of my knowledge not even Ugo Cerlettii, who was the professor of Psychiatry at the University of Rome, who had accidentally 'discovered' ECT by witnessing the effects of electric currents on pigs in a slaughterhouse in Rome, would have claimed that it was much good for the treatment of eczema or menstrual problems. But I was still worried – the acronym still made me slightly uneasy. I rang the therapist Pam Hampton for reassurance. She explained to me that 'small electric charges would be sent through crystals to rebalance the electric field around my body.' I cleared my throat – 'Small? How small exactly? Not ECT small? I'm not going to need tying down to the bed am I? I think you should know that I've seen *One Flew Over The Cuckoo's Nest* three times.'

I was, however, reassured that the charges were undetectable, 'and,' said Pat, 'I am a fully qualified practitioner. I have been trained by Harry Oldfield.' There was a long pause during which the full significance of this last statement was meant to sink in. It was the second time that night that I had cleared my throat. 'Er, um, Harry who?' 'Harry Oldfield is the originator of Electro-Crystal Therapy. He is the inventor of the therapy, the guru, and I have been trained personally by him.'

My mind, if not entirely at ease, was in a sufficiently relaxed state of equilibrium – some would call it a stupor – to proceed. I made my way cautiously to Lynthorpe Lodge, Natural Healing Centre – Pam's house.

Now, I've always thought that waiting rooms are important. It's the initial point of contact between the client and the professional. It provides an opportunity to use a variety of artefacts to build up an image – subdued lighting, and copies of *Tatler* and *Vogue* to show what an upper-class establishment the little back-street hairdresser's is. Copies of *Punch* and *Private Eye* to show what a jolly place the dentist's is. I quickly scanned all the available reading material to see what kinds of messages were being sent here. Here sat copies of *The Senaca Indians Foundation of Trust* competing for space with Sheffield's very own glossy magazine *WestSide*, the magazine all about glossy cars and holidays intended to appeal to Sheffield's WestSiders, those who live in the 'good' (i.e. rich) homes in the west side of Sheffield. I noticed the candles above the fireplace, and I started to think that this therapy was going to be more 'crystal' than 'electro' in terms of its particular bias. There wasn't a test-tube or a white coat to be seen anywhere about the place.

Pam Hampton greeted me and promptly explained that as well as being a qualified Electro-Crystal therapist, she was a clairvoyant, and could detect auras around *some* people. 'You can tell a lot about people from their auras,' she explained. Of course, I just had to find out if I was one of the lucky ones. Pam looked me up and down. Of course, I have been looked up and down before, but never, to the best of my knowledge, for someone to describe my aura. It really was rather a strange feeling. Pam smiled. I assumed that this meant that she had found one. It turned out that she had found a part of one. 'You've got a very bright aura around your head and shoulders,' she said, 'but not much from your waist down, I'm afraid. It's almost as if you're dead from your waist down.' I cleared my throat very forcefully this time and asked her exactly what she was implying here. 'Well, you've obviously got a very quick active mind, but could it be the case that you've got very tired legs. That could account for the lack of aura around that particular part of your body.'

Now, it just so happens that I did have very tired legs that particular day, because I had been on a fourteen-mile training run the day before. Pam, of course, didn't know about the run, but she did know about my active interest in sport. This was because when I had explained to her on the phone that I wanted to sample her therapy, I had also told her that I wasn't ill or injured – 'unless the odd sports injury counted.' You didn't need to be able to read auras, anyway, to tell that I had tired legs that particular day. The way that I was shuffling about the place would have given the game away, anyway.

189

So I shuffled off after Pam into the consulting room. A huge pink chair dominated one side of the room. 'This,' explained Pam, 'is the ultimate chair. It hugs you and it rocks you backwards and forwards. It's very much part of the therapy.' I tentatively sat not so much on it, as in it, but I still nevertheless managed to fall off it. The big pink chair appeared not to want to hug me. Indeed, it seemed to be actively rejecting me. I thought Pam was going to tell the chair off. Instead, Pam produced the equipment for the Electro-Crystal Therapy. It did not look terribly impressive. I asked Pam to talk me through it. 'The basic idea is that this device generates a pulsating electromagnetic wave of a certain frequency. You hold this glass tube of crystals in one hand, the electric current then passes through here and sets up a secondary electromagnetic field around the body. This new field is measured by this second piece of equipment. The basic idea is that we find a healthy frequency that becomes the standard, and then we look for deflections on the meter as the meter travels along the Shakras or energy centres of the body. Any deflection tells us that there is an imbalance or disease in that part of the body. The equipment can be used both for diagnostic purposes and for treatment.'

The whole thing really did smack of O-level Physics. I clutched the tube of crystals in my sweaty hand, and Pam travelled up and down and across me with her meter. Down the meter went to the dead region below the waist. I jumped. It wasn't that dead down there. 'Oh, I should have warned you about that,' said Pam. Then up my back, down my arms, and up to the top of my head. 'You're pretty much in balance,' she explained, 'except for your head. That's the only place where there's a deflection on the meter. Your head seems a little out of tune.' Now this seemed to me to be even worse news than the lack of aura from my waist down. I needed this clarified – urgently. 'Is it my head or my brain that's out of tune?' I enquired. 'Well, I can't say actually. The technique isn't perfect, and we do need a lot more research on it, of course,' I wanted to add 'you can say that again, if you couldn't even decide between my brain and my head as the source of fluctuation on the meter.' But, with some determination, I kept my thoughts to myself.

'Are there any differences in the readings between my two arms? I asked in a pointed and determinedly leading way. The meter again traversed my two arms, and some imbalance was noted on my left arm. 'Have you had any problems with this arm?' asked Pam. This was going to be my moment of triumph. 'Well, not exactly – I had my right arm broken in a judo contest some years ago,' I replied. I had been keeping this as a bit of a secret, you see, to test the diagnostic accuracy of the technique. I gave that particular little lopsided, unbalanced grin of mine. The grin that people say makes my face very smackable. I kept the grin up for about a minute.

My little ploy backfired on me, however, when Pam explained that all of the measurements that had so far been taken had been standardized with respect to my right arm, which she had assumed to be A okay, because it was the one that I had proffered. 'Now,' she said, 'we'll have to start the whole procedure all over again. This time we'll standardize the measurements with respect to your left arm.' This time she discovered more imbalance all over my body – especially from my head – or brain, whichever it was. But then again, if I had been making such measurements, I probably would have decided that someone who tries little tests in the middle of a consultation is slightly off balance.

I then enquired how one can become an Electro-Crystal therapist in the first place. Can just anyone make a little electrical box, and start running it over people's bodies? 'Certainly not,' said Pam, and she produced the training requirements and course syllabus for 'The School of Electro-Crystal Therapy – Harry Oldfield: Founder and Principal.' It spelt out exactly what is required to become an Electro-Crystal therapist in strong imperative language: 'Attend one Foundation Course. Attend one Intermediate Training Course. Attend a minimum of one Advanced Training Course. Attend one Anatomy and Physiology Training Course, unless written confirmation of previous training can be supplied. Attend the minimum of two Clinical Practices. Submit at least six detailed case histories.' And after all that apparently still not know whether imbalances in the head region are from the scalp or the brain.

Pam is down on the formal syllabus as qualified to teach the foundation course (Fee £50). More advanced courses can only be taught by Harry himself. The contents of the foundation course range from 'The psychology of illness and imagery' to 'Introduction to crystals and stones.' 'You can decide which types of crystals to put in the glass tube,' explained Pam. 'I use quartz myself.' The school produces its own code of practice. The printed 'Rules and Standards' warn sternly that 'Only equipment purchased from Harry Oldfield or his designated representatives can be used for Electro-Crystal Therapy,' and that 'Owners of equipment are not allowed to open the equipment cases or allow any other person to do so, as they contain no user serviceable parts.' I, rather uncharitably, could think of other reasons why one might not like people to look inside the equipment case, but I kept such uncharitable thoughts to myself. The punishment for anyone who does dare to peek inside can be severe – 'We reserve the right to recall certificates and equipment if we feel that a member has irrevocably breached the Rules and Standards of the school.' And where is an Electro-Crystal therapist going to be without his or her little box? I asked myself. I kept this last thought to myself, instead I asked Pam about her professional background. It turned out that Pam had been a biology teacher before she got into all of this – interestingly Harry Oldfield had also been a science teacher. It helped explain the emphasis on equipment and things with 'electro' in the title. 'My background is essentially scientific, but as a healer I'm more of a mystic,' explained Pam. I could see that Electro-Crystal therapy was just the job for her.

But Electro-Crystal therapy was only part of what was on offer at Lynthorpe Lodge. Pam also does healing without the help of little electric boxes which must not be opened. 'There's a universal healing power,' she explained. 'Some call it God, some call it God force, some call it life force. I like to sling out a lot of names, and hope that one hits the mark. I act as a channel.' When I asked about the evidence as to whether Pam's healing power worked or not, I was told, with some force by Pam, that she was a therapist – not a researcher, which is fair enough I suppose. Follow-up studies, needless to say, are not run. 'But,' added Pam, trying to conjure up some evidence of the range of her powers – 'I've even healed cars in the past. I got my husband's Marina Estate started once by just directing my thoughts at it.' I said that I was surprised that her techniques could work on cars. 'You would be surprised at the way the material and the spiritual worlds interact. I even have a tape recorder that responds to what is going on. Every time I discuss a particular problem with one patient, the tape gets all tangled up. It's fine on any other topic.'

It was clearly time to move off the topic of 'healing'. But Pam had not finished outlining the particular therapies she offers. 'I also practise "reflexology" based on the idea that reflex points on the feet correspond to parts of the body – the head is in the toes, the chest is the ball of the feet, the abdomen is the lower part of the feet. If you press on the reflex points of the feet, this has a beneficial effect on the associated organs of the body. I also practise metamorphic technique, aromatherapy, massage, astrology, counselling. I even give dietary advice. A full range really. Everyone has their own preference, of course. It's best if the patient chooses their own particular therapy. As long as they believe in it, there's a fair chance that it might work. In general, I find that those with a scientific background prefer Electro-Crystal Therapy, those into more mystical things prefer straight healing or reflexology.'

I, however, preferred just to leave, dragging what remained of my aura unsteadily behind me.

★ 10 ★
The upper crust

The country club

I've always wanted to be upwardly mobile, even before it was fashionable, even before there was a name for it. Well, when you start pretty near the bottom of the social heap, you do, don't you? I always wanted to get on, to socially climb, to become a bit of a nob. Now being a nob in my book was always fairly straightforward – big house, big car, good club. The car was easy, my father swore by Jags and he should know. He was a motor mechanic and he used to buy cars from scrap yards, and do them up. I spent my early childhood sharing the backroom, that is the downstairs room which was not the front-room, with assorted car engines. The backroom was the room that functioned as the kitchen, the dining room and the 'bathroom' (the room containing the basin to balance in while you washed yourself from the geyser) all rolled into one. The engines, always in the process of being 'done up', took pride of place in that room. My father was never really happy when he was driving. He would listen out in a compulsive fashion for any sounds in the car, any slight vibration, any rattle, any unprogrammed noise, and that would be it. The engine would have to be stripped down yet again. Indeed, whilst driving he would insist on travelling at speeds which would maximize vibration. My older brother would ask him if he was stopping. But at those speeds any slight mechanical defect could be detected. 'That's it,' he would say, 'the engine will have to come out again,' and for the next month you would have to thread your way rather carefully past the engine on the way to the toilet in the yard.

But when the car was on the road, and wasn't vibrating – then bliss. Trips down to Bangor to view those grand houses in Holywood. My father would drive even slower to give us a better view. 'Imagine living in one of those, Eileen,' my father would say to my mother. 'I can't,' she would reply. 'Look at those gardens, those rooms, those

194

curtains, imagine sitting there looking out. You'd feel like the queen. Look there's some woman there now. Money people, real money people, they're not like you and me.' 'No, they're not,' my mother would add.

Well times pass, and we live in different times now, or so they tell us. Mrs Thatcher says there's no such thing as class anymore. She's working class, she tells us, because she works. My mother disagrees, she's still not seen any of those big houses from the inside, and she still talks about membership of golf clubs as if it was a sign of nobility. You should hear the way she says that 'so-and-so plays golf'. It's the way she enunciates the word 'golf'. I don't quite aspire to 'golf', it's too value-laden, it's much too loaded a concept for the likes of me. I thought that I'd settle for a good country club instead, especially when an advert for a local country club in Sheffield, called Pinegrove, popped through my letterbox. 'It's a bit like a drinking club, but where they play bridge,' my mother explained when I told her that I was thinking of joining a country club. She didn't disapprove. 'That's where all the money people hang out, not like the snobs that you find in golf clubs, just the real money people, the nobs.' My mother, you see, draws some very fine distinctions in her lexicon of class-related terms.

So I went off to meet the nobs. It was about 9.00 pm, and the car park was full. I had to thread my way across the car park from some distance away. An S-reg Capri just missed me, and I jumped towards a Y-reg Vauxhall cavalier, the back seat of which was full of toilet rolls. Don't ask me why. And don't ask me why I notice the year of registration of the cars, it's probably always been important to me. Six years equals sixty thousand miles, which in turn equals perceptible vibration which equals the engine being taken out, which equals a stubbed toe when you go to the toilet in the middle of the night. Some associations are stamped into you early on. I walked past the cloistered walls of the country club, but when I looked closely I could see the columns of the cloisters were just piles of bricks cemented together and the roof was supported by a joist. I was not going to be discouraged, however, that easily. It turned out, by the way, that one of the owners of the club was in the building trade.

My expectations were still high. I had heard about Pinegrove's fabulous high-tech gym, its glass-backed squash courts, the magnificent snooker rooms, facilities second to none. I just wanted to meet the nobs, to see where they do their drinking. I was invited to wander around. There was the new badminton hall, but who was that nob resplendent in Fred Perry shirt and matching shorts. Why, it was none other than Honest Gerry, second-hand car dealer. The car dealer whose golden rule was that if you want to sell a car to a customer, go for the wife. This rule was backed by precise statistical information – 'only one per cent of men don't give a damn about what their wives say,' he had told me, 'seventy five per cent bring their wives with them.' But Honest Gerry's philosophy did not stop there. 'Men like cars that are faster than their mates. Women don't give a bollocks about that. But, do you know what women go for more than anything else? Heaters.' 'Heaters?' 'Yes, heaters. If a heater blows nice and hot they go for it. Don't ask me why. My own wife's just the same. So when I take them for a test drive, I make sure the heater's nice and hot.' I always expected that after hours, Honest Gerry would be found in some backstreet drinking club, playing cards, but no, here he was down at the country club playing badminton. 'My serve, Maurice, I think.' It was not what I had expected from Honest Gerry.

I hurried out, leaving Honest Gerry to his foot faulting. I made my way to the high-tech gym. Here indeed was the kind of weight-training facilities for the next century. The kinds of machines that exercise improbable muscles in even more improbable ways. The instructor spotted me trying to do bicep curls in the machine designed for exercising hamstrings. 'No, perhaps you should try it like this, Sir,' he said. The instructor turned out to be Chris, the bouncer, no let's be careful about such terms – the supervisor on reception from the local casino. The chucker-out. As he guided me around parts of my body which I had up to that point in time studiously ignored, he filled me in on the ethos of the place. 'A country club which appeals to the ordinary working man, the working man who's come on a bit. We have one or two money people, but then again we've got quite a few unemployed as well. They can spend the whole day here, one way or another. The really big boys use the free weights in the other room, this room's really for girls and those getting started.' And sure enough the room was occupied by an assortment of lovelies in pink leotards, and a few not-so-lovelies in 'I drank the world' T-shirts, covering the kinds of stomachs which would indeed suggest that there was some truth in the proposition. 'There's rarely any trouble here,' said Chris continuing again – 'we haven't barred anyone yet.' 'Don't you mean excluded from the club, Chris? Blackballed?' 'No, just barred,' said Chris.

'The biggest problem,' said Chris, 'is that it's now fashionable for ordinary working-class blokes and their wives or girlfriends to exercise, when it wasn't once upon a time. Some of these new fitness-conscious people aren't very fit to start off with. When a new client comes here, we take them on the exercise bike to warm them up. One guy in his forties came last week, he wanted to start training, but he was on the bike for just two minutes when his pulse rate climbed up to 180. There was no way we were going to let him loose on the weights, one of the instructors took him for a walk instead.'

After my hamstrings had been sufficiently 'worked', I limped off to the snooker room, decorated with huge portraits of those other working-class heroes – Jimmy White and Alex Higgins. A young Chinese couple were on one of the tables. They wore matching Mickey Mouse T-shirts. All of the balls were lined up against one of the side cushions in a way that I would have thought was technically impossible. 'There's a lot of money in chip shops,' said one regular when he noticed me watching the young couple play. 'They're the real money people about today – the ones with the Chinese chippies.' Diana Ross sang in the background. Two men in their late forties played on the table closest to me. They eyed me suspiciously, as if I was trying to pinch their table or their drinks. One was going for the brown. He missed. 'That were a double clanger,' said his friend. It was his turn, but the lights on the snooker table went out. He put another coin in the meter. He was talking to the balls – 'Get right up to that cushion, boy.' The ball might have heard, but did not seem to be listening. 'Fine hit,' said the wife sitting to the side. 'Did that go in?' said the other wife in the corner. 'Of course it did,' said wife number one. The pink had hit two side cushions and then had somehow miraculously dropped into the pocket. 'That were a good finish, well played, Arthur.' Arthur then took a long drink of his bitter, obviously very pleased with himself. The wife's conversation then returned to one of their daughters. '. . . all she spent on her holidays was what she brought with her. She only had twenty pounds left when she got back, no I mean twenty of them other things – Deutsche . . . marks, that's it. This German girl she met on holiday were a right nice lass.'

It was a night for name-dropping, and talk of foreign travel, for talk of all things foreign and exotic. A night for showing that you'd been 'abroad', and for looking the part. 'I got this leather belt in Spain, you know. I never take it off me. We went with Marjorie and her husband. You should see the tan she's got now, she's got one of them twelve-tube super-tanning machines. The one like the coffin that you have to climb inside. She keeps it in her front room.'

I even got a five-peseta coin in my change when I went to the bar, from the barmaid with the French knickers on under her tight, white cotton pants. I was joined there by Peter Hayman, one of the three owners of the club, and an ex-bookmaker. It was partly his vision to build a country club on the site of a rubbish tip in Sheffield. 'The basic idea was to attract the Rolls Royce set to a new better-equipped club, but unfortunately the Rolls Royce set stayed where they were, even though the facilities weren't as good. We tend to attract the local punter from Hillsborough. This is them going a bit upmarket. I don't think the council really liked us calling it a country club, it sounds a bit posh. Some people think that the working class should stick to flying pigeons. But this club is very successful. A lot of its members couldn't get in to some of the other clubs, which are a bit snobby. If you're in a golf club, if you get sent down, that's it. We wouldn't necessarily judge them that harshly. I even know of one bloke who had to resign from his golf club because every time he went in to the rough, he went in with a white ball and came out with a yellow one! Golf clubs can be a little strict. We're a different sort of club – here social status isn't a prerequisite. About 100 of our members are unemployed – it's hardly their fault after all, and they need the facilities more than most. We have an installment plan for them of a tenner a month. It makes it a bit easier for them to pay. It's not like the council's "Passport to Leisure" scheme, here they're still paying their own way. They can hold their head up high. We treat everyone alike.'

'It'a bit like the Thatcherite dream, here, I suppose,' said Peter – 'the dream come true – everyone who aspires to join a country club, now can. A bit of a classless society, if you ask me. Ordinary working people, who always wanted to mix with the nobs, can now join the executives for a quick game of squash and a drink in the bar. No social barriers exist any longer.'

'Just as long as they don't get blackballed,' I said.

'No, barred,' said Peter – 'just barred, we wouldn't ever go that far.'

A night in grand style

I'd passed the Grand Hotel in Brighton many times, but I'd never gone in. I don't know why I've always found it so forbidding. It's not the price, but at £145 a night for the cheapest double room with a sea view, I suppose it could be (the Presidential suite, by the way, costs £750 a night). Perhaps it's the name. A name I somehow associate, rightly or wrongly, with traditional upper-middle-class England – England when it still had an Empire, and the attitudes to go with it. And traditional values – very civilized, very proper, and very, very superior.

Indeed, I find that whole south coast of England a little bit forbidding for exactly the same reason. I went to Weymouth – just the once. I was working in a chicken factory just outside Chippenham at the time – during my holidays. My job was skinning the gizzards of chickens. I worked on a little machine at right angles to the endless conveyor belt of upside down chickens. Gizzards slid towards me along a metal chute kept slippery by a never ending stream of salty water. My job was to pick the gizzard up, turn it the other way round and press it onto a rotating wheel – thousands of times a day. The wheel tugged out the funny greeny bits, or most of them. The only breaks to go to the toilet were when the conveyor belt broke down. I was lucky, I just had to do this job for a few months, some people had to wait on that conveyor belt breaking down, year in, year out. I used to dream about gizzards at nights, and the smell clung to my hair and clothes. No matter how often you washed you still ended up reeking of dead chicken and salty water. It's not just prostitutes that have more than one bath at nights to cleanse themselves.

So one Friday I decided I needed a break from all this. I wasn't particularly bothered about where I ended up, so when one driver offered me a lift to Weymouth, I naturally accepted. I pitched my tent in the middle of the night, without the benefit of a torch, on what appeared, in the dark, to be right in the middle of some wild sand dunes. Sand dunes that I assumed were miles from anywhere. The North Antrim coast in Northern Ireland is full of such wild desolate places. For some reason, I thought that Weymouth would be as well. In daylight the wild remote sand dunes turned out to be no such thing. I'd inadvertently pitched my tent in the middle of a path on one low sandy hill at the back of someone's house. An old lady and her dog approached. It is often said that dog owners and their pets come to resemble each other through time, and this old lady and her Cocker Spaniel certainly did. They both looked at me and my tent with lofty disdain. 'Are you English?' said the old lady in a haughty manner. I shook my head. 'I thought not,' she replied and she and her dog continued on their way.

Needless to say I removed the tent before she returned, and I spent the following night sleeping rough on the beach in case I offended the sensibilities of others like her. But she had effectively put me in my place. I spent the rest of my days in Weymouth wandering around and looking in shop windows to try to work out how she could tell that I wasn't English so quickly. Perhaps it was the smell of the gizzards that lingered on my clothes. No proper English person would do such work.

I never made it back to Weymouth, and I certainly never made it to places like the Grand. Perhaps they would be able to tell that I wasn't English from one glance. Perhaps they would expect me to start pitching my tent in the middle of the foyer. I did once make it as far as the revolving doors, however. I was determined to have a cocktail, you see, but would I give myself away by ordering a cocktail at 6.30 pm? Would the nobs still be on afternoon tea at that time? What time did afternoon tea finish? What was it? Just a cup of tea, or something extra? In the end, I didn't dare risk it. The lady from Weymouth probably never had such self doubts in all her long life.

But it was a sort of ambition of mine to make it to the Grand one day. It was, as ambitions go, a very modest one. Some people want to scale Everest and look down at the world from this great peak, I wanted to get into the Grand and look down on the world from the sixth floor – sea view, of course, with separate bathroom. For once, I wanted to be on the inside looking out. I wanted to see the world from *their* perspective. I wanted to walk into the place as if I did that sort of thing every day, as if I owned the place.

So I did – well sort of. I strode purposefully from the train station and said to the Brighton taxi driver, 'The Grand, please.' He said, 'Do you mean the Grand Hotel?' I thought that he could smell the

gizzards from my brand-new jacket. As we pulled up in front of the
hotel, a man in a frock coat and top hat rushed to open the doors of the
taxi, and before I had time to savour the moment, me and my bag
were at the reception. Bell boys scurried about, one I noticed had
some muck on the backs of his trousers. Bags were placed on a trolley
with rails for suits and evening dresses. I never touched my bags
again, as the bell boy with the muck on his trousers escorted me to the
sixth floor. I looked down the magnificent staircase for a different
view of the foyer. One lone American tourist could see what I was
thinking. 'A suicide's dream,' he said. 'If it was a block of flats they
would have to put netting between the floors to catch the bodies,' I
added.

The key didn't turn in the lock, it lit up a green light and you then
pushed the door to open it. The room overlooked the sea. From the
sixth floor I looked way out on the grey sea rising and falling – for
miles and miles. It looked like a picture. Grey seas never look like
pictures from close up, on the promenade in the wind and the rain
and the litter. I looked down at the promenade I knew well, but no I
couldn't see any chip papers or ice cream wrappers. It was true, the
world did seem different from way up here.

Having rehearsed my room number and committed it to memory,
just in case I was challenged – 'Are you a resident? I thought not.' I
made my way more confidently to the foyer. Everything was brisk
and businesslike. The bar was full. The crowd assembled in front of
the bar looked like reps, but two old ladies like the one from
Weymouth sat in some armchairs. They looked disdainfully at the
reps over their Pimms. The reps were having some difficulty getting
served, the old ladies weren't. 'Get a move on, Fernando, for
goodness sake,' shouted one rep. Two solitary individuals in T-shirts
stood at one end, one wore a black T-shirt with no sleeves, they
definitely were not reps. One thin figure who I could tell at a glance
was not English made his way past. He wore tight black trousers and a
bright green sweater. He looked like a gigolo who was over the hill.
His black hair looked as if it was dyed, and he had a bald spot on the
crown of his head. He strolled around the bar, as if he might be
vaguely looking for somebody and then sat down with a glass of wine.
He eyed up all the older unattached females from his armchair, but
he never approached anyone. And most certainly no-one approached
him.

I could overhear the conversations from the reps around the bar. You couldn't help overhearing them, they were very loud, almost as if they were intended to be overheard. 'We work hard and we play hard in this company,' one female with a very posh accent was saying to her male companion – 'if you get my drift. But the whole thing is run as a very tight ship.' 'I certainly do get your drift,' the man replied – 'that's why I wanted to come aboard. I was in oil before but it didn't quite make the grade. Make the grade – geddit?' The female then did more than a passable imitation of a Sloane Ranger, with 'okay yah', as the universal punctuation mark. In fact, it sounded remarkably close. I got the impression that she was probably one (if they indeed exist) but pretending not to be, just to show what a good mimic she was. Or something like that.

Another rep with a pock-marked face approached the two. He was swaying a little bit on his feet. 'I was sending you all kinds of body language signals, but you were just ignoring me,' he said to the Sloane Ranger. 'I wasn't ignoring you, I just didn't see them,' she replied. 'Oh nonsense, you must have seen them,' the man with the pock-marked face complained. Another young member of the company joined them, but he was obviously more senior in terms of position, because they all immediately turned to face him. He leaned over and whispered in the girl's ear – 'tell him to bugger off, if you want rid of him.' Everyone could hear what he had said, even me. He presumably intended that this should be enough warning to the man with the pock-marked face. But the female took his advice, turned to the man with the pock-marked face and shouted, 'Bugger off.' There was a stunned silence. 'Charming,' said the man with the pock-marked face eventually and made his way unsteadily back to the bar. 'I never believed all that rubbish about body language anyway,' he said as he left. The man from the oil company that hadn't made the grade, decided to impress the senior executive. 'I used to work in Dundee, but it wasn't a piece of cake,' he told him.

I made my way round the bar. The reps were still having trouble getting served – 'Mine's a Tia Maria and brandy, Nick, a double, if you're buying.' Nick was talking about tomorrow's presentation. 'Have you used an autocue before? Maggie Thatcher swears by them. She uses two so she can look around more and appear more natural. I haven't quite got to that more advanced level yet. I write every word of my talk on them and every joke. If I didn't, I'm sure that my brain would seize up when I'm giving my presentation. It makes life a hell of a lot simpler.' The woman on the Tia Maria and brandy then outlined how she'd dressed up at her account meeting. 'I wore a cricketing outfit and used packets of the drug product as bales. I knocked them over with a ball to show that I was meeting my sales targets. Everybody wears costumes these days in their sales reports, but the product managers did think that mine was one of the more original ones. I'm going to stick with the cricketing theme for my next sales report presentation.'

I made my way back through the foyer, with my key in my hand. I wanted people to see it. The two old ladies were making their way out of the hotel into the wet, windy night. The concierge said, 'Good night, Sir' to me, and then 'Good night, madames,' to the two old ladies. But he seemed to bow his head as he said it to them. I felt like shouting, 'Hey, I'm the resident here, wack, remember that.' I made my way back to my room – for another view of the sea and another view of myself being seen. And sure enough I could see a young couple looking longingly at the Grand's magnificent façade. I stood gazing out of the window long enough for them to see me. Just another jetsetter, retiring to bed, after a hard day's work and a hard day's play. I somehow knew that my dreams that night wouldn't be about headless chickens and gizzards with greeny bits that wouldn't come off. They would be about cricket matches to be played with drug packets as bales, and bumper packs of assorted drugs as wickets, and fistfuls of money as balls. I had come a long way in one day, but perhaps still not far enough.

High table

They scurried across Great Court of Trinity College, Cambridge, wrapped in their voluminous black gowns. All going somewhere, all in a hurry. They traversed the inviolate lawns. 'Keep off the grass,' it said, but the notices were ignored. Only Fellows of the college are permitted to pay no heed to such warnings, and every Fellow did just that, to show the world exactly who they were – huge black, daunting figures wrapped in their gowns, and wrapped up in their own thoughts. Like huge crows. Ordinary mortals must never, ever step on that grass. Why Fellows are encouraged to walk on the grass, I'm not sure. Perhaps it's because it is recognized that they are always going to be in a hurry, perhaps they always need to take the shortest route – the diagonal, the hypotenuse, the path of the crow.

I wasn't busy. I was just passing time. Funny how the thought of dining at the High Table at Trinity makes me extremely nervous. They were all there once – Isaac Newton, Bertrand Russell, Ludwig Wittgenstein, Lord Byron sitting in those very seats, discussing – well God knows what. And that basically is the problem. What did they talk about? What do you talk about at High Table with the intellectual elite? This one college has produced more Nobel prize winners than France. I went off to the toilet in Angel Court *again*.

I was getting used to this particular toilet by now, it was fairly easily identifiable with the letters 'IRA' scrawled on the wall, behind the cistern. But this was respectful graffiti, respectful or recent. No-one had scribbled a reply. Kilroy was not here, Kilroy had never been, except perhaps the fawning Kilroy-Silk, as a guest of the JCR or as an invited speaker at some BA dinner or other.

But at least some graffiti had come to Trinity College, a sign that times do change – even in Cambridge, even here. Indeed, I could see some of the other changes in the college from my vantage point in that toilet. There was the evidence stuck up in front of me. A small white notice that someone had tried to tear off without much success – 'Please place your soiled dressing in the special chemical container provided.' The college now admitted women. Unfortunately, some members of the college evidently thought that things had gone too far, that things were getting out of hand. On top of the sanitary towel notice someone had written – 'What about Durex machines in the lavatory? The college has been taken over!' The same misogynist, and I assume that it was indeed a misogynist who had written this, had also chosen to display his wit and wisdom – 'All women are sex objects – they object to sex.' This, in fact, is a rather idealized version of what he had written, because in his original version, the word 'women' had been given a rather curious spelling.

Now before someone attempts to point out that in these modern times of ours 'women' is sometimes spelt in strange, idiosyncratic ways for all sorts of social and political reasons, let me say that I do know that. I do even understand it, even if I do not necessarily approve of the fact that 'women' sometimes appears as 'womyn' or 'wimmin', with its ritual deletion of men. I do not approve, by the way, because the same people who argue for 'wimmin', usually also try to tell us that we should have 'efemcipated' for 'emancipated' and 'womage' for 'manage'. And that's only the beginning, they usually then start on the homophones – 'himmicane' for 'hurricane', 'hersterectomy' for 'hysterectomy', and it goes on endlessly into new dimensions of semantic confusion, with 'ovarimony' for 'testimony' (where the balls are cut off quite literally) without any very good reason. I may not approve of all this, but at least I do understand. But here in this toilet in this great seat of learning was a new spelling, way beyond my comprehension – 'wemmen'. What strange significance lay within? What was this writer trying to provoke? What was behind it? Surely not dyslexia? Surely not here of all places? It was time to leave the safety of the toilet. The bells were calling me to dinner.

For a moment, I considered scurrying across the grass, like a Fellow in a hurry. But then without a gown, it would have had no dramatic effect. I would just end up looking like some Italian tourist who simply could not read the notices. I hobbled across the cobblestones instead, and pushed through the door ominously marked 'Private' into the Fellows' parlour. Now there is a lot to be said for not being too early for an event like this, for arriving with just a few moments to spare. But as I entered I could see this very elderly professor with a zimmer frame, also aided by his wife, trying to mount the last few stairs. I assumed that he was the last one just going in, and hurried up behind him, and waited and waited as he scaled each and every step. Before, that is, I was approached by the manciple – 'Excuse, me, Sir, are you aiming to dine? Then, perhaps you would like to make your way back into the parlour. We always let the professor go up first, because it does take him quite a bit of time. You'll be called when it's time to dine.' And I sheepishly descended the steps, each one requiring more and more effort, more effort in fact than the professor had needed to get up those stairs, my legs leaden with embarrassment.

I sank into the leather chair in the Fellows' parlour, avoiding eye contact, staring at the portrait of Isaac Newton. My eyes flitted to the back issues of Punch. What was thought to be humorous in 1859 I wondered? But, nevertheless, I did not dare to attempt to prise this particular volume out of the rather, full shelves. There was nothing else for it, it was time for reflection again. I wished that I had stayed in the toilet. The Fellows wafted in, just on time. Some wore their gowns directly over shirts that looked suspiciously like they had been purchased in Marks and Spencer's. But they still looked right. I had an Italian designer suit on, I didn't. A gong sounded. We trooped out for dinner, I hung back nervously, some would say suspiciously.

Trinity high table is lit by candles in beautiful, silver candlestick holders, the rest of this 400-year-old hall is lit by so-called electric candles. We trooped in behind the trestle tables, with the famous sixteenth-century copy by Hans Eworth of the painting of Henry VIII by Holbein, towering over us. The students rose as we entered, even though they were in the middle of their meals and in the middle of their conversations. They looked at us with mild curiosity. However, one seemed to focus on me with mild disdain, perhaps it was my imagination, perhaps not. A Latin grace was said, and the grace went on forever, beautifully enunciated by the Fellow who had needed the zimmer frame to enter. His wife was not dining with him. As a schoolboy I had studied Latin ('It's just in case you want to be a doctor,' my mother had explained helpfully at the time), and I can still manage to recite 'amo, amas, amat . . .' and 'dominus, domine, dominum . . .' with the best of them. But for me Latin, like French and Russian, and all the other languages that I ever learned, was a dead language – an intellectual puzzle, a series of memory tests, but nothing more. Here the Latin had a tone and a structure, and if you could not imagine it being used in conversation, then you could at least imagine it being spoken, and ringing out somewhere beyond the table, the old mensa, mensa, mensam . . . I started to feel nervous again, more than ever aware of my academic shortcomings, and the consommé had not even been served yet. I looked up at the minstrels' gallery for inspiration, but none came.

I could hear Pamella Bordes' name being mentioned on the next table. Typical Oxbridge high table, I thought to myself, always wanting to be in on the juicy gossip, always desperate to be at the centre of things, no matter what. I felt like shouting over, 'What about her relationship with Jim (nick, nick) Davidson then? That's the bit that really interests me.' But I didn't. I was just thinking how much I despise all this privilege, and all this elitism, when the Fellow next to me recognized me, despite a ten-year interval, as 'one of the best badminton players that the college had ever produced.' Suddenly, my mood started to change, despite the fact that I wanted to point out that I, and any skills that I may have had as a badminton player, was more a product of Legmore Street, Belfast, than Trinity College Cambridge. But at least I had been identified as somehow being connected with the place, not an interloper, not just a visitor. I brightened up, for a moment.

The conversation was starting to sparkle. 'Do you know,' said one female Fellow to my right to the male Fellow sitting opposite her in the Marks and Spencer's shirt, 'what this dock dispute is really all about – the dockers want to be paid in cash, so that they don't have to show their wives what they're earning. Who, if they knew the truth, would have any sympathy with *that* position?' The man in the Marks and Spencer's shirt grunted meaningfully. I sighed, but no-one took a blind bit of notice. Talk ranged across matters weighty and worthy – Pamella Bordes, the dock strike, Pamella Bordes again, the Hillsborough disaster. It turned out that the female Fellow's father had been at Ibrox *once* – 'he was really working-class, you know, he lived on a council estate.' But, no, she had never visited it. One Fellow opposite wore what looked like a Marks and Spencer's suit under his gown. 'I come from Huddersfield – the jewel of the North,' he told his neighbour, and they both laughed in a kind of embarrassed way.

The consommé had been swept away, and the gammon had arrived. I hesitated before taking a third slice. The Fellow, who had recognized me, urged me to go ahead. I said 'cheers' to the man who proffered the food, everyone else served themselves in silence. Talk was now all about rotation – 'rotate an A, and you find . . .' The Fellow beside me turned out to be a mathematician. 'Yes, that is an interesting problem that they are discussing, but it is rather well known I'm afraid,' he explained. Meanwhile, the main course had finished, and I was now busy shovelling cream on to my fresh fruit salad. The only snag was that I managed to ladle so much on to the rather flat dish that the cream was starting to trickle over the side. This was a rather well-known problem of a different sort. I tried to direct the rivulets of cream down off the trestle tables, into the little lake of cream that was forming between me and my neighbour. This occupied most of my attention. Suddenly the meal had ended, and we ascended more steps to an even darker room, lit again by candles in beautiful silver candlestick holders – 'for port,' my neighbour explained.

We sat in silence as three decanters were passed around. One of them was labelled 'Madeira', port was probably in one of the other two, but what was in the third, and which drink went with which of the three glasses. It was guess-work from here on in. The wine waiter, who I happened to notice was wearing a rather chunky gold bracelet on one wrist, and a very flashy gold watch on the other, looked rather amused by my efforts. The fruit, then the crackers, then the Stilton followed. I tried to scoop the crumbly bits off the Stilton, because I didn't fancy digging too deeply into it, but all the crumbly bits shot off on to the shiny polished table. Indeed, so highly polished a table was it, that one Fellow had already joked that it was kept in this condition so that any drinks sitting on the table would all slide to the Senior Fellows at the other end. It was now, however, a highly polished table dotted with large crumbs of Stilton. The mysterious three decanters circulated again, and circulated right over the Stilton, leaving large skid marks on the highly polished table just in front of me. The talk was now of lepidoptera, and now Rs, rather than As, were being mentally rotated. My thoughts, however, were confined to the skid marks on the table. There was nothing else for it. I hit the port, or whatever was in that third decanter. But suddenly, and without any warning, the decanters had gone. 'Oh, the port and the Madeira only go round the table twice,' said the Fellow beside me, sensing my puzzlement – 'the claret remains until it is finished, if you would like to help yourself to some claret.' Then he explained that some of the Senior Fellows like to engage in a bit of game playing, by filling their glasses up right to the brim, so that the decanters are refilled on their two rotations. 'Perhaps that's what the Fellows had been discussing earlier, with all that talk about rotation,' I suggested, but the joke fell rather flat.

The port had now been passed, the cigars smoked, the coffee consumed, or in my case spilt. It was an end to a perfect evening. I wandered out, back into Great Court, trying to imagine what Newton, what Russell, what Byron had felt and thought, when they felt the fresh spring air hit them after dining in Hall. I watched the Fellows hurry back to their rooms, their gowns still flapping majestically, back to their great private thoughts, no doubt.

There was no other way to end such a perfect evening, I thought to myself, as I started to stride purposefully across the grass. The only problem was that it turned out to be a lot soggier than I had anticipated.

Summer Balls

The summer ball – strawberries on the lawn, a moonlit night, a punt on the river. A magnum of champagne, and another one please. When *Brideshead* comes to life for one evening at least – the wild excesses of youth and privilege. Just look at the colleges the next morning. Discarded teddies everywhere. Yes, some of them are very short of ideas. A walk along the backs – with wild flights of fancy, or should I say wild flytes of fancy. 'Oh Sebastian, where are you now? See how we play – forever, and ever,' or so it seems. And half remembered lines – 'If it could only be like this always – always summer . . . the fruit always ripe and Aloysius in a good temper.'

And see how they swim through the less than hygienic Cam with bundles on their head – containing all of their earthly possessions, like some fleeing refugees searching for a promised land. But these bundles are different, here we find dinner jackets, wing-collared shirts and black trousers all neatly folded and wrapped around the obligatory black shoes. And then the music – string quartets and reggae, jazz and scratch music. Wildly different. The last big bash after the exams before being pushed out to confront the real world. Some day you're going to be stuck in a boring job – with the BBC or the Foreign Office, so enjoy your last days at Cambridge or Oxford. Just enjoy yourself, just be yourself, let yourself go, really go.

But you can't let yourself go too far, dinner jackets are compulsory, so the trendy ones try wearing their dinner jacket back to front, upside down, or inside out. They wear bow ties that revolve or light up or squirt water, but only with recognizably expensive DJs. Rebels without a cause of complaint. And the punts drift dreamily along and ever onwards in the moonlight.

That is one sort of May ball, which occurs in June. But there are other sorts as well. England has, after all, many fine universities of which it is justifiably proud. 'Summertime Ball' said my ticket – this was definitely not 'Oxbridge. The name of the ball reminded me of 'summertime blues', an old song by the Who, and I think Eddie Cochrane before them, but perhaps that was the intention. 'Oh, I'm going to raise a fuss and I'm going to raise a hollerin',' if I remember the words correctly. Although, perhaps I should add that my memory of pop lyrics is definitely not to be trusted – for years I sang the Bryan Ferry line 'like a Friday, you're so cool' as 'like a fried egg, you're so cool.' I still think that my line makes more sense. I thought that I might sing my line at the 'summertime ball', this proletarian alternative to the May ball. Perhaps. Or, if not quite proletarian, then somewhat less elitist. 'Well, we haven't all got three As at A level, you know, or attended schools that just automatically send you to Oxbridge, but should we miss out?' Quite, I said. 'Grosvenor House Hotel – 7.00 pm for 7.30 pm. Formal Wear.' The ticket seemed self-explanatory.

'What does formal wear mean in this context?' asked one student. 'You see the problem is that my boyfriend has only bought jeans since he left school. The smart clothes that he had when he was back at school won't fit him any more – he's lost so much weight since he got here. Does formal wear mean a penguin suit, and where do you get penguin suits from?' We discussed formal wear and I explained the system of frequenting Oxfam shops to buy old dinner jackets, but I could see that there was a further question building deep inside. 'But will my boyfriend be *allowed* in if he hasn't got a dinner jacket. That's what I really want to know?' This to me signified a great deal. I had a friend who once went to a Trinity May ball in a long, black velvet dress. Nothing unusual in that, but the friend was a man. And no, he wasn't allowed in. However, he was so full of confidence and self-assurance that he could take no for an answer. When he was forbidden entry, he merely returned to his rooms in college and borrowed a friend's dinner jacket for the evening, his was at the cleaners – he'd been sick on it again. But he was the kind of person who had lots of friends who could lend him a DJ at the last moment. It was no big deal for him to be turned away, once. Presumably if the student who had last worn trousers at school was refused entry, it would have been more difficult for him to correct the mistake.

The Grosvenor House Hotel is in the centre of town, near the city centre pubs. There was no place to park, so I got there late. The second floor, said the notice board which had been strategically placed in the foyer of the hotel. Students were already leaving the bar when I got there, and carrying their drinks into the main dining room with them. The favourite tipple seemed to be lager. Rather surprisingly, nobody asked to see my ticket. There would be no-one trying to swim here tonight, I thought to myself. The women were in long evening dresses, or rather most of them were. Some wore short frocks, some trousers. 'That's from Dorothy Perkins,' said one female at the bar, pointing at a short pink dress – 'I nearly bought it myself. There's no point in buying one of those elaborate velvet affairs when you'll only get one chance to wear it.' The men were in dinner jackets or lounge suits. A number wore penguin suits. They thought that they looked special, and they were probably right. There was no champagne to be seen. A string quartet played in the centre of the room.

The guests were already seated, when I got in. There was a general air of expectation as the students surveyed the range of cutlery laid out before them. Just to confuse things – a fish knife had been laid out for the first course – paté. The guests hesitated. The room was generally silent as some guests tentatively made their first moves in the conversation. People talk about the art of conversation, but it is not so much an art as a game. The opening gambits are important because they tell you what rules the participants are planning to play by. In more familiar language, you might say that the opening moves set the tone for the evening. The professor seated next to me made his first move. He explained to the first-year student seated next to him that if you analysed the first-year feedback results from a slightly different perspective, 'taking care to separate out the effects of the intrinsic interest of the course material from the evaluated interest of the style of presentation, then my course which is intrinsically rather difficult and rated overall as not that interesting, actually emerges as very interesting in terms of style of presentation. I've done rather well after all. You see the problem with the feedback questionnaire is that it confounds two quite separate variables.' He started drawing a graph on his napkin to illustrate the point further. The first-year student nodded nervously.

The first-year student decided to engage in some self-presentation of a different kind by announcing that she was addicted to the soap opera 'Neighbours'. Perhaps she hoped that she could somehow turn the conversation. But it turned out that the professor had a daughter who just happened to have a friend at Oxford who also watched 'Neighbours', and through this rather circuitous route he had come to understand that it was something of 'a cultural phenomenon where groups of students gather together at set times to watch this drama and indicate their attitudes to what is happening on the screen, rather noisily I hear. Is that the same here? Well if it is, I hope that any analysis of the appeal of the programme takes these aspects into account.'

The string quartet played on in the background. Every table was engaging in what it took to be civilized conversation, with words like 'delightful' and 'splendid' just discernible above the music of the string quartet. Every table except one that is. On this one table all the guests leant inwards, as if subject to some enormous conspiracy. There was complete silence then a massive guffaw, usually followed by the loud chink of very full lager glasses.

The dinner passed and the wine waiter came around taking orders for liqueurs. Except there were no orders. This most definitely was not a night for excess. Instead individual guests made their way to the bars for the now customary pints of lager. The chief careers officers of the university rose to make the one after-dinner speech. 'Anybody here from Lancashire? Anybody here from Oldham? How can you tell when the M62 gets near Oldham . . . the road becomes cobbled. Why did God make Widnes? – so that people from Oldham would have something to look down on . . .' He finished with a plea to students to make better use of the career's service and told them that prospects were very good at the moment for graduates. Even on this night there was no forgetting the outside world, no possibility of hiding inside the ivory towers, even for a minute.

The disco started and the professor and students did their own thing, as usual. And very similar it was, if the truth be known. A group of Australian cricketers who just happened to be staying at the hotel, wandered in on the proceedings. Although they were wearing sweatshirts and jeans, no-one challenged them, or indeed took much notice of them. Rather surprisingly they didn't look out of place among the dinner jackets and penguin suits of these particular students. Someone in the corner started hiccuping and it seemed to go on for ever, as between each record you found yourself listening out for it to pick up where it had left off. The sound suddenly shifted position as this individual started trying to make his way to the toilet. On the way his hiccups stopped rather abruptly, so he sat down just by the toilet for the remainder of the evening, staring morosely at the passers-by. He threw all passers-by a kind of malevolent and challenging look as if he wanted a bit of bother but couldn't really summon up the energy for it. They do say that drink affects people in very different ways, and here was someone who clearly wasn't getting a very positive buzz from it.

212

The group of Australian gate-crashers was making many new friends, still completely unchallenged. One student came up to complain that he hardly recognized anybody in the room – 'it's like a ball rent-a-crowd in here, are these all professional ball-goers or what?' I hadn't the heart to point out the large posse of gate-crashers to him.

In many ways the whole evening resembled an evening at a nightclub rather than a ball. An orderly sort of evening, the whole pattern dictated by the DJ's choice, the DJ being the man who plays the records rather than the individuals in the black tie ensemble. As the midnight hour approached, the professor and his wife made their excuses and left. The last dance was to 'Loadsa Money', which seemed appropriate somehow. Not because the students had loadsa money, but because they aspired to having loads – some day in the not too distant future when these golden days of youth and learning would be just a blur. 'That's what being a student is all about nowadays, ain't it?' one said – but then again he may just have been an Australian gate-crasher.

The revellery continued until 2.00 am, and then everything stopped dead. Then women in long dresses, and men in dinner jackets and penguin suits made their way out to queue for taxis to long remember this long night of mid-summer madness. Among the debris there wasn't a teddy bear to be found.

★ 11 ★
Blind mobility

The pensioner living alone

My directions had been extremely precise: 'Just opposite the gasworks in Garston in Liverpool. The flats that used to be lovely before the cockroaches came. Just ask anybody, everybody knows the flats, and the cockroaches. When you get to the flats, it's number . . . You have to ring the bell outside, Lizzie will be expecting you.'

Lizzie's daughter-in-law had given me the directions. The daughter-in-law was sixty-six. My anxieties had started even then. Who's going to believe an article about an old age pensioner living alone, when her flat is situated opposite a gasworks, for goodness sake? It's too much of a cliché. But it was a good landmark for direction finding, if not scene setting.

I approached the front door of the flats' complex with some trepidation, careful not to step on any cockroaches. I read the large yellow sign – 'Beware. During the hours of darkness, these premises are patrolled by guard dogs.' There was no sign of the guard dogs, or the cockroaches for that matter. An old grey-haired lady watched me approach from a window on the first floor. She was staring at me in a kind of vacant way, as if she stood there all day staring at the strangers come to visit. Always waiting expectantly, but not quite. Always standing there, just in case. A look of very mild expectation laced with resignation etched on her face. It reminded me of the look you get from those old ladies you see in hospital during visiting time, the old ladies that nobody ever visits. The creatures that time forgot. They watch the daffodils and the grapes being carried to all the other beds. They pretend not to mind.

I pressed the combination of keys corresponding to Lizzie's number and waited for the voice to come over the intercom and the front door to open. But they didn't. I tried once again and then again. The old grey-haired lady, from the first-floor window, stared harder

214

now, and suddenly her body jolted into movement. It shuddered as she started to hobble down in my direction. Many minutes later, the front door opened. There stood the old lady with that same vacant look on her face. 'If you're looking for Lizzie, she's gone out – hours ago. It's such a lovely day to go out into the country. Her son took her out. It's such a lovely day to be out and about.' I asked if I could check Lizzie's flat just in case. And for the first time the face of the old lady showed some real undiluted emotion – fear. The security of the flats complex had been increased recently, even she knew that. I had been told that previously you could just walk straight into the flats. The only problem was that burglars were doing just that, and removing anything that wasn't nailed down, and several things that were, including the coinbox of the public telephone, the clock on the wall and most of the prints used to decorate the place. So what had I come for? The old lady's expression said it all. She stepped back as I seemed to push in past her. I passed one print on the wall – that dark swarthy girl with the big watery eyes and the strangely Caucasian features that they used to sell in Woolies. Her big doleful eyes seemed to follow me as I made my way on to the first floor with the old lady hobbling behind me, trying to keep up with me to see what mischief I might be getting up to.

I rang Lizzie's door, and I could just about make out this very quiet shuffling noise coming from behind it. The old grey-haired lady could hear it too, and she hobbled off, talking to herself as she went – back to her watchtower, back to her lonely vigil. Lizzie opened the door about a minute later. The first thing I noticed was her eyes, they had this sparkle in them. They were the eyes of a young girl, and a very mischievous young girl at that. They weren't like the eyes of the old lady that had seen me to the door. 'You're an hour and five minutes late,' she said. 'Is that how you do things these days.' Having put me firmly in my place, for I was indeed exactly one hour and five minutes late, she motioned me into the living room. She walked in front and you could see that she could only move with the greatest difficulty, using a stick. Her body had been bowed by her eighty-six years until it looked ready to snap, like a bow that had been put under too much strain. But when she sat down, she sat upright, and her eyes dominated the conversation once again.

I looked around the flat. The living room had a curtain at one side of the room which covered her bed. You could just about make out her pink nightie folded neatly on one side of it. 'Not far to go to retire for the evening,' she said – 'just as well. The nightie's see-through, by the way, if you're interested.' And she squealed with laughter. 'I'm looking for a toyboy, at the moment.' I could see that Lizzie was going to be calling all the shots in this interview. 'Now what can I do you for?' she said.

I told her that I was doing a series about what people did after dark, and that I wanted to include an old-age pensioner living alone. She looked at me as if I and the rest of the world had gone mad. 'What's the matter, isn't there any news in the world anymore? Isn't anything happening out there?' she said. I asked her to humour me by telling me anyway.

'Well, I can't cook for myself anymore, ever since I scalded myself with the kettle, so my daughter comes around every day and makes me dinner, and cleans. I have one daughter and four sons still alive, and they come to visit me as does my daughter-in-law who lived with me for nearly eighteen years. We're more like sisters really, she's sixty-six, it keeps me young having young people about the place. But I'm one of the lucky ones, I had a big family, some of the old people here never have anyone to call on them. Never ever. You know, this place used to be a lovely place to live. I was on top of the world when I got this flat. But all the nice old people have gone. They've moved some old confused people into the flats, and to be honest they don't make very good neighbours. One of my neighbours called Billy comes and sits with me for an hour every weekday from five o'clock to six o'clock. He's one of the ones that isn't confused, as bright as a pin he is. But I don't invite many people into my flat. We like to keep ourselves to ourselves here, that's the way we all like it. But Billy is an exception – I'm trying to get him married off to my daughter-in-law, but I wouldn't want him. I'd want somebody that was a bit more capable, if you know what I mean.' And she squealed with laughter again.

'Apart from my family, I've got the telly for company.' The telly was on in the background, as we spoke. 'My favourite is the wrestling. I love the wrestling, particularly the big men. If Big Daddy was to lose a bit of weight, he'd not be so bad, you know. But all women love the wrestling. It used to be on later on a Saturday afternoon. But they moved it to an earlier time and now I hear that they're going to take it off altogether. It's terrible news for the likes of us. When the wrestling was on later in the day, all the men would go off to the football, and all the women would settle down to the wrestling. I used to go and watch the wrestling at Garston baths. They'd cover the baths with floorboards. One night this big Canadian was wrestling. God, was he handsome. All the lights went out and he took his dressing gown off and you know what? He didn't have any trunks on underneath. I don't know whether it was an accident or not, but I had a good look. I'll tell you that for nothing. He was fighting Billy Pie that night. He's probably dead and buried as well now. I'll tell you what if I could walk without my stick or without my wheelchair, I'd liven up some of these young people about today.'

Her wheelchair sat in the corner of the room, Lizzie needs it to travel more than a few feet. But, rather unfortunately you might say, she lives on the first floor of the flats. There's no lift. She only gets out of the flat therefore when one of her sons comes to visit and physically carries her down the stairs. There's a public phone in the corridor of the flats so that she can keep in touch with her family, but Lizzie can't get the money into the coinbox any longer. She doesn't want to be moved to the groundfloor because the flats down there are infested with cockroaches. So she's stranded on the first floor, waiting for someone to arrive to allow her out. 'Billy is a little past carrying me and the chair, otherwise I'd be in clover,' she said with a great smile on her face. 'Now my nights, I go to bed every night at about 10 o'clock with my Ovaltine and my tablets. Ovaltine always does the trick and sends me off to sleep. I wake up at about 2.30 am to see what's going on. I always have a good look through the window. There's a good view of the gasworks from my window. During the war, the Germans, and I don't mean Stan Boardman's Germans, dropped a landmine on a little parachute that landed on the gasworks. If it had gone off, the whole area would have been devastated, me included. I can't look out without thinking of what has happened and what might have been. Such memories.

'After my little quiet think, it's time for bed again, and up at 6.30 am. I have to get up early, it takes me nearly two hours to get dressed in the morning. I have to have a little rest after I put on each item. But I'll do it if it kills me. I always say that I'll die getting myself washed. There's a bath in my flat, by the way, but I can't get into it myself anymore, so I have to wait for my daughter to come around on a Friday night to help me into the bath. There's also a shower down the corridor, but there's no shower rail to hang on to, so I can't use it. It's such a pity, because I bought a shower cap and everything.

'I've had a good life, the thing that I always loved, though, was the singing. People always told me that I had a lovely voice. And every Saturday night I'd be in the pub with the relatives for a sing song. But I stopped singing when my oldest son John died seven years ago. No matter how old you are it breaks your heart losing a child.' And she motioned towards an old photograph on top of the cabinet where a big proud woman was surrounded by boys in caps and girls in smocks. The big, proud woman had the same fiery eyes as Lizzie. 'That's my John there, and that's him when he got back from Burma after the war. He got £16 for the six years he served in the army. His wife bought herself and me a blouse each with the money.' And her eyes started to sparkle a little bit more, with tears this time. All powerful emotions seem to light the eyes up – one way or another.

Up to that point my own background had been studiously ignored, but Lizzie began to focus in on my accent. 'What part of Belfast did you say you were from?' she enquired. 'My brother-in-law was in the Black-and-Tans, you know,' she told me. 'He met a neighbour from Woolton, the village where I grew up, when he was over in Ireland, and he was ready to kill him. It's a powerful thing religion. I have a neighbour from a few doors down that's turned her little flat into a chapel, with an altar in one corner. Billy says that he can hear her praying at nights. But I'm a Protestant, like yourself. You know we had religious trouble in Garston before there was trouble in Ireland, and we've always celebrated the twelfth of July. Every Twelfth the Orange Lodge would go on a day trip to Southport, a bit better than just marching through the centre of Belfast, if you ask me. We used to follow the band and sing all those Orange songs.'

I asked Lizzie to sing me just one, but she just looked at the photo of John, as a young lad, and said that she couldn't. 'What's a mother got to sing about when she loses her son, tell me that?' I asked her to hum one of the songs then instead, and tell me the words afterwards, if she liked. She broke into a half-singing, half-speaking voice – 'Billy came from Ireland/A Protestant to be/He brought with him a root/Of the good old Orange tree . . . We used to sing at the top of our voices as we passed the old chapel in Garston.' And her eyes sparkled once again, as she remembered the long nights of passion in those days. Passion that stirs the soul – be it love, hate or sheer bloody-mindedness. Passion in the days when Lizzie had to wait on no man.

And as I left her little flat I could still hear her humming above the noise of the television, and the old confused people still talking to themselves.

A man on a Treadmill

It was 8.45 pm, and Steve Moorhead, a 22-year-old medical student was just getting changed for his nightly eight-mile run. He never misses it. Such dedication is not that unusual these days, not even in students. Steve had, however, been weight-training for the previous forty-five minutes, and completed ten to fifteen miles on a bicycle just before that. This would take his total training session that night to well over two hours. But that was only the evening session! Steve's training starts at 5.50 am, when he goes out for an hour and a half on his bike, which for him represents riding between thirty and thirty-five miles. As soon as he gets back he goes straight out for a run – 'five miles at a nice steady six-minute-mile pace. Then it's time for breakfast.' And that's only the morning session. At lunchtime Steve swims 2,000 metres – that's sixty lengths of his local pool non-stop in about twenty-eight minutes. Then he can look forward to the evening training session all over again. This routine occurs every day, without fail.

Steve is a triathlete, one of the new breed of supermen and the odd superwoman, who compete in events where they have to swim, cycle and run in that order without a break. This event can sometimes involve a swim of two and a half miles, a cycle ride of 112 miles, and then a full marathon with no gaps in between any of these events. 'I've recently been involved in the National Long Course Championship – this involved a 2,000-metre swim in open water, then fifty-six miles on the bike followed by a half marathon. It does tend to put marathon and half marathon running a little in the shade,' he said with just a little understatement.

In more ways than one, I thought to myself. I had been along to watch the National Long Course Championship held in late July at Rother Valley park, near Sheffield, having run a half marathon myself that morning in nearby Rotherham. I can sometimes struggle around a half marathon in 1 hour 26 minutes (but not that morning, I'm afraid), the best time for the half marathon in that day's triathlon championship was 1 hour 8 minutes. That time would win many half marathons in this country, and that is after an exhausting swim and cycle ride. Although I suppose that the swim and the cycle ride cannot be that exhausting for these people or they wouldn't be able to do the run in that kind of time. But it's not just the times that are impressive, its the aura that surrounds them. The half marathon that I'd run that morning (wearing I must confess a friend's number who couldn't make it), was the Prince of Wales half marathon, which is organized by Rotherham Harriers. This is an extremely well-organized event, but hardly glamorous. No TV cameras, but plenty of drizzle that particular morning. The drizzle had managed to dye my body and feet a number of rather different colours – my feet were blue from the colour of my running shoes, my chest red from my running vest, and my groin region a funny pink colour – not from my underpants! I looked a somewhat sorry sight when I finished, and I wasn't alone.

Over in Rother Valley park, things were different. First of all, the sun was mysteriously shining. And who were these apparitions gliding effortlessly along the roads, and running in cut-off vests and swimming trunks? Apparitions with shoulders and well-developed quads. One of the most disheartening things for me about running marathons and half marathons is being passed on some hill by someone whose body looks quite frankly incapable of propelling them at any speed what-soever. You do see people with the most improbable bodies running some very good times. And as for the men and women who actually win marathons! As one marathon runner I interviewed put it, '. . . good marathon runners are like match-stick men, you've never seen such a sickly looking lot in your life – all they consist of is lungs and legs and all the rest is just holding them together.' The Rotherham half marathon is an out-and-back course, so you do get a chance to see the sickly looking winners of these events, something I usually seem to miss – for some reason. You really do wonder who would want to end up looking like that. But the triathlon is different – shoulders well-developed from swimming, quads well-developed from cycling, and even the ravages of the marathon cannot reduce all that muscle to mere string.

And then there is the gear to go with it. Steve talked me through it: 'Most triathlons involve an open-water swim, so you are allowed to wear a wet suit. The maximum thickness is, however, 3 mm which is a lot thinner than the kinds of wet suits that you wear for something like wind-surfing. The argument is that thicker wet suits provide too much buoyancy. The wet suits have special zips so that you can get out of them very fast. Then it's on to the bicycle. Cycles can cost up to £2000. I was part of a team that was sponsored last year by a bike manufacturer from Manchester called Harry Hall, but the team has disintegrated this year, so there's been no sponsorship. On the cycle ride I wear swimming trunks and a cut-off vest, which I run in as well. Spectators don't seem to mind, because when they're watching an event, they've already seen enough half-naked men.'

As a boy, Steve had swum for Yorkshire, he had also been a keen cyclist since his father, a Consultant in a local hospital, bought him a racing bike for his eleventh birthday. At seventeen, he started running half marathons. The triathlon was a fairly natural next step. He did his first triathlon when he was eighteen. 'It was on the 29th of December. It was an indoor 800-metre swim, thank God, because it started at 7.45 in the morning and it was dark when I got there. All the swimmers start together, and the only way that I can describe it was it was just like eels in a bucket. There were a lot of punches thrown in the water. Coming from a swimming background, I couldn't believe it. I dived in there, and there were bodies everywhere – it was just like Zeebrugge. I was very inexperienced, so for the cycle ride I wore cycling tights, a T-shirt, a balaclava and gloves. The only problem was that it took a long time to put all this gear on – I probably wasted about five minutes getting changed. I still couldn't feel my feet for the first three and a half miles of the 28-mile cycle ride. It was freezing. Then this bloke zoomed past me, and he was just wearing a pair of swimming trunks. I thought that this was an event for loonies. There was a seven-mile run to finish off. It was a fairly short course and I finished in sixth place overall out of about 120 competitors. But it encouraged me to get involved. My best time at the moment for the long course is now 4 hours 8 minutes, and I made the National squad last year.'

I was intrigued as to how the training for such an event could ever be incorporated into something approaching a normal style of life. Having to train for a marathon by going for a run every day can be anti-social enough, as anyone who has ever done it will know. But how on earth do you fit in all this other stuff? 'Basically, by getting up very early every day, and training every night. When I'm on call at the hospital, which is one day in seven, I run down to the hospital in the morning with a bag full of clothes on my back, and run home at night. I took a year off last year to concentrate on the triathlon to try to make the National squad, which I did, but I had to take the year off anyway because I failed an Anatomy exam. Luckily I've now passed it, so I'll be entering my fourth year at medical school. Medicine must come first, I realize that, but I give myself entirely to Medicine and the triathlon. I have a girlfriend, but I only see her once a week. She understands my dedication. She realizes that when she's not seeing me that I'm out burning rubber on the road, not elsewhere.'

All this burning of rubber requires a lot of fuel, and the way that Steve talks about his daily intake of 9,000 calories, fuel is perhaps the best word for it. He had begun telling me about his diet by explaining that he ate most of his food at the end of the day, and only 'a light breakfast' at 8.15 am – 'I have a large tin of beans with eight rounds of bread followed by a bowl of cereal and plenty of dried fruit and a pint of milk, followed by two cups of coffee with three sugars in.' The light lunch sometime later was half a loaf of bread with jam or cheese. I didn't have the heart or the stomach to ask him about his big meal in the evening.

'It depends, of course, on what you're used to,' added Steve. 'You get used to such a strict training regime. It's amazing what the body can cope with.' I nodded thinking of the large tin of beans for breakfast – before the cereal. But what about injury? Surely all this training must produce a whole host of sports-related injuries. 'Well, the funny thing is that I do have problems with my back. In fact, I have got Ankylosing Spondylitis, which basically means inflammation of the spine. This condition is aggravated by sitting around, and in fact it's eased by training, which is one reason why I like to do so much.'

It was beginning to seem that triathletes were a breed apart – none of your marathon men here who go down to the pub the night before an event. The triathlon seemed to be a total way of life, even if you do have the rather unpronounceable 'Ankylosing Spondylitis' to blame it all on. I was starting to wonder how Steve would describe other triathletes – apart, that is, from the gentleman on the bicycle who had passed him just wearing swimming trunks at the end of December, and who he had already described as 'a loony'. 'Well, in my view, triathletes are a little eccentric. A lot of them are squaddies and they seem to have this amazing dedication to push their bodies to the absolute limit, to see who really is the fittest of all.' But didn't he see anything unusual in his own behaviour? Wasn't he himself pushing his body to the absolute limit with all the training that he did? 'I don't really see my own behaviour as eccentric at all. If I didn't do well at the event, then fair enough, I suppose. But the triathlon doesn't seem that strange if you do well somehow.'

The interview was over now. It was time for the evening's cycle ride, the second cycle ride of the day. Then it would be time for the weight training, and then time for the second run of the day, in this never-ending cycle of painful activity. Any hamster on any wheel would feel relieved if they could just look in at Steve in his own personal cage of dedication.

As a postscript, perhaps I should add that in this year's national championship, Steve Moorhead was in twenty-fifth position after the swim (out of approximately 400 competitors), and in eleventh position overall after the cycle ride. Unfortunately, he then had to drop out of the run after three miles because of problems with his back.

★ 12 ★
Darkness at noon

Have you got what it takes?

It was midday, and I was standing in the blinding spring sunshine looking for the security agency offices. This was where the interviews were to be held. 'Opposite the skating rink, and upstairs from the car hire business,' the voice on the phone had told me. Just next door to Cee Bee (busy, busy, busy) variety agency. I spotted the sign on the window and went into the hallway. It took my eyes a few minutes to adapt to the dark, after the bright sunshine. All other senses, however, were working overtime. The damp, dank smell hit my nose first, the sun had never had a chance to dry out this carpet. I made my way up the stairs, they creaked below my weight. There was one other candidate outside the door, sitting on the stairs and gripping a pink form. He was wearing a denim jacket and jeans. He looked strangely proportioned, but I assumed that it was just the way that he was sitting. He eyed me up as I approached, as if to say 'no chance mate'. I asked him if he was waiting to be interviewed. He said that he was, but that you just had to wait.

There was a notice on the door. It said, 'Please knock and wait. Thank you.' So I knocked, and waited, and nothing happened. So I knocked again, and still nothing happened. So I stuck my nose around the door. Two women stared at me through a cloud of smoke. 'Would you mind waiting *outside* please?' said the woman from behind the desk. 'You've come for the interview . . . Fill this in and wait *outside*.' 'Yes, but . . .' I tried to reply before I was pushed back on to the stairs. I was gripping my pink form, as if it was a comforter.

'That's just what happened to me,' said the other occupant of the stairs. 'I don't think we've made a very good start so far. You'd better start filling your form in. Look I've started mine already.' And sure enough he'd already got to question 4: 'Marital Status . . .' and 'Husband's Occupation . . .' I didn't know how long it had taken him,

224

but he seemed to have been there quite a while already. 'Hey, I think this form's just for birds,' he said suddenly. '"Maiden Name, Husband's Occupation," do you think this is part of the test.' I said that you couldn't be sure, indeed anything was likely in a place like this. Just then someone from the Cee Bee Variety agency opened their door, knocking me down a few of the stairs. I thought that this was more likely to be part of the test, as I hauled myself back up, staring at the offending door. It too had a notice on it – 'Sorry but due to increased work load visits by prior arrangement only (THIS MEANS YOU).' It wasn't a very welcoming place.

Suddenly we heard the stairs creaking. 'This must be the bloke coming to do the interviews,' said my companion hopefully. Or another candidate for the job, I thought to myself – the top stairs were cramped enough as it was. It turned out to be a woman in her thirties wearing a bright yellow sweater and sunglasses. She greeted us, and my new companion sprang up to say hello. If we had been standing outside at the time, it would have been quite likely that he would have blocked out the sun. I couldn't see round him. The woman in the sweater looked impressed. When he eventually stepped aside, she looked me up and down. I could see her disappointment even through her shades. She told us to hurry up with the pink forms. I hadn't started mine yet. The man who could eclipse the sun was writing very slowly indeed. The other two women left the office, they said nothing as they passed.

My new companion was called first to be interviewed. I was pleased, I wanted to hear the type of questions which were to be asked. I listened through the door which wasn't properly closed. I discovered that he was nineteen years old, and had been unemployed for six months since the fitness studio he worked for had gone bust. He had no criminal convictions and could start straight away. And then the really tricky question – 'Do you have a dark suit?' 'No, I can't get one to fit me,' he said – 'I've got a 54-inch chest, you see.' The woman in the yellow sweater sounded most impressed, and she was just in the process of recommending a shop which produced suits for men 'with a good build', when another candidate made his way wearily up the creaky stairs.

This one was in his mid-forties, with receding hair. He was wearing a green Parka jacket and grey flared trousers, the trousers had a patch on the inside of the thighs. He eyed me up and down as well, and this at least seemed to give him a little confidence. I nodded towards the door, on which he then knocked. A pink form was thrust his way. He glimpsed the young man being interviewed, through the crack in the door, and his confidence seemed to ebb again. 'Jesus, look at the size of that thing in there. I hope they're not just looking for blokes like that.' There was a bit of a gap in the conversation, which he proceeded to fill, he clearly needed to talk – 'Oh well. I've got a job already, you know, I'm not unemployed, I work in an engineering firm not far away. I'm just looking for a bit of extra cash. I saw the advert in the paper. I've always fancied a bit of security work on the doors of clubs or pubs or whatever. I really wouldn't mind a job with a uniform, even a dickie bow. But I thought that bouncers were changing their image lately. I thought that they wouldn't be looking for heavies anymore. But I wouldn't fancy having to throw five of somebody like that animal in there out of a pub.'

Just then the young man with the 54-inch chest made his way out. He threw me a confident smile. The man in the Parka jacket looked even more crestfallen. I told him that he could go first, that I was in no hurry. 'Better to get it over with, eh?' he said as he walked manfully through the door.

This time the rate of pay was explained at the beginning – £10 a night on the door of pubs, working from 8.00 to 11.30 pm, £16 a night for clubs – working from 9.00 to 2.30 am. 'How do these rates of pay strike you?' enquired the lady in the yellow sweater, who I couldn't help noticing was chain-smoking. 'Magic,' said the man in the Parka. 'Right, now some questions to assess your suitability for the position,' said the interviewer. 'Say there were five lads in the club, and it was after 2.00 am, and you wanted them to leave. How would you go about it?' The man in the Parka jacket looked pensive, this was his opportunity to show that brains were better than brawn, and that a little initiative can go a very long way. 'Well, I'd not go in heavy, that's for sure.' 'Fine,' said the lady interviewer. 'What would you do instead?'

'Well, I'd ask them to drink up please, and say something like, "Would you mind making your way out of the club, thank you very much indeed." The man in the Parka looked satisfied with his answer, the interviewer didn't. 'What if they still didn't move?' she enquired. There was a very long pause, during which the man in the Parka moved forward in his seat, and started twisting his own ear. 'I'd say to them – "come on lads, haven't you got any beds to go to? Move along."'

'But what if they still didn't move?' asked the interviewer again. The man in the Parka slumped back in his chair.

'Look,' said the man in the Parka, 'I'm not desperate. I was just looking for a nice cushy job on the side. I don't want a load of bloody hassle. I thought that it might be simple security work. Would you mind if I had my application form back?'

'I would,' said the interviewer.

'Why?'

'We just want to keep it, in case you apply for any other security jobs.'

'I don't want any other security jobs, I just want my form back.'

'Why?'

'I just want it.'

Things were now turning decidedly nasty.

'Okay,' said the interviewer, and she started to tear the pink form up right in front of him. 'Is that better?' she asked sarcastically. The man in the Parka grunted and pushed his way out. He didn't say 'cheerio'.

It was my turn now. The interviewer was reading some notes, it gave me a few seconds to look around the office and get my bearings. I was trying to compose myself. I could just make out the little notice on the wall – 'This job is so secret that I don't know what I'm doing.' It sat above a tyre in one corner. There were press cuttings about the woman in the yellow sweater – 'A normal day for the danger girls,' ran one headline. Below it was another headline – 'Why a shy guy stole sexy gift for bride.' Was she the bride? Did she catch the shy guy? What was the sexy gift? What was I doing here? My eyes flitted to a pile of application forms. I could make out the form of the man with the 54–inch chest – '54 inch chest' had been written in red ink at the top. The one just below it, and visibly jutting out of the side of the pile, was covered in a childish scrawl. 'Why would you like a job as a Store Detective?' asked the pink form, even though the interviews were for positions as bouncers. 'I WUDE LIK A JOB AS A STORE DETECTIVE BICOS I LICE IT' was the reply. All printed in thick capitals. The 22-year-old respondent, who had last worked on a Community Programme, had lived at his current address for '4 MUMFS', the form said. Unfortunately, it wasn't a joke, although I did start to laugh just a little hysterically.

I thought that I'd take the initiative. 'I've got a thirty-eight-inch chest,' I began, 'and if I was in a club and the five lads refused to leave, I'd leave instead. Okay? With any luck they'd follow me out.'

On that cue, I got up and skipped down the creaky stairs and ran back into the bright, fresh spring sunshine, passing one more hopeful on the way in.